F   NEWTON
GIL

Giles, Janice Holt
40 Acres and No Mule

2-12-00
9-14-09

40 ACRES

AND

NO MULE

40 ACRES

AND

NO MULE

✓✓✓✓✓✓✓✓✓✓✓✓✓✓✓✓✓✓✓✓✓✓✓✓✓

JANICE HOLT GILES

With a Prologue by the Author

THE UNIVERSITY PRESS OF KENTUCKY

Copyright © 1967 by Janice Holt Giles.

Published by arrangement with Houghton Mifflin Co. by
The University Press of Kentucky

Scholarly publisher for the Commonwealth,
serving Bellarmine College, Berea College, Centre
College of Kentucky, Eastern Kentucky University,
The Filson Club, Georgetown College, Kentucky
Historical Society, Kentucky State University,
Morehead State University, Murray State University,
Northern Kentucky University, Transylvania University,
University of Kentucky, University of Louisville,
and Western Kentucky University.

Editorial and Sales Offices: Lexington, Kentucky 40508-4008

Library of Congress Cataloging-in-Publication Data

Giles, Janice Holt.
    40 acres and no mule / Janice Holt Giles; with a prologue by the
author.
        p. ca.
    Originally published: 2nd ed. Boston: Houghton Mifflin, 1967.
    ISBN 0-8131-1792-5 (alk. paper)   ISBN 0-8131-0809-8
(pbk.: alk. paper)
    1. Giles, Janice Holt—Homes and haunts—Kentucky—Adair County.
2. Adair County (Ky.)—Social life and customs. 3. Novelists,
American—20th century—Biography. 4. Giles, Henry, 1916-1986—
Marriage. 5. Farm life—Kentucky—Adair County. 6. Adair County
(Ky.)—Biography. I. Title. II. Title: Forty acres and no mule.
PS3513.I4628Z4618   1992
813'.54—dc20
[B]   92-20034

Again, *TO HENRY*

40 ACRES

AND

NO MULE

Prologue

This book, *40 Acres and No Mule*, was written during the winter of 1950–51, sixteen years ago. I had lived a year and a half in the hills of my husband's homeland. I had been a good observer of my new family and neighbors. I saw what went on around me and was watchful of ways and customs, the social pattern of behavior, and I was beginning to learn some of the rules of the behavior. To the extent of faithfully relating these things I saw, the book is as valid today as it was in 1950. What I was ignorant of, however, and what it took long slow years to learn, was the basis for the whole social structure, its history, the reasons *why* the people acted as they did, believed as they did, felt as they did.

I did not know, for instance, that I had come into a little corner of Appalachia to spend the rest of my life, nor would it have meant much had I known it, for I did not know Appalachia was unique. I had come to live on a small farm in the poor, rocky steep hills of north Adair County. Having lived most of my life in cities, I thought that the strangeness, uniqueness and differentness I found was only the difference between urban and rural living anywhere. It took years of living within the framework of an Appalachian family-clan, with its courtesies and loyalties, its economics, religion, politics, for me to begin to absorb the uniqueness and differentness. It took years because I had first to shed my own preconceived ideas and break the mold of my own cultural background. I had to *become* Appalachian myself, for not even my husband could bring himself to be rude enough to correct or teach me much, nor could he understand how strange it was to me and how much I had to learn. When I stumbled and offended, he comforted and explained, which all too often did not keep me from stumbling and offending again.

Not until I began to have some dim comprehension of the religious concepts of the Appalachians did I begin to understand the pattern of social behavior or to realize that the whole social structure is based upon these religious concepts. Not until I began to do intensive research on the American Indians for use in my writing did it become clear to me that Appalachia was not a subculture of American society, a folk class, but an island long isolated in the middle of America, a primitive society with its own mores and norms, its own peculiar ways and customs, its own social structure, its own legalistic and biblical religion.

I wrote what I saw and it was true. I also wrote what I felt, my own horror and revulsion, my own emotions, and they were true. But essentially I wrote without deep understanding because I was still an "outsider." I wrote as so many have written since, the missionary, the minister, the teacher, the sociologist, the researcher, with the only measuring sticks I had, and the only ones they have — the intelligence, the education, the class consciousness, the culture which bred me. This is not to say they were wrong. It is only to say they are not enough and that they have several built-in factors which almost always lead to error. They cannot produce in-depth understanding.

The only valid measuring sticks to an understanding of Appalachia, the Appalachian's religious concepts and his close, tribal family life, are very difficult to obtain because of his inherent dislike, distrust and resentment of the outsider. Living *among* Appalachians, even for many years, is not enough to overcome these things. One must be born "inside," descend from "inside" or marry "inside" before the door is open. The Appalachian is courteous and hospitable, and, in these days of intensive research into Appalachia following John F. Kennedy's discovery of the area in 1960, he allows himself to be interviewed, surveyed, measured, charted, polled and tabulated. But behind his courtesy and hospitality he remains inscrutable and his very courtesy and hospitality are themselves his barrier and protecting wall. He uses an affable manner and agreement in all that is said as a shield for his own integrity, and as a mask for his contempt for the questioning outsider.

Nearly every Indian tribe speaks of itself as "the People." The Indian ways are the "right" ways; his mores, norms, standards are the "right" ones. All other ways are foreign, alien, barbaric. All other peoples are inferior. So with the Appalachian. He feels superior to any outsider. He considers the outsider to be inept, ridiculous and foolish, does not like him, and the sooner the outsider goes his way the happier the Appalachian will be. To the Appalachian the outsider is ignorant of all the simplest, most basic things. And he is so ill-mannered. He comes breezing in, too hearty, too familiar too soon. He is "talky" and "pushy" and "nosey." He is "braggy" and "thinks himself something" when he is not. He is full of energy. He comes rushing in turning things upside down, and he continues to rush around and ends up making a complete idiot of himself. In precisely the same ways the American traveler abroad creates resentment and makes a bad impression with his money and his manners, his brashness and loudness, his unconscious arrogance and presumption to superiority, the outsider does the same in Appalachia.

In the north end of Adair County we are not the deep mountains of Kentucky Appalachia, or the coal-mining regions. But Appalachia is made up of many parts and regions. It is not one amorphous mass. Some of it is coal-mining country. Much of it is marginal farmlands. Some of it is ridge-and-saddle, some of it "up-the-holler," and much of it is spur and fringe, as we are. Each region may have some individual characteristics because of its own peculiar conditions, but there is a consistency of certain traits and characteristics, certain mores and norms, which run through all the counties and the various bordering states like a common cord. Thus Appalachians from West Virginia and North Carolina moving into Adair County are comfortable among us, and those of our

3

people who go among them feel at home. Indeed, it is the very consistency of the religious concepts and family ways in all of Appalachia which makes it possible to speak of "Appalachia" at all.

We are hill-and-holler, farm and timber people in north Adair County. We live in the intricately tangled hills and hollows of a broad, long, fingering mass of spurs and foothills of the Cumberlands. Here there is a pocket of pure Appalachianism and our older people still speak the tongue.

My mother-in-law, for instance, telling me of a bad cold said, "It served me ill." She saw a snake and it was "quiled" ready to strike. A dog is told to "begwine," or begone. A neighbor comes to "holp" out until the work is "cotched up." Livestock is called "property" and house furnishings are "house, plunder." Not even my husband speaks of a bull. It is a "brute." A person in ill health is said to be "drinlin'." A man who is able or capable is said to be "witty" or "clever." A child is told to mind his manners with the admonition, "Be smart, now." Young couples do not go together. They are said to be "talking" to each other. An ill-tempered person is "tetchy." A spotted cow or horse is "piedy." If one is uncertain about the length of time since an occurrence, it is "untelling" how long it has been. A thing which lasts is "enduring." Something very old has lasted "forever and enduring." The envelope for a letter is not addressed, it is "backed." It is not mailed or posted, it is "started." Anything different from the usual is "quare" or "goes foolish." To the day he dies a man's son remains his "boy" though he may be an old man himself. Thus my husband, in his fifties, is still Frank Giles' "boy." A woman's husband is her "man," and a man's wife is his "woman."

My husband's people have lived in this same community for seven generations, and we live within two miles of the spot the first of his people settled in 1803. When he brought me here to live in 1949, I groped and fumbled in the new environment, and the first few years caused him and his family much embarrassment. But slowly I was instructed in the right ways, the right language, the right behavior. I was told not to talk so much, not to ask personal questions, never to dispute or argue, or quarrel, or correct. I was taught never to offer advice or counsel. I was told if I did not agree with someone to keep quiet. It was not mannerly to disagree. I was told I must never act as if I took pride in anything I had done or owned. I would be "putting myself above others." I was taught that it was all right to tell news but that gossip was frowned on and the difference between news and gossip was a very fine line. If one always added the phrase, "Now, that's the way I heard it," it remained news. It was gossip if one expressed personal opinion or judgment. To my chagrin I learned that allowances were made for me because I was "from off," I had not been properly "raised up" and I therefore could not be expected to know much.

THE RELIGION

Slowly, very slowly I realized that nearly everything the Appalachian is proceeds from his religious concepts. The Bible was quoted to me so constantly as the basis for all behavior that it was impossible not to understand eventually that in everything that matters the Appalachian actually lives in Thessalonica, Philippi, Corinth and especially in Ephesus and Galatia. The apostle Paul writes letters to him. He tells the Appalachians what they should believe and down to the minutest detail how they shall behave. No aspect, no intimacy of their life escapes his instruction. He admonishes them, chides them, he grows impatient with them, he warns and encourages them, he guides and directs, and he promises them the kingdom of heaven if they are faithful. They strive to understand him and to obey him, and they wait for the chariot to swing low and carry them home. In the whole pattern of his life the Appalachian is an Early Christian.

This did not tally at all with what I had always read, that the Appalachian is irreligious. There were even statistics to prove it. Only 10 per cent to 15 per cent of all Appalachians belonged to churches. But no society is entirely irreligious. In the whole recorded history of man no society has ever been found in which there were not religious concepts of some sort which bound it together, informed and furnished its habits and customs. Why, then, was the Appalachian, so biblically religious that his entire society was based on it, considered irreligious? *Because he did not join churches.* And the facts were incontrovertible.

In almost a hundred years of effort, the established and organized churches have made so little impression on him that the percentage of those belonging to churches in Appalachia has risen only a meager amount — from around 5 per cent to 10 or 15 per cent. And if that final figure were broken down it would undoubtedly show that fully half of it is concentrated in the towns, that 5 per cent would still be a truer figure for rural and village Appalachia. Why? There had to be a reason. The Appalachian was religious, rigidly religious, but *he would not join churches.*

The truth was slow in unfolding as I pursued this study, but it finally became clear. The Appalachian is a Pauline Christian, a biblical Christian, but he is not only non-denominational, he is violently anti-denominational. He will have nothing to do with organized churches — that is, the established churches with a central organization, church membership rolls, a literature and an educated ministry — because the organized churches are "denominations."

Many Appalachians believe the denominations had their origins at the tower of Babel and have been scattering confusion over the face of the earth ever since. To him, the denominations not only have no scriptural authority but, far worse, they have "added to" the Bible and are thus actually guilty of "going against the Bible." To many Appalachians it is *a sin to belong to a denomination.*

The only "denominations" he will have anything to do with are those which claim *not* to be denominations — such as the splinter groups which have broken away from the established churches, the many Baptist splinter groups, the various primitive groups which have also arisen from rigid Bible interpretations. These groups rarely have a central organization, do not insist upon church membership rolls, do not have an educated ministry.

Every census year for generations, therefore, the Appa-

6

lachian has replied to the question concerning his church affiliation, the denomination to which he belongs, "I don't belong to none." This was my mother-in-law's reply in the census year of 1950 which, made in my presence, set me to thinking and studying. She had added, "I don't hold with the denominations."

There is no more deeply, devoutly, truly religious person in the world than my mother-in-law. She is the purest example of the Appalachian Christian I know, yet all her long life she has replied to any question about her church affiliation, "I don't belong to *no* church." Her tone of voice as she replies indicates her affront at even being asked if she belongs to a church. Multiply this by hundreds of thousands of Appalachians, over many generations, and there is the statistical assumption that because so few belong to churches the Appalachian is irreligious.

The early Appalachian brought at least some vague denominational concepts and theology with him into Appalachia. Harry Caudill in *Night Comes to the Cumberlands* says it was mostly Calvinism, because the early Appalachian was largely Scotch-English in origin. This is further proved by the fact that, separated from society as he was, as he slowly developed his own Bible-based religion he founded it on the remembered scriptural basis for the doctrines of Calvin — the Pauline epistles. As all denominational concepts slowly faded and were abandoned, using the Pauline epistles for guidance, interpreting them as best he could for himself, the Appalachian became wholly nondenominational.

There was no ministry. Paul enjoined him that any man led of the Spirit should be heard, so he raised up his own lay ministry. Paul had taken no pay except hospitality in his ministry, he had earned his living in other ways as other men did, therefore a preacher should not be paid for preaching. He should be given hospitality, a collection might be taken to pay his expenses, but he should never make his living by preaching. To this day the Appalachian has a built-in dislike for the educated minister who has made of the ministry a paid profession. Preaching is a grace, added to a man by the Spirit, and

7

he should not cash in on it. The educated, denominational minister has a harder row to hoe in Appalachia than almost any outsider, because he violates so many of the Appalachian's long-held traditional religious concepts.

The Appalachian's religious concepts have dictated the social patterns for him. Much of his social behavior is grounded specifically in the apostle Paul's letter to the Galatians. He is told here not to indulge in backbiting, and that all works of the flesh are to be avoided. They are spelled out in detail for him. He is to avoid adultery, fornication, uncleanness, lasciviousness, idolatry, witchcraft, hatred, variance, emulations, wrath, strife, seditions, heresies, envyings, murders, drunkenness, revellings, and suchlike. He is told not to be desirous of vainglory, provoking one another, and that if a man thinks himself to be something, when he is nothing, he is deceived. The Appalachian strives to avoid these things.

He is also reminded here to love his neighbor as himself, to honor his father and mother, to do good. He is told that the fruit of the Spirit is love, joy, peace, longsuffering, gentleness, goodness, faith, and that if he lives in the Spirit, he must walk in the Spirit. He is promised a place in the kingdom of Heaven if he is faithful. He believes these things and he strives to abide by them.

The outsider coming in thus finds a society in which a man does not seek leadership, in which individuality is sunk and any singularity is frowned upon. These things would be desiring vainglory. The Appalachian would be thinking he is something. He would be putting himself forward, he would be elevating himself above others, he would be acting as if he were better than others. He would be "walking proud."

The outsider finds men who will not engage in free debate. It is argument and variance. It is provoking one another. It generates wrath, hatred, strife. It is troublemaking. Feelings get stirred up. People are hurt and there is general unpleasantness. Except in matters of religious and biblical interpretation, so important to the Appalachian because it concerns his immortal soul, he is not generally disputatious. He strives hard to be pleasant, agreeable, to give no offense.

The outsider finds a people who are remarkably honorable, good and decent personally and in their dealings with each other. In a day when all the corruption and evil of which mankind is capable seems to be oozing like pus out of its pores, it is healing to find a people, still, who so honor the Commandments that they do not, generally, lie or cheat or steal. Even a white lie comes hard to the Appalachian and stealing is held in such abhorrence that it is not necessary to lock one's doors.

In Appalachia a man's word, in personal dealings, is as good as his bond quite literally. "Thou shalt not bear false witness" is taken seriously. From the sale of a cow or a car, a tract of timber, or house and land, the Appalachian does not knowingly misrepresent anything about it. Every trade or sale is concluded, "Now, if it ain't just like I've told you, let me know and I'll make it right." He does make it right if some error has crept in. To a great extent it was this honesty which made him such easy prey for the unscrupulous mining and timber people who cheated him so badly. Honorable himself, he believed all men were honorable. He had to learn the hard way that it was "ignorant" to be honest.

The outsider will find a people whose men and women honor their marriage vows and whose divorce rate is very low. He will find a people who honor their parents. Not even an adult Appalachian will argue with, quarrel with, or speak disrespectfully to his parents, and in their old age parents are cherished and cared for in the home of a married son or daughter. He will find a people where youth, yet, minds its manners and juvenile delinquency is almost unknown.

Not organization-minded, the Appalachian does not channel his good works through the church or the community. He is personally committed to being a good neighbor. With his own kind he is generous to a fault, his hospitality is boundless and no call for his help goes unheeded. The opposite of more sophisticated people who do not like to be personally involved, the Appalachian feels he *must* be personally involved.

The outsider coming in will find a people so courteous, in whom courtesy is so practiced and ingrained, that it has become almost the gentle Oriental art of saving face. Never do you expose a man to ridicule or humiliation or embarrassment.

As a woman, I have often wished the apostle Paul had not been a bachelor and, I strongly suspect, a dyspeptic one at that. He might not have made a wife's place so lowly had he been a husband. But the place assigned to wives, accepted and practiced by generations of Appalachians, is found in Paul's letter to the Ephesians, in particular the fifth chapter.

> Wives, submit yourselves unto your husbands, as unto the Lord.
>
> For the husband is the head of the wife, even as Christ is the head of the church: and he is the saviour of the body.
>
> Therefore as the church is subject unto Christ, so let the wives be to their own husbands in every thing.

In all ways a husband was the head of the house. He made every decision, he did not share his opinions with his wife nor ask hers. His will was the only will. A wife was silent, obeyed her husband and served him. She did not ever in public dispute him, cross his wishes, or in any way cause him embarrassment or humiliation, with her tongue or by her actions. She did not eat at table with him. She and her daughters served the husband and sons. When the men had finished, the women ate. In church she sat apart from him with other women. She was allowed no voice in "meeting." In walking together a wife walked behind her husband.

I have vivid memories of my first years on "the ridge," when I watched my husband's old uncle — the patriarch of the family-clan — walk down the dirt road to "meetin'" every Saturday evening. It would be "first dark," or dusk. In one hand he carried an unlit lantern to be used going home. In the other was his Bible. He walked exactly in the middle of the road. If he met a car, it went around him. He never gave ground. Behind him, six paces perhaps, dutifully followed his tough little knot of a wife. In all the years I knew them, I never knew her to speak directly to him or to call him by name in speaking of him. He was always "He." "He says," "He wants," or "He don't want." Her sole purpose in life was to make him comfortable, to obey him and to serve him.

He was the last of a long, long line to adhere so rigidly to the tradition. But to the day he died, a few years ago, he and his wife followed the old way. I am grateful that she outlived him and is having some years in which to bloom and enjoy life.

Slowly the Pauline conception of husband-wife relationships has been ameliorated, but there are still many holdovers. Appalachian wives still wait on their husbands more than most wives, still defer to them publicly, still teach their children to honor their father as the head of the family even in the increasingly frequent cases where the wife is the wage-earner. I saw a mother slap a teenage son's face hard recently, because the boy spoke disrespectfully of his father who had done nothing all day while the mother was at work in a factory in town. "He's yore *father*," she said, "and you'll not speak of him so!"

In the early days, struggling to interpret the Bible, to determine the right ways and the right behavior, the recognized most purely religious man became the most respected man. To this day the man most respected and most honored is not the man who acquires the most education, riches, possessions. He is the man who, according to Appalachian concepts, is the most religious man — the best Christian. There is little emphasis on upper, middle, and lower classes. There are primarily only two classes — sinners and Christians. A man is a sinner until he has the mystical experience of being "saved." He is then a Christian.

As civilization encroached upon Appalachia, denominationalism came with it. The organized church discovered Appalachia and began to send in its missionaries and to establish its missions, and denominational evangelists and preachers found their way in, gathered a handful here and there, built churches and preached their particular convictions.

It has been said that religion is the most divisive element in Appalachia. It is. But it has not been understood that the organized churches have themselves caused it. Denominational concepts have always occasioned differences and divisions, but in nondenominational Appalachia these differences and divisions became convulsive. Quarreling about religion became a commonplace as some Appalachians began to be converted to the denominations. Those not converted, by far in the majority, were bitterly antagonistic, as neighborhoods, communities, even families were split over the problem.

The Bible, the Appalachian Christian said, did not say anything about organizing churches, having church membership rolls, central organizations, using church literature, and the like. All these things had been "added to." Jesus said simply, "On this rock I will build my church." The Appalachian Christian, instructed further by Paul, construes this to mean that "the church" is the body of people who have faith. "The church" has nothing to do with an organization.

The basis for this stricture against "adding to" or "taking from" the Bible is in the eighteenth and nineteenth verses of the twenty-second chapter of Revelation:

> For I testify unto every man that heareth the words of the prophecy of this book, If any man shall add unto these things, God shall add unto him the plagues that are written in this book.
> And if any man shall take away from the works of the book of this prophecy, God shall take away from his part out of the book of life, and out of the holy city, and from the things which are written in this book.

These are strong words for a man who believes literally, and they are a strong deterrent from having anything to do with the denominations. In particular, the Appalachian Christian inveighs against anything printed or written out, such as printed orders of worship, litanies, creeds, catechisms, church literature, even sermons written out, or notes used in the pulpit. These are all "added to." The preacher should preach from the Bible only and he should be "led by the Spirit."

Try to convince the Appalachian Christian that he is interpreting this passage in the wrong context and he will tell you that you are "taking from" the Scriptures. *The Bible says!*

That is the end of it. "Do you believe in the Bible?" he will ask. "Yes, but . . ." There are no ifs, ands, or buts about it to him. He cannot rationalize about it. It is too important. For as he believes literally in the Bible, so he believes in a literal heaven and hell. The sinner is doomed to everlasting torment. His only salvation is to "know the truth" and be "saved."

The Appalachian is "saved" when, in public meeting, through the leadership of the Spirit, there is no doubt left in him that God is speaking to him, that he has "broken through." He makes a public confession of his sins followed by a public profession of his faith. He is then baptized. He is now a Christian, but he has in no way joined a church.

Since the Appalachian's religious services are highly emotional, with much singing and richly cadenced preaching, it is possible to think that this mystical experience is as much the result of overcharged emotions as of the leading of the Spirit. But what man is qualified to judge? I do know the experience is not often faked. Nobody wants to fool God. That would get a man nowhere. So the Appalachian deeply desires this experience and strives to have it. Some men never have it, and it is a matter of grief to them and their families. There is a shred of hope for them in a scriptural passage which says some things not forgiven in this world may be forgiven in the next. My husband's father, so good and honorable a man, is one of those who cherishes that particular passage, for he has never been able to be "saved."

When the denominations came in, *anti*-denominationalism became rampant. Splinter groups broke off from parent denominations in an effort *not* to be denominational. Basic, was no central organization, but there began to be a great splitting of hairs over a great many things. Baptism to the Appalachian had always been simple immersion in some creek or river. Now there was quibbling over various forms. Communion had always been held when a group of elder Christians decided it was time. Now there was quarreling over how often to have it and in what manner. The Appalachian had always used a "dulcimore" and later a "banjer" and still later a "gittar" to accompany his hymn singing. Now there was strife over whether musical instruments of any kind should be used.

Two missions were established in our community in the late 1920's. They made some converts, and the divisiveness and strife they caused in families, neighborhoods and communities has lasted to this day. I doubt if any minister or worker in either mission ever knew, or knows, the extent of it, nor the deep resentment felt against them, for they were unfailingly treated with courtesy. One denomination practices plain dress and the women wear small white caps on their heads. A neighbor stood beside me not long ago watching a woman of that faith walk down the road. "If I could," she said bitterly, "I'd gather up every one of them white caps and burn 'em, and I wish there was a law to make all them people git out." By their singularity this sect offends not only the religious concepts but the social pattern of the area.

Both of these missions established social programs including nursing clinics. The people placidly made use of the nursing clinics and almost entirely ignored the religion. When good roads made it possible for the people to get to the county towns and to doctors, they quit using the nursing clinics and both missions closed the services. Both missions reached a peak of membership and influence in the 1940's and have been steadily diminishing ever since.

A multiplicity of denominations, which are *not* denominations, have now sprung up. Anyone who can find a few followers can set up another splinter group, and anyone "led of the Spirit" can be heard. No wonder the sensible Appalachian holds to his biblical Christianity and refuses to commit himself to any of them. It has become the tower of Babel all over again.

The biggest appeal any of the organized or established churches has for the Appalachian is its security. Paul laid down for the Appalachian Christian what he should do and should not do. The difficulty is that in this modern day there are many things Paul never dreamed of. All things worldly are to be shunned. The Appalachian sensibly knows that he lives in the world and must take heed of his basic needs. Things worldly relating to them, or making his living, are not barred.

14

But what would Paul consider "lusts of the flesh" today? One family may be so strict that radio and television are permitted only for hearing the news, weather, religious services. Another family, able to rationalize more, will not prohibit so rigidly. One woman may decide she may use cosmetics, cut her hair, wear modern dress. Another will do none of these things. The prohibition against "revellings" naturally includes parties, dances, skating rinks, bowling alleys, but does it also include movies, lodge meetings, certain kinds of community meetings? If he wants to be absolutely safe, the Appalachian Christian will bar everything but family gatherings and church meetings.

He is far from perfect in these things naturally, and when he errs he is said to "backslide." He slides back among the sinners, loses his place among the Christians. The Appalachian Christian feels that the denominational Christian has an easy way of it. He can sin and sin and sin and he does not lose his church membership. So if the Appalachian can bring himself to break with his age-old belief that it is a sin to "add to" the Bible and "join a church," he may go into one of the established churches. It is so comfortable to know that he cannot fall from grace. He can now relax and sin a little.

As with all primitives, who use a self-deprecating laughter as an armor against life's small tragedies, the Appalachian will joke about backsliding. "Well, I've done backslid," he will say and make a jest of it. "I knowed I would when Jim broke out that deck of cards." But it is not really a joking matter and he knows he must some time make amends. He *can* be saved again, by confessing his error and professing his faith again. The Appalachian Christian is required to forswear practically all pleasure, however, and it comes hard. Not yet, he says to himself, not yet awhile. But he does truly believe he will burn in hell if he does not at some time do it and make it stick.

The Appalachian must, too, please the Lord. Over the years he has adopted certain expressions which he uses almost as incantations. For instance, not wanting to give the slightest degree of offense by appearing ever to question the will of the Lord, or to seem rebellious against it, he says of all misfortune, big or little, "It was the Lord's will." "The Lord meant it to be," or, "It's hard, but if it's the Lord's will, His will be done."

One of the most maddening things about the Appalachian is his reluctance to commit himself definitely to any thing or any course of action. He will not do it if he can possibly avoid it, not even to a given chore or task or piece of work, or even to a definite appointment. For operating deep within him, elementally within him, is an uneasiness that by committing himself he may be tempting fate. He wards off any possibility of not fitting into the Lord's plans by saying, if reluctantly he must commit himself, "Well, if nothing don't happen."

Women are often more explicit. Sometimes I leave my mother-in-law at the end of a visit by saying, "I'll see you again next week." Invariably she replies, "Well, if the Lord's willing and nothing don't happen."

One never knows *what* the Lord has in mind and it is best, just in case He might mean for your old car not to start, or for you to be sick in bed Monday morning at ten o'clock, to genuflect a little in His direction.

The death ritual is very like that of all primitive societies, also, in particular the American Indian's. It is a time of very noisy mourning. The family will relive, over and over again the death scene. They will tell it in all its details. Much importance is attached to dying words. Prophecy is often read into them and many dying are believed to have a vision of heaven. "He knowed he was going," they may say, "and he seen a great light. With his last words he said the light would lead him home." Promises to the dying are *never* violated, no matter how inconvenient or uncomfortable they make those who promised. "I promised my mother on her deathbed . . ." "I promised my daddy as he lay dying . . ." These promises are sacred.

After a death, friends call in the home and there is much weeping, somber sympathy, long details of the illness and death, efforts at comfort — the most effective being, "He died a good Christian."

At the funeral, in the home or church, during the hymns and the preaching, the family often cry out, sob and moan.

But it is when the casket is opened for the "last look" that the most emotional scene takes place. Every member of a bereaved family will cry and scream and pray, but the nearest relative, the husband or wife, mother or father, will throw himself on the casket, tear at it, kiss the dead person, plead and pray and moan and sob, even sometimes tear at their own hair or dress. Often they collapse, faint, must be carried out.

This is ritual. For days those present will recall it and speak of it, saying approvingly, "She taken it hard." To take it hard is the last, final and best tribute the Appalachian can pay. There is criticism if it is not done. A young friend of mine lost her husband. A college graduate, she had learned more subdued ways. It was said, "She shorely didn't love him much. Nobody ain't ever seen her cry. She stood there like a stone by the grave. She never shed a tear."

A child is mourned forever, and an aged parent, a sister or brother is grieved for always. A husband or wife may remarry shortly, but no dishonor to the dead is meant. An Appalachian husband is so pampered that he is helpless without a wife to "do for him." An Appalachian woman especially with children needs help. One old man told me in sweet confidence, in the presence of his third wife, that he looked forward to living in heaven with all three of his wives. "I have been blessed," he said, "with three good Christian wives. I hope to spend eternity with them." The third wife looked placid about it.

The ritual of noisy and emotional mourning is slowly changing as the Appalachian becomes more and more exposed to other ways. Funerals are being held in funeral homes more often nowadays, and the people feel inhibited in the presence of outsiders.

The most tragic thing about the Appalachian's religion is that by its very lack of organization, the thing he most abhors, it has no order, no coherence, no authority except the Bible. It is without much comfort or solace to him. He has no real security in it. The religion itself makes him deeply apprehensive. He must take daily and constant care, and he lives in perpetual fear that he may in some way violate, or has in some way violated, the biblical laws and that he is eternally doomed. In our American society, in trouble a man may turn to his minister and be at least a little comforted. But Appalachia has rejected the minister. He has only friends and family who believe as he does. They turn ceaselessly to the Bible, but it is a melancholy consolation.

But however unattractive the Appalachian's religion may be to those accustomed to more austerity and dignity in their own, to ignore it is unrealistic. To assume that, because census statistics show that only 10 to 15 per cent of all Appalachians belong to churches, they are irreligious is to be statistically irresponsible. The figures prove only one thing — the Appalachian is not given to joining churches. To call an Appalachian Christian a "so-called" Christian, as some people do, is to be presumptuously arrogant.

A religion so basic and central that it informs, shapes and directs an entire society must not only be recognized, it must be reckoned with if genuine understanding of that society is to be achieved.

THE FAMILY

The Appalachian family is unusually close-knit, far more than the average American family, and the influences of the family, to a remarkable degree, endure all of an Appalachian's life.

In the beginning the closeness was inevitable, because in his deep isolation the family, in all of its ramifications, was the only society. With families staying rooted for nearly two hundred years, opening to receive and absorb influxes of newcomers, the society enlarged, but to an unusual degree it stayed family-connected. The habits and ways in the family, developed early, have come down very little changed through all the generations.

The immediate family is by no means an Appalachian's entire family. With seven, sometimes eight or nine, generations behind him in one small area, he has an enormous family-clan. The Appalachian has always delighted in big families for precisely this reason. Through many children who in turn married and had many children, he was furnished a community, a tribe or clan, which guarded against loneliness, was loyal in trouble, helpful in work, was his security against the helplessness of old age and was pleasant in social contacts. Besides, he had good scriptural authority for multiplying.

It is almost impossible now to untangle the interweaving of clan and family marriages. Second and third cousins frequently marry. Occasionally first cousins marry but not often. First cousins grow up so close to each other that they regard each other almost as brothers and sisters and the idea of marriage between them is not attractive.

My husband's family-clan is a good example of the intricacy of relationships. He is the seventh generation in one community. He has nieces and nephews who make the eighth generation. There is hardly a family, even with the slight influx of newcomers, in an area involving a dozen square miles to whom he is not related by blood or by marriage. One of the first lessons I learned upon coming into the family was never to venture an opinion about anybody. "That man is my third cousin," I would be told. Or, "She is my sister's sister-in-law." After putting my foot in a dozen or so times I learned to keep my mouth shut.

The immediate family is usually so close to aunts, uncles, grandparents, first cousins, that they are practically a part of it, but there is a clan closeness to every relative, there is clan pride and there is clan loyalty and helpfulness to the second, third and even fourth generations. What it amounts to is that all of Appalachia lives within the close ring of some family-clan. Within the immediate family the closeness is intensified. The homes are crowded with people and the Appalachian is never out of sight or sound of his family.

The Appalachian loves babies and small children with an abandon which is common to all primitive societies but is seldom seen elsewhere. Deep inside all primitive peoples is the instinctive knowledge that life is tragic. Life is hard and unpredictable and death is always the victor. In sophisticated society many intellectuals arrive at this same conviction, but it is elemental in the primitive.

The small child will be innocent, helpless, wholly happy only a brief time, then he must begin to assume life's hard load. The Appalachian treasures the brief, happy time. He and everybody in the family adores, pets, pampers, spoils, humors babies and small children until they often become young tyrants. Small mischiefs, rages, whims, are all indulged. The baby is offered food. He rejects it. Gentle laughter follows and he is not required to eat it. Medicine must be given. He spits it out. Only the knowledge the child is desperately ill will make the parent force the medicine down him. Otherwise he is allowed his way. He is humored in practically all of his wishes. He is never allowed to cry. A crying Appalachian baby will bring the entire family to see what is wrong, to try to pacify him. A sick Appalachian baby can throw the entire family into panic. He is the dear precious love of them all.

The Appalachian keeps his children small as long as he can. Before compulsory school age was set at six, Appalachian children were often kept at home to seven or eight. "He's too little," it was said. My husband was not allowed to go to school until he was eight. Children are allowed the bottle or breast until they themselves break the habit. I have seen children of three or four years come in from play, run to the mother, stand beside her to take the breast, then run back outside to play. Children are carried until they are physically too large for it. My husband's sister swung the last family baby onto her hip to carry until he was six years old.

The Appalachian has constant body contact with his baby. The Appalachian mother does not carry her child in a cradleboard, or make a sling for him from her shawl, but she or some member of the family does carry him. An Appalachian baby is held or carried constantly. He is always in body contact, warm, comforting, assuring, with someone who loves him.

The baby sleeps with the father and mother. No Appalachian mother would think of putting her baby into a bed alone. He is kept with her so that she may feed him in the night, change him, know that he is warm and safe. When he is supplanted by a new baby he is moved into a bed, usually in the same room, with an older brother or sister. Or, as the family grows, the father and mother may cease sleeping with each other and each may take a room and a child into bed with him. My husband slept with his father until he was twelve years old.

It is necessary eventually to put children into another room. It is always the oldest who are moved and always, if possible, both the room and the bed are shared with a member of the family. "I wouldn't want him to be skeered," the parents say. Few Appalachian children ever know the terrors of the child alone in the night. There is always the blessed warmth of a mother, or father, an older sister or brother, grandmother, aunt, uncle. This habit of body touch, body contact, makes for an extremely close-knit family.

To the sophisticated man the lack of privacy would be unendurable. To the Appalachian, privacy would be loneliness. It is this very closeness he cherishes. When you are never alone, when the family is all around you, touching, talking, working together, a great feeling of security builds up. This is the reason the Appalachian child can get so dreadfully homesick away from home at night. We all know the feeling of homesickness, but the Appalachian child can feel it so deeply that he can become actually physically ill, have nausea and fever. The Appalachian never entirely outgrows this homesickness for his family.

As the Appalachian child grows older he begins to shape and form in the mold of his society. To an outsider it might seem as if he had very little training, but he has been taught many things and he has been steadily admonished in how he is to behave. He has learned even more from watching his parents, older brothers and sisters, the rest of his family-clan. He absorbs as much by example as by precept.

Appalachian families visit much together. "Taking the day" with each other, and the church meeting, are the only social affairs. Inarticulate with outsiders, in a family gathering there is enough chatter to last the week, news is exchanged, family jokes are told, there is laughter. With the family the Appalachian is gay. He has a fine, dry wit and a way of turning a phrase pungently and effectively. He especially loves an inverted joke on himself. He misses a shot at a rabbit. He goes into great detail to tell how stupid he was. He makes a trip to the city. It will take him an hour to recount all the disasters that happened to him — all, naturally, because he was a hillbilly in the city. With his own kind the Appalachian is genial, warm, full of fun and comfortable laughter.

All of this the growing child takes in, listens to, absorbs. It becomes part of him, the way he is going to be. His growing up is so wholly understood by the child and parent and family that a look, one murmured word, the tone of voice, the bodily stance, the set of mouth, the way a comment or question is framed, all can give him instantly a clue as to what is expected of him, what is thought of him, whether he is being approved or disapproved. He becomes by the time he is grown one of the most sensitively perceptive human beings to be found, a person who seems able to absorb the climate of personal weather almost through his skin.

Appalachians do not often resort to physical punishment with their children. They use instead something perhaps more cruel — shame. A child is "shamed" out of bad habits, or bad behavior. He is made to look foolish and ridiculous before others. This is so crushing to him that he never in all his life outgrows his shrinking from it. He cannot bear to be made to look ridiculous, even as an adult, and knowing how he shrinks from it himself he will inflict it upon another only if that person is his enemy. It is the surest weapon he has with which to cause hurt.

All of this, the closeness, the immediate and mutual understanding, are blood, body ties never to be entirely broken. All his life the Appalachian feels safest when close by his own people. My husband feels like a displaced person if he must live more than three miles from his parents. And these ties even enshrine the homeland. The Appalachian knows every rock, every tree, every riffle in every creek, every hole in the river, every path up the mountain. They are all family-connected, family-associated, family-dear.

Though he is an obedient child when the parent sets his foot down, the lack of discipline in his formative years contributes to some lacks in the adult Appalachian. Allowed his whims as a child, the adult is impulsive. Not required to stick to things he does not like, or in situations he does not like, the adult lacks self-discipline. Having been allowed to follow and drop interests at will, his time-span of interest as an adult is brief. He recognizes none of these things in himself. The phrase the Appalachian uses constantly for his shifts and changes is, "I didn't like." Whatever the adult Appalachian does not like, he does not often do if he can help it.

Our people are trying to go to the cities — Detroit, Chicago, Indianapolis, Cincinnati. Some of them stay. Many, however, come back in a few months. "He didn't like," the people say. No other reason needs to be given. Everybody understands that if you "don't like," of course you "don't stay." And then they say, "I knowed he wouldn't like. It goes so foolish off there."

He didn't like. To a man whose feet are used to walking on the earth, city pavements can be very hard. To a man used to the quiet of the hills, city noises can be maddening and wearying. To a man used to the warm closeness of family and clan, strangers and strange customs make the soul sick. To a man used to choosing what he will do this day, the assembly line is death itself. No amount of money, no job, no added conveniences in living, can make up to him for what he loses. Like the Cheyennes who sickened and died removed from their homeland, the Appalachian is only half alive away from Appalachia.

So he comes home and his homecoming is an occasion for joy. He has come back, where he belongs, whence he should never have strayed. There is a saying about those who leave and come back. "Well," it is said, "he had shoes, so he left out." Which is to say he was restless, he had to go out and try, but he came to his senses and came home.

And he *can* come home. That is why the Appalachian will give up a job another man might hang on to for dear life. There is a little piece of land, there is a rooftree, there is the family, the clan, the tribe. He can pull in his belt and "make out." If it takes public assistance to do it, all right. Many

23

would far rather take it than to wither, soul- and heartsick, away from home. The youngest generation has the best chance of making the transfer less painfully, but even for them it is a dreadful wrench and they make long trips home for holidays, birthdays, and any weekend they can get away. Like Antaeus, the Appalachian must renew his strength by touching the mother-earth. Not until there is a new generation, born out of Appalachia, will the transplant be complete.

If it is understood how enormously the Appalachian is influenced by his religious concepts and his very close family ties, it will be understood that he is not at all the individualist legend has made him. He is actually one of the most conforming conformists to be found, but he conforms to something so different from what the average American knows that it cannot be recognized.

Even his freedoms are conforming freedoms in his own society. For generations he has been free to hunt and fish, come or go, work or visit, when he pleased. In his entire society it was customary. The man who did not would have been the individualist, the nonconformist. So, when the condition of the river and the weather of the day are right for fishing, he drops everything to go. The same is true of hunting. For generations he has supplemented his diet with fish and game. He still does, and when the time is ready to hunt squirrels, rabbits, birds, ducks, deer, nothing is more important than to go hunting. It is time, and the old instincts go to work and the gun and the dog and the man are ready.

The Appalachian has had very little experience in planning for the future, or even very far ahead. In the long experience of his people it was never necessary. The land gave him what he needed. If it was marginal, out of touch as he was with anything better he was not aware of it. He had no need to plan for the future because it was right there, where the present was, and it was safe and secure. In the mining regions when the coal companies came in, the Company took the place of the land. The Company took care of him. It, too, would always be there.

Until the last fifty years the Appalachian had very little need of money, did not have much, set no great store by it. It was primarily for buying things he could not grow or make at home. He tried to keep a little by for paying the doctor if there was illness in the family. He did not need it when he died. Friends prepared him for burial, built his coffin, dug his grave, and buried him in the family burying ground or the neighborhood burying ground where burial was free.

To this day he is not realistic about money. Money and basic needs have been slow to make a connection in his mind. It has never been a status symbol with him and it is still to buy what he wants and to spend generously on his family and friends. When he has spent his money, he does not value greatly what it has bought. An Appalachian does not take good care of a car, or any expensive equipment for the home, or for that matter good clothing. He has no acquisitive sense nor does he treasure or guard what little he acquires. For so long he did not need it and he can still do without much of it. What is standard for the average American is luxury to him, pleasant to have if possible and convenient, but in no way essential.

His long years of self-sufficiency on the land developed in the Appalachian a reluctance to ask a favor, except in kind. He did not need favors and, if he did, he felt he should not have and he felt shame for it. To have to ask a favor filled him with such discomfort and humiliation that he would suffer almost anything rather than endure it.

Asking for work is asking for a favor. The average American can walk into an office, apply for a job, give his qualifications and feel no sense of humiliation. His need for what the Appalachian contemptuously calls "public work" and his pride in his own qualifications make it an acceptable thing for him.

With the Appalachian it is different. Under no necessity to do "public work" generally, when or if he had to work "out" it was an admission that he had failed in his own work. He had not made enough to provide for his family that year, so he had to go out and do "public work." It was humiliating because he had it to do, it was humiliating when he stood before a foreman or "boss" and asked for work. Many who needed the work could never force themselves to endure this crawling, raw sense of shame and humiliation felt in asking for it. The Appalachian could not see it as a creditable thing to do. To him, it was failure, a public admission of failure.

He still does not like to apply for work. The old discomfort holds over. With our people who do go away to work nowadays this discomfort is eased by an intermediary. A few brave souls, mostly of the younger and television-educated generation, pave the way. They go first, find employment, and they then bring in their relatives and friends to work in the same great factory, plant or industry. I have never yet heard one of our people leave to go out to work without the explanation, "My cousin has got me a job where he works," or some other relative or friend. Slowly whole colonies are built up in one city, usually in one area of a city, so that friends, neighbors and relatives do not give up all their ties with home. Such colonies frequently become known as "Little Kentucky," and all too often they are grievous problems to state and civic organizations.

In the mining regions, the first Appalachians to go into the mines were sought. The companies needed them. The jobs were opened to them. Once employed, the people brought in their family and friends. The mines affected the economy of dozens of counties in eastern Kentucky and western West Virginia, but it should be remembered that even in the times of their peak operation they did not employ more than one tenth of the total population of those counties. It should also be said that it was mostly the already victimized Appalachian who went to work in the mines. To this day the Appalachian with a "scope" of land his own, able to manage yet for himself, calls mining "hand to mouth" work. In our section of Appalachia "sawmilling" is in the same category.

The Appalachian has never had any experience in getting out and bucking for work in a competitive society. And I have never heard an Appalachian who has gone outside and gotten work speak with pride of it, as he often did of his fine burley crop, or his corn or his wheat. He is working for money now, doing what has become necessary, since he has become an anachronism. Many, who cannot bring themselves to go out to work, sit and wish for things to be the way they used to be, and, in order to live at all, many go on public assistance.

Let me make it clear immediately that not all of Appalachia is on public assistance as would seem to be the case by the television and newspaper coverage of the area. There are many, and they are in the majority, who manage, somehow, never to take public assistance. Proudly, stubbornly, they hang on. They feel very much about any interference with them as the Boston West-Ender did who voiced his protest to urban renewal so vehemently that all of America heard it over television: "It is my Constitutional right to be ignorant and poor if I want to be!"

Deep inside their hearts many Appalachians feel like that. They wish to be let alone. They do not want to be done good to. There is in them still the old independent spirit. They take care of themselves, pay their way, and ask no more than any other American from their government. And they are deeply ashamed of the kind of picture and kind of story that television, magazines and newspapers have given to the nation, for they know how these have been deliberately slanted to portray the worst to be found in Appalachia. And the worst is never typical of the whole.

In addition to the miners out of work, who, the rest of us are the first to admit, need help badly, we have also in Appalachia the permanently poor who are to be found everywhere, in all societies. They are the unemployables, the hopeless, the broken poor who crowd city slums and the rural south as well by the millions. They are permanently on welfare here as they are everywhere else. They have always had to be helped and I am not hopeful that any time soon they will not have to be helped. But however badly off they may be here, they are not nearly so hopeless and badly off as they would be in slums, for here they have friends and relatives and neighbors who do care and who do help as much as they can.

It must be admitted, however, that we do have now in Appalachia a growing attitude of cynicism and chauvinism. It took the Appalachian a while to catch on to what every other American has known for generations — that government is the biggest employer, the biggest benefactor, the biggest business in America and that there is a nice, big, fat public trough out of which the shrewd man can feed, on the county, state or federal level, for most of his life. The Appalachian sees it being done all around him on the local, county and state levels. He has long had experience with the political patronage jobs in his county, and he has done his part to get as many of them for himself and his family as he can, through his vote.

Especially in the last decade the Appalachian has come to look on public assistance as that part of the public trough most readily open to him. He lumps them all together, county, state or federal, from public commodities to Social Security, from old-age pensions to farm subsidies, as "giveaways," the big governmental grab-bag into which it would not be realistic of him not to plunge his hand.

Behind the desk to which he must apply sits most often a person he knows to have ties with some political power, who is rewarded through kinship, through political pull, through political patronage, with the job he holds. The Appalachian does not rate that kind of patronage, perhaps, but with hard-nosed realism that same man who would not tell you a lie, who will not misrepresent one slightest thing about a property he sells you, who would cut off his hand before he would steal, is not too scrupulous about how he gets his share. He often gets it through his own small political pull — his vote. Through his family-clan he may control as many as twenty or thirty votes. He may, in some cases, control an entire precinct.

It has been said that the Appalachian is keenly interested in politics largely because it affords him a respite from boredom. Respite from boredom indeed! On election day the Appalachian who controls a clan vote is a very valuable man. He has long ago picked his candidate, he has literally "run" with his man with much and wide use of bumper stickers, campaign buttons, his influence in the neighborhood. He has a very real stake in a campaign, for he knows perfectly well if he scratches a winner's back, his back will be scratched in return.

It is difficult to understand why this is condemned in the Appalachian and so approved in the rest of society. This philosophy is operative throughout the world. Practically everybody who goes to the polls casts his vote in self-interest. What will it get me? My family? My business? My power group? My union? My race? This philosophy even underlies our foreign policy. We win friends with foreign aid. But hands are held up in holy horror over the single-vote Appalachian, the "floater" who is given a half-pint of whiskey or a couple of dollars when he "votes right." He does not feel he has sold his vote. This is his tiny bit of patronage. The big clan-vote Appalachian can expect more, a patronage job or — and it amounts to precisely the same thing in his eyes — eligibility to be put on one more "draw" for him or some member of his family.

In the seventeen years I have lived as a Giles in the Giles-ridden north end of Adair County I have witnessed some changes. We have electricity now. We have a road-net of paved roads. The long generations of isolation are ending. Our people can get in and out of the area now and can move around more freely within it. We even have telephones. With good roads the school system is slowly doing away with the little one-room schools. Children today ride to the consolidated schools over the new paved roads in big yellow school busses. Hot lunches are served in the cafeterias. No child takes his "dinner" today in the old-fashioned lard bucket. How much virtue there is in the consolidated schools will take another generation to determine. Something good, intimate and small, has no doubt been lost. It is to be hoped something better has been found.

But the greatest change in the ways and habits of our people has come about through a strange medium — television. Almost every home has a television set nowadays, and its visible, tangible impact has been greater than a hundred years of preaching and teaching. Not all of its impact is good, but it has helped change diet, habits of dress, it has brought new

29

standards of beautification around and inside the homes, it has brought a different kind of speech and music into the homes, even a different concept of religion. Bought for entertainment, television is a most subtle and powerful educator. In one decade, ten short years, I have seen our people changed more by television than by any other medium.

Whether these changes will create a happier, more truly abundant life for Appalachians remains to be seen. For a long time they had something very beautiful and something intrinsically very valuable. They were a beautiful people. But it is axiomatic that a strong, dominant culture, such as that of the Great Society, cannot tolerate an alien culture within it. It is beside the point to regret change and to lament the loss of old values and old ways, the profound sense of human dignity, the gentle courtesy, the strong family love and loyalties. This nation, for some reason, cannot abide differentness. Every one and everything must adjust, conform and be standardized. The Appalachian may soon be standardized into another American legend.

For myself, I am glad I had some years as a member of this society before it began to change. I am glad I saw it lit by kerosene lamps and warmed by wood-burning stoves. I am even glad I made use of an outdoor privy and walked a dirt road. I am glad I helped spring-pole a well and raise a tobacco crop. I can, if it is necessary, do these things again without feeling the least bit underprivileged or substandard. My standards are entirely my own, not those of the Great Society, and they do not necessarily include central heating, modern plumbing, electricity and paved roads. They do include woods and hills and living water, books and open fires, excellent home-raised food and work that challenges. All else can be used if available and done easily without if necessary.

Chapter

1

ᕙ ᕙ ᕙ

I want to be as honest as I can in telling this story of our first year on the ridge. I would like to avoid a too rapturous description of the beauty and peace of life in the country. The beauty is certainly here, and the peace, but they are not the whole story, and if I dwell on them at too great length and too nostalgically I shall not be telling the truth. There are practical, even harsh things, about country life, and they must be told too.

And there are all kinds of people here, just as there are everywhere else. Some are good, some are bad, and I've mixed them all in, in a sort of high, wide, and handsome way with the account of our own activities. The story moves rather loosely through that first hot summer when we labored so terribly over our house, garden, and tobacco crop, through the fall with the cutting and stripping of the tobacco and the building of our fireplace, into the cold and mud and isolation of the winter, back around to tobacco time again. One year on the ridge. Not exactly a typical year, for we were not a typical ridge family. But a year of backaches, fun, low ebbs and high tides, and above all a year of eminent satisfaction.

I turned my face toward these Kentucky hills and set my feet on the old dirt road that winds and twists down Giles Ridge in the summer of 1943. But I didn't know it. I thought I was starting to West Texas.

It was July. Hot, sticky, and steamy as it usually is in Louisville in July. I was secretary to the dean of the Louisville

Presbyterian Theological Seminary, and I was starting my vacation. Because of a mix-up in office schedules I had been compelled to cancel my train reservations, and, taking my courage in my hands, I was going by bus. I checked all my luggage through except one small bag, dressed comfortably in a cotton dress which had a jacket for cool nights, stowed my mile-long ticket in my purse, and crawled on the bus at two o'clock on the afternoon of July 12. The bus was full, but not crowded. I thought maybe it wasn't going to be too bad.

Bowling Green was the scheduled supper stop, although we got in there at five thirty. I remember seeing a soldier standing nearby when the bus nosed into the dock. I remember also thinking how clean he looked in his summer tans, and thinking too how differently individual soldiers wore the uniform. Some were never neat, never clean-looking, always mussed and rumpled. This man was one of those who wore the uniform with distinction. All of that flitted through my mind and was gone in a second. After all, I lived in Louisville, and there had been a deluge of soldiers in that city since the fall of 1941. One more soldier certainly didn't make too much of an impression on me.

The soldier was the only new passenger getting on at Bowling Green, and there were only two vacancies on the bus— one on the long seat across the rear, and the seat by me. He grinned at me and took that one.

Well, that is how I started my journey toward the ridge. For the soldier was Henry Giles. When he wants to tease me now, he tells people he picked me up on a bus. That's as may be. For a pickup I must not have been very promising. I was in my middle thirties and looked it. There wasn't a thing girlish-looking about me. As a matter of fact I was the mother of an eighteen-year-old daughter, whom I had reared alone. On top of that I have always had a certain dignity in my bearing which does not encourage brashness. But, my goodness, you can't be seatmates with a person on a forty-eight-hour bus trip, sitting beside him, eating beside him, even sleeping beside him, without settling down eventually into a sort of friendly familiarity.

Before we got to Dallas, where Henry had to branch off to go to Austin and Camp Swift, we had gone through everything but a major catastrophe together. He had even passed me off as his wife in order to get me on a special bus with him, and I had rifled his pockets to find his pass when the MP's checked the bus once when he was asleep. When we said good-by in Dallas, I felt as if I were leaving a very old and dear friend. He had told me about his home, his people, some of his experiences in the Army, and many of his wants and desires in life. I suppose I had told him much of the same sort of thing.

We promised to keep in touch with each other, and of course one thing led to another, and by the time he went overseas we were planning to be married. Two years and 769 letters later we were. That was October of 1945.

Chapter

2 ↙↙

The first time I saw the ridge I didn't believe it. I was like the man who stood on the rim of the Grand Canyon. I saw it, but I still didn't believe it. And you wouldn't either. It was the summer of 1944. Henry and I were engaged. He was overseas, but he had written his people about me and they had invited me to visit them when I could. The first good chance was my vacation that summer. I arranged to spend the first week of it on the ridge, and they wrote me to take the bus to Campbellsville and said someone would meet me there. I had never seen any of Henry's family, but he had sent them my picture, and, " We'll know you the minute we see you," they promised.

Henry's oldest sister, Irene, was the one who met me. She and her husband and three small children lived in Detroit, but when Charlie was called into service, she took the children and rented a small house near her parents on the ridge. There were two reasons for this. She didn't want to be alone in the city while he was gone, and she thought she could stretch his allotment check farther in the country. I think I should have known her, although I had never seen her before. She looked quite a bit like Henry.

She led me to a car parked across the street. I should say she led me to what had once been a car. It must have been at least twenty years old, the doors wired shut, most of the upholstery gone, and I couldn't tell whether it sagged from the load it was carrying or from a couple of broken springs. It belonged to a man who ran a tiny store on the ridge and it was packed with bags of feed, flour, meal, and other supplies for the store. Perhaps this is as good a place as any to explain the transportation system on the ridge. There isn't any. If you have a car, well and good. If you don't, you hitch rides with people who do have one. And in emergencies or crises you get anyone who will go to drive you to the doctor or wherever you must go. In that case, when you ask a man to stop work and make a special trip for you, you pay him, of course. Not much. I think the folks paid this man one dollar to bring Irene to meet me. For the round trip, that is, and it's twenty miles from the ridge to Campbellsville. You can see that no one gets rich running a taxi on the ridge.

But I didn't know anything about the ridge taxi system then, so I eyed the car distrustfully, hoped I was mistaken, then accepted the inevitable and crawled into the back, wedging myself down between two sacks of feed which I knew were going to play havoc with my black linen dress. I was lucky, had I but known it. The way I went back to Campbellsville a week later was on a truck with six goats, a cow, and two pigs!

We left Campbellsville on a black-top highway and I chattered away with Irene. She was friendly, warm, and sweet. I liked her a lot. I had to keep shoving the feed off of me, for every time we went around a curve — and Kentucky highways are all curves — one sack or the other fell over on top of me. But I didn't truly mind. I didn't even mind what was happening to my black linen dress.

I noticed that the farms were fairly large, the valley we were following was broad and swelling, and the land looked rich. We went through two small villages, then abruptly the

34

black-top gave out and we were on a graveled road. It was washboardy, rutted, and very, very dusty. There were chuckholes big enough to bury a horse in, as the driver said — one of the two remarks he made on the entire trip. The other one was when the car door came unwired and flew open, spilling out my bag, several sacks of flour, and a carton of snuff, which broke and sent the little round boxes flying in every direction. After he had picked up everything and stored it back inside, he said mildly, "Got to git that door fixed one of these days."

The graveled road wound around the base of the hills very intimately, for the valley had narrowed and the farms were getting progressively smaller and poorer-looking. Back up in the hollows I saw occasionally a tired-looking little shanty perched on the side of a hill, never underpenned, never painted, barely roofed and holding together. Then we went through Knifley and I knew we were only a few miles from the ridge. For Knifley was the post-office address of Henry's family, and he had told me the ridge was only five or six miles beyond.

We came to the top of a long, winding hill, and here we turned down the final lap of the trip — the ridge road. You may think you have seen bad roads, but unless you have driven down our ridge road, you haven't seen anything! It is so narrow that you can't pass at all. When you meet someone, you must pull off into either a field, the woods, or the precarious edge of a hollow. If you have just passed a house, the simplest thing to do is to back up until you can pull into the yard. The road is deeply rutted where there is soil enough to rut. And rocky, with small sharp-edged boulders, where the soil has washed away. In the summertime it is churned to a fine, powdery dust which sifts over the trees and bushes, into the houses, and even into your hair and clothes when you are in the house. In the wintertime it becomes a sea of mud, hub-deep on a wagon, and all passenger cars simply have to quit traveling.

When we started down this road, Irene turned to me and grinned. "Hold onto your hat!" she said. And believe me I did. I have heard Henry say since we ourselves moved to the ridge that in the two and one half miles from our house to the pike you have to change gears exactly twenty-four times. I don't drive, so I wouldn't know, but the only thing that surprises me about that figure is that it isn't larger. That first day I just held on grimly and felt like the old woman who awakened with her petticoats sheared off and cried, "Lawkamercy, me, this is none of I! "

We crawled along in and out of the ruts, the car never on an even keel. When we hit bottom the first time, I bit my tongue. The next time, one sack of feed toppled off the seat and the other one fell on me and jammed me up against the side of the car. I thought I had cracked a rib, and the whole week I was on the ridge my side was black and blue and very sore to touch. I took my hat off. There wasn't time to be grabbing at it. I needed both hands and feet to take care of myself.

Even so, the beauty of the hills made me catch my breath. We are not in the mountains of Kentucky. They lie far to the east of us. At no place in our hills are we more than seven or eight hundred feet above sea level. But just the same it is rough, rugged country. As you drive south from Louisville you wind through the beautiful Bluegrass country. It is rolling to level. And then in Marion County you come into that narrow ten-mile strip known as the Knobs. This is a band of sharp, conical hills which surround the Bluegrass. You climb steeply out of them up the main escarpment, Muldraugh's Hill, and you are then on what is geologically known as the Pennyroyal plains. There is nothing plainlike about this section, except that it is higher than the country through which you have come. Our hills begin now. And they grow progressively rougher and more rugged the farther south you go. They are tumbled closely together, with deep, steep hollows gashing their sides, and the roads must wind around and between them. Only little dirt roads like ours venture off down the spiny backs of the ridges. Every spur, every hollow, every ridge has its name, but combined they form the Tennessee Ridge, which is like long vertebrae snaking slowly southward into Tennessee. Giles Ridge, then, is like one little bone in the spinal column, and a very small one at that.

I don't know how to tell you of its indescribable beauty. You

36

are in the midst of hills in every direction. There seems no end to them. And as you drive slowly down the road there are openings in the trees through which you look off over sweet, swelling valleys. The Green River valley is to one side of our ridge and the Crooked Creek valley to the other. And there is one place where the road is merely a saddle across the narrow hump of the ridge so that you look down in either direction onto farms and homes and the green fringe of trees down the watercourses. On a clear winter day, when the trees are stripped bare of leaves, I can climb the slope back of our house and look out across five ridges, each rising a little higher than the one before, and I can see the sun glinting on the tin roof of a barn over on the last ridge. In between, the mists will be rising, like pale smoke, hugging close to the streams down in the hollows.

Clutching as I was any stable thing in the car to hold onto, I was aware of this beauty around me. Henry had been right. He had told me the ridge was so lovely it hurt. But I was also aware of other things, and he had told me about them too. Most of the houses were slatternly, unkempt things sitting sullenly beside the road, yards grown up in weeds, roofs sagging, broken windows grinning like snaggled teeth, chimneys tumbling down. Occasionally there was a better house, but on all the ridge there is not one home that by modern standards could be considered a good one. Electricity has come now, through the rural electrification program, and many of the houses are wired for lights, and most of them have refrigerators and washing machines, but to this day, and this includes our own home, there isn't one that has water in the house or any form of central heating. The largest homes have four or five rooms. The smallest have one. It is a poor, poor section of the country.

What disturbed me even more than the homes was the people. Too often we saw hordes of dirty, unkempt children playing about in the yards with ragged, moth-eaten cats and dogs. Too often they stared at us with the vacant look of malnutrition and the blank stare of stupidity born of low mentality. Too often the women and the men did the same. A great many of the women I saw were thin, stooped, gaunt, and haggard-looking, breastless and paunched, blear-eyed and snaggle-toothed. And the men were as gaunt as the women, as stooped and paunched. But men fare better in this country than women do. The greater burden of poverty seems usually to fall on women.

The home of Henry's people was not as large as the better homes we had passed on the road, but neither was it anything like as poor as some. It was old, for Henry's grandfather had built it, but it had a clean, curried look about it. It was uncluttered and tidy, and when I stepped inside I was carried right back to my grandmother's fireside. There was the same mingled smell of fresh-scrubbed floors and wood smoke. The same slow-ticking clock on the wall. The same spaciousness in the rooms. And there were Henry's people. From the first they were like my own folks to me, and I felt at home with them.

There was Henry's mother, whom I call Miss Bessie, thin and stooped like the women we had passed, but dark and beautiful. Sometimes when I look at her I think she is the most beautiful woman I ever saw. She has long hair which has never been cut, and she wears it drawn severely back from her face and wound into a heavy knot on the back of her head. When I first saw her it was as black as a raven's wing. Now it is turning gray, but it is still so smooth you want to run your hand over its shiny, glossy surface. The severity of her hair makes the bone structure of her face stand clean and clear, exactly as if it had been carefully chiseled. Her eyes are brown, fine, clear and deep, speckled a little with green, like the sides of a speckled trout. In the middle of her chin is the same deep dimple she passed on to Henry. The minute I saw her I loved her.

There was Henry's father, Mr. Frank. White-haired, round-shouldered, bulky and big. All his goodness and tenderness shines in his face, with its shy, habitual half-smile. But his mischief shows in his eyes, which twinkle with a deep-blue glint. In the years since, I have never known him to say a cross or ugly word, nor to show a moment of impatience or intolerance either with persons or with situations. As a matter of fact, I have never seen his slow-moving body hurry but once. That was when the old cow fell over the cliff and got wedged in the bottom of the hollow. He made tracks mighty fast that time!

There was Robert, the second son, who had polio when he was a baby and has never walked. Robert, the omnivorous reader of the family, who is widely traveled through his books and radio, and who can tell you at a moment's notice the population, the form of government, and the customs of the people of any country in the world. He has been to Campbellsville twice in his life. But he will talk to you by the hour of the history of Thailand. He reads encyclopedias as other people read fiction.

There was Cora Mae, the second daughter, beautiful, shy, awkward, timid, and with the loveliest cloud of silvery-yellow hair curled about her face I had ever seen. She was fifteen then, and sweet beyond words.

And then there was Kenneth, the baby son. He was just starting to school that summer. Kenneth is what is called around here a "change baby." Long after Miss Bessie thought her childbearing days were over he made an unexpected, and it may be even an unwelcome, appearance. But that was only temporary. He became the darling of the family at once, and he has always been our special pride and joy.

When I wrote to Henry that night, Kenneth asked if he might write him too. I said yes, and added that I would enclose his letter with mine. He got down his first reader, and he painfully copied the first page in large, block-printed letters. He didn't separate the words, or punctuate. When he came to the end of a line, it didn't matter if he was in the middle of a word. I remember "you" being divided "y" and "ou." Henry said it was worse than a Chinese puzzle, but it had been an eminently satisfying effort to Kenneth. I can see him yet, sitting in the middle of the floor, his face red and sweating, his tongue bitten between his teeth as he struggled to make the letters.

He walked with me the half mile to the mailboxes the next

morning to take the letter. It was in my purse. Shortly after we left the house he looked up at me. " I kin pack yer purse," he said.

" Oh, it isn't heavy," I answered, but when his little face settled with disappointment it dawned on me why he wanted to carry it. The letter, of course. So I surrendered the purse at once, and he gripped it proudly the rest of the way in his small, sweaty hands.

He is a great talker, Kenneth. I remember Miss Bessie warned me he would talk my arm off. That morning he got started on sweat bees, for they were thick along the road, and it took him clear to the mailboxes to tell me what he knew about them. And don't think he didn't know. For not only was he a great talker, he was unusually observant, and he remembered and thought about what he observed. At six he knew more about the wildlife all around him than most ridge men know in a lifetime.

He had no sense of time yet, and he began looking for an answer to his letter the next day. And because he did not have any sense of distance either, we could not help him to understand how far away Henry was and how long it would take for his letter to reach him. He continued to be bitterly disappointed each day when there was no letter for him. I was not there of course when the answer finally came, but I know it did come, for Miss Bessie wrote me that Kenneth had got his letter, addressed to him, and that he carried it with him constantly. Henry had written him as seriously as if he had been his own age, thanking him for his letter and not once suggesting that its subject matter had been unusual, and telling him about a little French boy who came to their camp for gum and candy.

The thing I loved Henry's people most for, however, was a tact born of inherent courtesy. However much they may have wanted to know about me and my life, about how Henry and I had met, about any plans we may have made for the future, not one question was ever asked. They surrounded me with a gracious hospitality, a glad welcome, and listened carefully to anything I wanted to tell them. And that is still true. My mother-in-law is the perfect mother-in-law. She pours out her love and devotion to us in the most unselfish sort of way. If we needed the roof off her house, she would not hesitate to give it to us. But she leaves us entirely and completely free. She does not bind us to her with obligations, and she does not probe into our affairs. Not once has she ever given me a word of advice, except when I asked for it. That is good breeding. And that is selfless love.

No, I did not feel strange with Henry's people. They were too close kin to my father's. But I did feel strange when we went out someplace. I had never seen hill farms before, with corn and tobacco slanting down the steep sides of the hills. There were few tractors here. There was a man and a mule and a plow. And beside the road there were the battened houses, with dogs and children and chickens sprouting from every square inch of yard. There were the women with their starched sunbonnets, their feed-sack dresses, their lips of snuff and cuds of tobacco. There were the men with their sweaty bodies and dirt-stiffened overalls, and their week's growth of beard. Men shave only once a week on the ridge, Saturday or Sunday morning usually. There was the queer, drawling speech, the primitive household ways, the outspoken curiosity about my job, my clothes, Henry and me. I did indeed feel strange then as if I had been set down in a different world altogether.

And one night we went to meetin'. We walked three miles down the hollow by lantern light, the girls and I giggling and stumbling along behind, Miss Bessie and Mr. Frank upholding the dignity of the family up front. Miss Bessie frowned on us equally when we came in sight of the tent. " Now you girls jist settle down. I'm not aimin' to have you actin' up in front of folks! "

It was a White Cap meeting. The White Caps are a small group of people who migrated into Kentucky some thirty years ago from Pennsylvania, taking up a sort of mission work among the hill people. They came to America originally from Switzerland in 1770, and they are descendants of the Mennonites. Their official name is the Church of the Brethren in

Christ, but we call them White Caps because of the small, sheer white bonnets the women wear constantly. The women also dress uniformly in long-sleeved, round-necked dresses, wearing no jewelry of any kind, not even wedding rings. The men wear sober, plain suits, with vests and no ties. Doctrinally they believe in the imminence of the Second Coming of Christ and live in constant readiness for it. They believe in baptism by trine immersion, and in the washing of the feet of the saints.

I have seen the Negro camp meeting in the South, and a few times I have attended a Holy Roller meeting. But I had never seen anything before like the White Cap meeting that night. Not only was there the emotional release of shouting, singing, praying, and crying, but to me there was a new type of preaching. Here in the hill country a preacher is considered good when he works up to a pitch of speaking that to the uninitiated is entirely unintelligible. It is delivered in a high monotone, in rapid, running form, punctuated with "ahs" every few words. "I tell you, ah, my brethren, ah, that the time, ah, is coming, ah, when every man, ah, shall be judged, ah, and be found wanting, ah. . . ." There never seems to be a period or a paragraph. The faster he goes, the more "ahs" he gets in, the higher and shriller his voice becomes, the more emotional the congregation becomes. They begin to swing and sway and to chant with him, crying, "Yes, Lord!" and, "Amen!" until finally the tension becomes unbearable and someone "gets happy." Then pandemonium breaks loose. I lost track of the preacher's subject after the first five minutes when he was still working up steam. After that, and I do not mean it disrespectfully — I am trying to tell the truth — it sounded to me exactly like the chant of a tobacco auctioneer.

That is the kind of preaching the hill people want and understand. That kind of preaching is not reserved wholly to the White Caps. It is also true of the primitive Baptists and the Church of God. The people expect to be stirred emotionally. They have no use for the calm, quiet delivery of the city minister. They do not want a learned exegesis of Scripture. They know their Scripture, thank you, and they'll make their own interpretation of it. They want to be lifted out of their seats, made to feel guilty for their sins, made to sing and shout, made to repent and to weep and wail. They want to "get happy" with their religion.

I was fascinated by it — fascinated, truth to tell, by the whole ridge, and from then on I fairly haunted it.

Chapter

3 ↙ ↙

But there is a vast difference between loving to visit a place, being fascinated by it, being interested in it, and living in that same place. And well did I know it.

Henry had come home and we had been married nearly four years. We had a very pleasant sort of life in the city. Both of us worked, we made fairly good salaries, we had a comfortable, even luxurious small apartment, and we had a circle of friends whom we enjoyed a great deal. But there was always a nagging discontent running an undercurrent to it. There was a fretful frustration at not being able to make it count for more. We were so hurried all the time. Hurry to get breakfast and get off to work in the morning. Hurry to snatch a quick lunch at the noon hour. Hurry to get home in the evening. Hurry with dinner and the dishes, and then only a few free hours afterward and we were back on the treadmill the next morning. Hurry, hurry, hurry. There never was any rest at all. Even on week ends it was hurry to clean the apartment, do the marketing, wash underwear, stockings, blouses to get ready for another week at the office. And Sundays we were always so tired that we slept half the day and were sluggish from so much sleep the other half. We paid a tremendous price for everything the city had to offer.

And I had my own personal problem. I had reached a place where I was beginning to have a stagnant feeling about my work. I had come to Louisville in 1941 to work with Dr. Lewis. J.

Sherrill, who at that time was dean and professor of religious education. In 1943, Dr. Sherrill began to lose his vision through macular dystrophy and the nature of my work was radically changed. From then on it became largely serving as eyes and hands for him. I was not unhappy with that change in the beginning. It opened doors of research and reading which in all likelihood I should never have had opened otherwise. It stimulated my thinking, taught me discipline in both method and practice of work, and helped me to mature in many areas of thought.

Anyone who knows Dr. Sherrill is aware without my saying it that it was a privilege to work with him. I could not have had a kinder, more thoughtful, more concerned employer. But it was Dr. Sherrill himself who, in the long run, was responsible for my growing discontent. You see, with a spark of intelligence of your own, you couldn't spend eight years under his tutelage and not reach a place of growth where you wanted to stand on your own feet. He chuckled over that, when I pointed it out to him one day, rather ironically. But I think he wouldn't have changed it, for he had the ability to be genuinely glad for another person, selflessly glad, and when I began writing, I think he foresaw that the time would come when I would give up office work. Neither of us foresaw how soon it was to be.

Henry's tension was more easily explained than mine. He simply did not like the city. He yearned for the kind of life he had always known, and dreamed of the freedom and independence in which he had been nurtured. He was ill-adjusted to the kind of work he had to do in a large industrial plant, and there were few times when he could take any real pleasure in it. We felt that in our own ways we had become the cogs in the wheel, the stenographic symbols at the end of the letter.

Even so, when Henry talked of buying a farm on the ridge, I was apprehensive. What I had in mind was a little place out on the edge of town — say, fifteen or twenty miles from Louisville — where it would be easy to run into the city to shop, to visit friends, to use the libraries, and to hear the concerts. Of course such a place would also have all the conveniences of the city: plumbing, central heating, electricity, and so forth. My idea of living in the country was simply to remove the body to a small acreage and to continue holding tight to everything the city had to offer at the same time. It wasn't mutual. Henry had a very different idea. The ridge was pulling hard at him, and he talked about it constantly.

I talked all around the subject with him without ever believing it would actually happen. But it did. One day when we were spending the week end with his parents, he heard about a little forty-acre patch of scrub brush for sale, about a mile and a half down the ridge from them. The owner wanted $1,100 for it, and before I could take a good deep breath, I found myself signing on the dotted line, and we went back to Louisville that night poorer by $1,100.

Still, we were not going to move to the ridge for several years, we said. Not until we had saved back that $1,100 and some more to go with it. We had to remodel the house, be able to buy farm equipment, and have enough cash on hand to see us through the first year. In April we said all that. The first of June we unloaded our furniture into the house that came with the forty acres and I, for one, watched the moving vans hurry back to civilization with dismal eyes.

Two things had happened. For six months Henry's work had been interrupted by constant strikes and the final blow fell when the plant closed down for an indefinite period. We knew we should have to eke out my salary with what was left of our savings in order to sweat out the time until the plant reopened. And then, just as we were thinking we might be able to do it, I came down with ulcers. I was really laid low. The next thing I knew Henry was packing. "We're going to the farm," he said grimly. "The hell with this kind of life!"

Miserable as I was, it was something of a relief not to have any choice in the matter. But I was miserable — make no mistake about that. I was all mixed up inside, all my emotions tied in knots. I suddenly loved Louisville devotedly. And I wasn't sure at all, now, that I wanted to leave the office. Maybe I didn't want to write after all. Maybe I *couldn't* write but the one book I had already written. And I surely didn't like the idea of living on the ridge. But . . . "whither thou goest," and so forth, so I dragged myself out of bed and helped pack, looking around at the comfortable, pretty apartment we were leaving, shuddering already over the ugliness to which we were going. I was homesick before I left for everything I was saying good-by to.

I know just how Frony, one of my neighbors here on the ridge, felt when her man brought her to Kentucky from South Carolina forty years ago. "I could of jist laid down an' died," she told me, "I hated so to leave. I jist felt the heart inside me was goin' to bust wide open. An' the train made me sick to my stummick. I jist laid there with my head out the winder, athinkin' how fur ever' turn of the wheels was takin' me from home an' my mammy an' pappy. The conductor, he come along oncet, an' he said, 'Lady, you'll git yer head cut off alyin' it out the winder that-a-way.'

"'I don't keer if I do,' I says to him, 'I don't no more keer! I'd ruther to be dead than feel the way I do.'"

I looked back once as we drove off. It was a mistake. It made me feel as if I'd "ruther to be dead."

"You did learn to like it here in Kentucky, didn't you?" I asked Frony a little anxiously.

She looked at me in surprise. "Like?" she said, "why, Lord love you, child, they ain't nothin' in South Caroliny as good as these here hills. They ain't no folks in South Caroliny I love so good. I'd shore hang my head out the winder if I was to have to go back there now!"

I was vastly comforted.

Giles Ridge is but a piece of the whole. A friend of ours once, trying to find his way to our place, kept inquiring for "the ridge" for I spoke of it that way in my letters. My soul and body! There must be a thousand ridges such as ours in these winding, twisting, overlapping hills. Each ridge, and frequently each section of ridge, has its own particular name, usually that of the family most numerous in population. Our ridge, for instance, is variously called Giles Ridge, Caldwell

Ridge, Blair Ridge, and probably several other names with which I am not familiar.

It runs, roughly, in the crescent shape of the new moon, beginning at one end at the top of Dunbar Hill, where the road angles off from the pike, and ending at the bottom of the Ray Williams hill, where once again it joins the pike. Our place lies almost exactly halfway in the crescent, and you can take your choice which end you want to use to get to it. In good weather we come and go by Dunbar Hill. In bad weather we use the Ray Williams hill for the road is, if possible, a little rockier that way and therefore there may be a mite less mud. In really bad weather we don't go either way, period. The only things that can traverse the ridge in the middle of the winter are a mule, a jeep or tractor, and a helicopter. Unless we get a graveled road down the ridge pretty soon, we are going to be compelled to buy a jeep, although since the war Henry has had an understandable aversion to them.

Giles Ridge is named for Henry's family, of course. There are literally dozens and dozens of Gileses on the ridge and down in the hollows and valleys. I am never called Mrs. Giles. What would be the use? No one would know which Mrs. Giles was meant, for there's Luther, William, Walter, Russell, Wesley, Owen, Lee, Milt, Fred, Welby, Charlie, Dewey, Sammie, Johnnie, Elby, Edgar, Frank, and Van. No doubt I've left out as many as I've named, but those are the ones I know. I am either Henry's woman, or Janice, Janet, Jenny, and even, heaven help me, Jennet!

But, for that matter, no one is ever called Mr. or Mrs. here on the ridge. It is such an intimate, closed circle of family and neighbors that it would be silly. The smallest child calls the oldest man by his given name. And no outsider ever moves to the ridge. If one does come, as I did, he is connected by some tie to a ridge family, and naturally he becomes "John" or "Richard" or "Janice" at once.

There is a family legend about the way the Gileses came to this part of Kentucky. It is said that the first Giles, Henry's great-great-grandfather, came over into these hills from the settlement near Crab Orchard in Rockcastle County on a

47

hunting trip. Doubtless even a hundred years ago good hunting was getting scarce in the settled parts of the state. So the first Jeems Giles came ahunting into these hills. He fell in love with them, and, according to the family story, traded his gun for something like a thousand acres of land. A thousand acres for a gun! But I suppose it wasn't too bad a trade at that. Land hereabouts used to sell for a nickel an acre, and that would make the thousand worth around fifty dollars. There might even be those who would say Jeems Giles got gypped. For I suppose a good gun cost as much as fifty dollars even a hundred years ago.

That first Jeems Giles had three sons, and as each of them married, he gave him an entire ridge for himself. But even a sizable inheritance dwindles as the family tree branches out, and Henry's father inherited less than a hundred acres. And when we came to the ridge to live, we had to buy back a piece of land that had belonged to Gileses a hundred years ago. Most of Henry's cousins have had to do the same.

When Henry was a boy, there weren't more than a dozen families the entire length of the ridge. Now there must be at least two dozen of us, each family living within shouting distance of the next. We are strung like pearls on a necklace, rubbing elbows and able to exchange next-door gossip together. There isn't a house that sits lonely on its own piece of ridge, unable to see the lights of a neighboring house or its supper smoke curling from the chimney. We are all knit together, and when Henry gets up at three thirty on a foggy morning to go duck-hunting, Lutie down the way asks me sometime during the day who was sick at our house during the night. She says she "seen" our light. When I have written the morning away and don't get around to cooking dinner until the middle of the afternoon, Sereny, up the other way, is likely to say in passing, "You git yer story done yit?"

"How did you know I was working today?"

"I seen yer dinner smoke along towards three o'clock. I knowed in reason you'd done fergot to cook agin."

My goodness, you can't even have an upset stomach without the grapevine knowing it. "Is Henry feelin' pearter today?"

"Much better. How did you know he'd been sick?"

"Seen him make five trips to the outhouse yestiddy."

But I think the very ultimate in the ridge way of putting two and two together was the time my brother drove by, most unexpectedly, to spend a week end with us. Lutie knew he was coming. "Seen you git a long white envelope outen the mailbox. Figgered somebody was comin'."

Dorothy Canfield was right when she said that when you live in the country you are married to humanity . . . for better or for worse. Truer words were never spoken. For better or for worse the ridge knows every move you make. Accustomed to the anonymity of the city, at times I resented it. But it does no good to waste energy resenting it. If you're going to live in the country, there's nothing to do but accept it, for you certainly can't change it. Where people live so close together, thrown back upon themselves by their isolation from civilization, it is natural for the happenings of each family to have importance to every other family. What else is there to think about or talk about? There is only one point at which Henry and I are adamant. We will not discuss financial matters with others. The first question asked when you buy something is "What'd you have to give fer it?" We have a stock answer. Either we say, "Quite a bit," or, "Not very much."

When my first book was published, people asked, "How much you reckon to make on it?"

"A lot, I hope," was my reply.

If this seems rude, I hope we may be pardoned. But you have to remember that you are not sharing a thing with one person. You are telling the whole ridge, and from there it goes to the village, and it even manages somehow to seep on into town. And it gets woefully distorted and multiplied before it stops.

I ordered a new pair of moccasins from Sears, Roebuck once. Frony came to see me several days after they had come. "Oh, them's the purtiest shoes!" she said. "I wisht I had me a pair. What'd you have to give fer 'em?"

Now Frony is one of my favorite people. I am willing to tell Frony almost anything. So I told her, "Four ninety-five," which you must admit is a very reasonable price for a pair of moccasins.

Two weeks later I was in town and met a friend on the street. " I hear," he said laughing, " you're just throwing money around right and left. Paying twelve dollars for your shoes! "

There is no way of knowing how it got to town. It just traveled from Frony down the ridge grapevine to the village, and by osmosis no doubt on into town. It didn't matter about the shoes, but you can see what would happen if you ever discussed things such as royalties, income tax, insurance, and the like.

But the nosyness on the ridge has its good side too. You don't have to wait very long for help when you need it. If you're sick, Frony or Sereny or Lutie shows up mighty soon and takes over for you. They know that when a woman's sick abed, the household sort of goes to pieces, and they don't waste time waiting for you to send for them. They come, and between them they keep your house going, meals cooked, and chores done. If you're very sick, someone stays with you day and night, never leaving you to the loneliness of long night hours of pain and fear alone. You awake from the fitful, fevered sleep of flu or childbirth or some remote virus infection, and there sits Frony by the fire, nodding a little maybe, but alert when you stir and by your side instantly to know your wants. It's a comfortable feeling then, the close-knit neighborliness of the ridge. It holds you up and sustains you when that's what you need.

Or something goes wrong with the old car. Henry is working over the engine, the hood propped wide. Someone passes on foot, speaks, and goes on. Thirty minutes later here comes Johnnie in his car. " Havin' trouble, Henry? Jessie seen you workin' on yer car." And Johnnie pitches in and spends perhaps the entire balance of the day helping Henry find the trouble. If it's something they can't fix, then Johnnie tows Henry to the village, or drives him there in his car to get the part they need.

My family were coming to visit us. They had never been to the ridge before. I had only a few short days of notice, and

Here is a rough church-shaped outline of our forty acres:

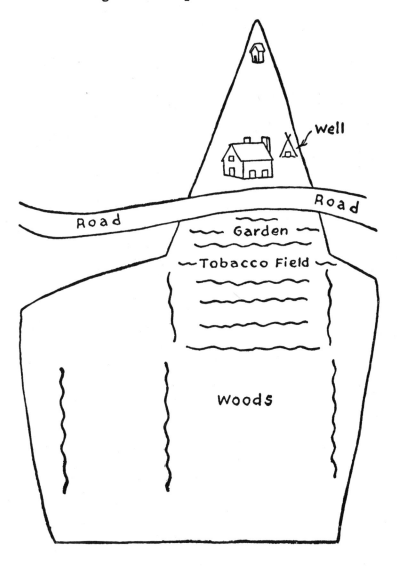

suddenly the house looked very shabby to me. I was so accustomed to it that I paid it little attention, but when I looked at it with their eyes, I was afraid they would all be horrified. So I bought wallpaper and paint. And I sent out word that I was going to paper and paint. Every woman on the ridge not sick in bed dropped what she was doing and came to help. In one day we papered the house and painted all the doors and window sills. I say "we." All I did was cook dinner for the others. They took over the job and before dark it was finished.

At the very last minute before the family arrived, Sereny brought down two bouquets. One was roses and honeysuckle, with a few sprigs from her potted fern. The other was a dozen of her very best handmade crepe-paper tulips. She didn't know which I'd like best, so she brought both.

Oh, yes, that person who counts the number of trips you make to the outhouse is right by your side when you need her. You can depend on that and bank on it. And you never have to ask.

You can see that our house sits up in the steeple of the church, and except for the seven or eight acres directly in front of our house across the road, the land is uncleared. And I might add that I strongly suspect it is unclearable. For within the boundaries of the thirty-four or thirty-five acres of timber stretching out in front of us are three separate and distinct ridges, with a steep hollow dividing each one of them. That makes three ridges and two hollows to which we have title, but it doesn't make any cornfields or pastures.

We do have a pretty good stand of timber on those ridges and down in those hollows, and if we ever *had* to, we could sell it for a right smart. It hasn't been cut over in some seventy-five or hundred years, so there are some big board trees — oak, ash, poplar, beech, walnut — and there is plenty of hickory. During that first hard year Henry occasionally cut enough hickory to make up a load of ax handles. You'd be surprised how handy a good hickory tree or two can be!

It was a Sunday that we moved to the ridge, May 30, 1949 — Sunday because that was the only day the movers would take an out-of-town job which promised a deadhead trip back to Louisville. And it was one of the hottest days on record. We were about an hour ahead of the vans, but because we had decided and moved so hastily, the house hadn't been touched. It was *not* clean and ready for us to move into, and there was no time to get it ready.

When we drove up, I was a battleground of emotions. I could not help taking a little pride in our ownership of the place. I remember that as I stepped out of the car I thought, This is our own land! And there was a sense of miracle in the thought. It was the first time in my whole life that I had ever stepped foot on land to which I had clear title. My father and mother had been teachers, and we had moved constantly. They did not buy their first home until long after my first marriage, so that their home had never been my home. Libby, my daughter, and I had lived in apartments, moving as my work took us to different cities. And in the years of our marriage Henry and I had lived in an apartment, so that, even in the midst of being ill physically, the appalling heat of the day, the desolation of the house and yard, I had a brief feeling of permanence, of coming home. But it passed as I viewed the unutterable ugliness before me.

The house sits about halfway down a gently sloping hillside. The back of it hugged the ground, and the front reared back on its haunches like a dog about to bite. It was not under-penned, so that it had no secrets from passers-by on the road. Plainly in view was a litter of broken bottles, old papers, rags, bits of lumber, and refuse. And cans. I am not exaggerating when I say that we picked up and hauled off over a *ton* of tin cans! Apparently the only method of disposing of tin cans during the entire occupancy of the house had been the simple one of stepping to the back door and heaving.

The yard was grown up in weeds, and back of the house was a thicket of sassafras and persimmon trees, matted with grapevines until the whole was a jungle. That thicket had served as an outhouse for the various families who had lived there. For there was not an outbuilding of any sort except a very small chicken house across the road. No barn. No woodshed. Not even a well house, for there was no well. People who had lived there had carried water from a spring in a hollow about a quarter of a mile away. Or had made use of a neighbor's well.

The house itself looked as ancient as time, but that was only because it had never been painted and was merely weathered, for it was actually only about twenty years old. It was a thin, spindling house, fifteen by thirty feet. It had two rooms downstairs, and one big room upstairs which had never been finished. Finished? It had never even been begun! It had a roof over it and that was all. It was neither floored nor ceiled.

Each of the downstairs rooms had an outside door to the front and a window. In front of the door leading to the kitchen was a sort of stoop supported on rotten stumps. That served for a step. The door from the living room simply opened into space. And the back kitchen door stepped down directly onto the ground. Not a porch, not a step. Just doors and gaping windows.

Inside, the house was even more dreary than outside. It had been built of green lumber — the rough, undressed kind you buy cheaply at a sawmill. In seasoning, the floors had buckled and sagged. The walls had come apart in wide cracks and the corners had as much as two inches difference sometimes. Various women had made valiant efforts to paper the walls. None of them were successful, although we tore off four or five different layers of paper before we got down to the bare boards. Then we saw why. You could see daylight between the boards. The wind simply whistled through and ripped the paper right off the walls.

A steep boxed stairway climbed up from one corner of the kitchen, and a pantry of sorts had been made underneath it — a pantry that only mice had inhabited for a long time. The risers on the stairway are a good nine inches, which makes it like climbing a ladder to begin with, but to add to the difficulty, the treads themselves all slant outward, so that not only do you have to climb the stairs, but you have to climb up the treads themselves. What it amounts to is crawling up.

The movers dumped the furniture and crates and boxes into

the two rooms and took off. We had had a four-room apartment in the city, so that literally there wasn't even space to take a deep breath by the time they had piled everything into those two rooms. I sat down on one corner of the couch and looked around. I was hot, dirty, and ill. The house was hot, dirty, and cluttered. Outside was the dusty road, the weed-grown yard, the stretching woods. I ran my hand over the upholstery of the couch. It came away gritty with the fine, powdered dust sifted over it. And then, just as I thought I couldn't bear one more thing, Henry came in whistling. "The first thing," he said happily, "the first thing is to get a garden planted and the tobacco crop out."

That was the last straw! I looked at him with loathing and then I simply closed my eyes and had hysterics.

Chapter

4 ↙ ↙

Frony didn't come to see me for three days after we moved to the ridge, and she was practically a " door neighbor " too. But I didn't miss her. Lord love you, no! For everybody else certainly came.

It began with the children the day we moved in. Where they came from I don't know, and even now when I do a mental census, I don't know how so many could have sprouted so suddenly. They appeared, a head here, a head there, and they just sort of seeped through the doors. They didn't say a word unless we spoke to them, and then rather shyly they mumbled a " howdy." Henry pressed two or three of the larger boys into helping him move the furniture around, but other than that they merely came, stood and looked, and then vanished silently. " What do they want? " I asked Henry.

" Nothing," he said, " they just want to see."

The next day the adults began to come. An introduction is unknown on the ridge. There is so rarely any need of it. So I don't remember who came and who didn't. They didn't tell me who they were, and Henry was busy outside. One or two of them I knew from having seen them at Henry's parents'. The rest were perfect strangers. They came, said "Howdy," sort of wandered through the house, and left. And they left me so confused I didn't know whether I was coming or going. I tried to be courteous. "Won't you sit down?"

No, they didn't have time to set. Jist thought they'd come say "howdy." They had to be gittin' on back. And as they left, "Jist go up with me."

"Just go *where* with them?" I asked Henry.

"Nowhere. It's the polite way of saying, 'I've got to go now.'"

"What am I supposed to say?"

"'Cain't. You jist better stay.'"

I tucked the phrase away in my memory to use in the writing. But I needn't have been afraid I'd forget it. It soon became a part of my own vocabulary. It's the ridge folks' way of saying, "Good-by now." And I don't know that I ever heard one I liked better. It implies: "Your hospitality has been so gracious and your company so pleasant, I am indebted to you. Come, go with me and let me try to repay my debt."

I know of only one other farewell that is as charming, the Japanese "Sayonara." It says sadly, "Then, good-by, if it must be so." But there are so few times in my life when I can say, "Sayonara." And just any day of the week I can unwind myself from a hickory chair, squint prophetically at the sky, and bid my host, "Jist go with me."

"Why is everyone drifting in and out of the house like this?" I asked Henry then. "They don't seem to be calling. They just come in, look around, and leave. I can't get anything done!"

"Don't stop for them. They don't expect you to. Mainly they're just looking you over. They want to see what kind of furniture you've got, see what you're doing to the house. The kids yesterday spread the news that you have some things they're not used to seeing — the piano, the desk, rugs, the couch. People on the ridge don't have furniture like that. They've come to see for themselves. But if you need help, all you have to do is say so. They'll pitch in. Mostly, though, they've come to look, and later they'll get together and talk. This is a field day for the ridge!"

I was labeled and tagged "quare" from the beginning of course. On account of my furniture, on account of the way I talked, on account of my city ways and city clothes. And especially on account of the writing. No one ever heard of "sich." George Trotter, the editor of the *News-Journal* at Campbellsville, was in Knifley one day, and he mentioned knowing me. One of the women in the store at the time spoke up. "I knowed she was quare, but I jist figgered hit was natural to her. Never knowed hit was writin' done it."

But when Frony came, she stayed awhile. Frony was almost, but not quite, a "door neighbor." A door neighbor, of course, lives right next. She is the one who can tell when your light goes on at three thirty in the morning. Who knows by your chimney smoke what time you're having dinner, who can count your trips to the outhouse. She is your nearest link in the ridge necklace, the immediate joint in the ridge grapevine. Frony was around the bend and across the hollow.

She came right after the noon meal on Wednesday. We had moved on Sunday. And she came bearing her apologies and a hot apple pie. "I've not come sooner," she said, "fer I've been puny an' couldn't of helped. I hadn't no intentions of jist comin' an' settin'. I aimed to help when I come. Now jist tell me what to do an' I'll pitch in."

There is no excuse for what I did that afternoon. It was just plain snide. No amount of heat, or dirt, or tiredness, or illness should have made me ill-mannered. And I was just that to Frony. More, I even patronized her. "Oh, no," I said to her kind offer to help, "let's just sit and talk awhile. I'm tired of working anyhow."

Well, I was. But the polite thing for me to have done would have been to think of some small task we could do together as we sat and talked. That would have been as kindly and generous as Frony's offer. No, I turned it back on her. "Let's just sit and talk," I said. "I'll put the kettle on and make some tea." And I knew very well that ridge folks don't take tea. Henry had told me he had never tasted it until he went into the Army, and I had seen Miss Bessie's wry face the only time she tried to drink it at our house in the city.

Frony's eyes slanted around the room frankly, taking in everything. "I've not never tasted tea," she said. "Don't know's I'd keer fer it."

"Would you rather have coffee then?"

She rebuked me. "In the middle of the afternoon?"

I murmured something about hoping she'd like the tea and put the kettle on the little kerosene stove to boil.

Frony was a tiny woman, weather-beaten and old, thin as a bed slat, brown as a berry, and neat as a pin. From under her starched sunbonnet her eyes peered, black and beady-sharp. Her snuff was well lipped and under complete control. Around her waist was tied a fresh apron. The apron is the badge of ridge womanhood. I have never seen one without her apron. Except, of course, in town. And Frony told me once she "allus felt more'n half nekkid" when she went to town without her apron.

When I came back from the kitchen, Frony was quiet a moment and then she said: "I knowed in reason them kids was alyin'. They said you had *two* dressers! As I told 'em, what would you be wantin' with two!"

"We do have two," I said, "one for Henry and one for me."

It was simply a matter of fact to me. Little did I know that word was going to be spread around that I bragged over having two dressers!

Frony humphed. "Jist plain wasteful, seems to me. Where is the other'n?"

I waved vaguely toward the upstairs. Henry had managed to get a makeshift floor laid across the rafters up there and we had shifted most of the excess furniture out of the lower rooms. "I never put no dependence in what them kids said," Frony went on, "but I reckon they was right. I see you been tearin' down the old paper. I'm a right good hand to paper. When you git ready, jist holler."

"We haven't decided whether we want to paper again," I said. "I'd like to panel the walls and then paint them."

"With wood?"

"Yes."

Frony humphed again. "Hit'd go awful quare, I'd think. Allus paper here on the ridge. Likely the wood'd sweat, come winter. An' be cold. Paper keeps out a sight of cold."

I said nothing and Frony's eyes roamed around the room again. "Kin you play that there organ in the corner?"

"That's a piano . . . yes, I play a little."

"I thought hit looked uncommon different fer a organ. Never seen no pumps on it, neither. I'd like a heap to hear you play a piece on it."

The last thing I wanted to do was to play a piece for Frony. But grudgingly I moved to the piano. It wasn't exactly arrogance that prompted me to do what I did. At least I don't think so. It was a sort of desperate last stand. A kind of flag-raising of independence. All my dislike for this move to the ridge, all my feeling of self-pity, all my homesickness for the city, lay back of it. And my determination to retain my own identity, to remain myself. So when I went to the piano instead of playing something Frony would enjoy I turned to a Chopin prelude, the little Tschaikovsky "Humoresque," and something of Schubert's. That was all I could manage, for the music itself made me heartsick.

When I turned from the keys, Frony smoothed her apron, her eyes on her fingers. "Kin you play 'Lord, Build Me a Cabin'?"

"No."

"Kin you play 'We'll Soon Be Done with Troubles and Trials'?"

"No."

"Kin you play 'Angels, Git My Mansions Ready'?"

"No."

She sighed. "I was ahopin' you was real good at playin' an' singin' when I heared you had a organ. But as I told 'em, likely you hadn't never had much time to be alearnin' on music, aworkin' like you done in the city an' all. Hit wouldn't be expected you could play an' sing like them that follers it regular."

I was so flabbergasted I couldn't think of a thing to say. That was the first time Frony ever put me in my place. But it's certainly not been the last time.

One of the things which I thought the ugliest about the ridge was its music. The old ballads have long since died away. Only a few people even know them any more, and they consider them old-timy and you can rarely find anyone who will sing them. Henry's brother Robert knows most of them, and if persuaded will sing them. Henry knows them too, and occasionally when he and Robert get out their guitars and sing them, it's wonderful to hear. Such ballads as " Lord Lovel," " Barbry Allen," " Black Is the Color of My True Love's Hair," and the others which are so old and so lovely. But there is no folk music left on the ridge. And, strangely enough, ridge folks have not taken to the rowdy hillbilly music of the radio either. Typically the music of this section of the country has become the religious song of the shaped note revival meeting songbooks. Frony mentioned two or three that are favorites. And there are literally hundreds of others, of which any ridge person can sing all four stanzas and almost any of the four parts. For everyone on the ridge can sing. That is, he knows do, re, mi, and he can carry the part for which his voice is best suited in harmony.

The principle of shaped note singing is a little difficult to explain unless you were " brung up " with it. I certainly can't apply it to this day, but at least I have a speaking acquaintance with it. The notes of the scale, instead of being C, D, E, F, and so on, are Do, Re, Mi, Fa, Sol, La, Ti. When written the notes are shaped for purposes of identification, for while they may be played on a piano or organ, just as round notes are, primarily they are shaped so that singers may recognize them without benefit of instruments. Thus:

Do   Re   Mi   Fa   Sol   La   Ti   Do

If it sounds terribly confused I am sorry. But it must actually be very simple, for the least young'un on the ridge can read music. I have seen Hazel Giles's least one, who is barely four years old, pick up his father's hymnbook, clear his throat, sound off with a very treble " mi, mi, mi," and then, beating perfect time with his baton hand, launch into " Lead Me Home" with complete confidence. He can't read the words yet, but he sure can read the music.

There seems to be a natural ear for music. But the quality of the voices is something else again. When I first began to hear the kind of singing hill folks love, I thought the songs were a travesty, and the voices were worse. And the inevitable guitar that accompanied them. Whang, whang, whang was all I could hear. I'm not a complete convert yet. And I don't know exactly when I began to change at all. There is still a lot of the singing that is just plain not good and never will be. There are people who go to the radio station in Campbellsville and sing over the air that ought to be throttled on the first note. But I think I first began to sense a difference in good and bad hill singing the first time I attended the Adair County Singing Convention. Until then I had never heard anything but the bad. But that day I heard a choir from one of the small churches nearby sing " I Know My Lord's Gonna Lead Me Out " with such sure harmony and such fine feeling that I broke out all over in goose bumps. That was a choir of sixteen voices. But there was a quartet! They called themselves the Jubilee Four. I've heard them many times since and I give you my word I'd rather hear the Jubilee Four sing " Jesus, Hold My Hand " (see the two pages following), than to eat fried chicken on Sunday.

Take a good, strong lead, a dash of second tenor, a low rumbling bass and a sweet first tenor, mix them, stir them, give them hearty 4/4 time, and you've got a song. And the Jubilee Four can sing you right out of your seat any time you want to listen. They're wonderful.

I ordered several shaped note songbooks after that first singing convention and started to work. I don't care how good a pianist you are, I dare you to sit down and swing into 12/8,

JESUS, HOLD MY HAND

A.E.B.

Albert E. Brumley

1. As I trav-el thru this pil-grim land There is a Friend who walks with me, Leads me safe-ly thru the sink-ing sand, It is the Christ of Cal-va-ry; This would be my pray'r, dear Lord, each day To help me do the best I can, For I need Thy light to guide me day and night, Bless-ed Je-sus, hold my hand.

2. Let me trav-el in the light di-vine That I may see the bless-ed way; Keep me that I may be whol-ly Thine And sing re-demption's song some day; I will be a sol-dier brave and true And ev-er firm-ly take a stand, As I on-ward go and dai-ly meet the foe, Bless-ed Je-sus, hold my hand.

3. When I wan-der thru the val-ley dim To-ward the set-ting of the sun, Lead me safe-ly to a land of rest If I a crown of life have won; I have put my faith in Thee, dear Lord, That I may reach the gold-en strand, There's no oth-er friend on whom I can de-pend, Bless-ed Je-sus, hold my hand.

Chorus

Bless-ed Je - sus, hold my hand, Yes, I need Thee
Je - - - - sus, hold my hand, I need Thee ev - 'ry

ev - 'ry hour, Thru this land, this pil - grim land
hour, Thru this pil-grim land, Pro-

By Thy sav-ing pow'r; Hear my plea, my fee - ble plea,
tect me by Thy pow'r; Hear my fee-ble plea,

O Lord, dear Lord, look down on me, When
Lord, look down on me, When I kneel in

I kneel in pray'r, Bless - ed Je-sus, hold my hand.
pray'r I hope to meet you there,

63

9/8, or even 6/8 time, with gobs of sixteenth and thirty-second notes without running into trouble. If you can sight-read boogie, you might be able to do it. But I'll have you know that after patience and persistence I can now swing into "Angels, Git My Mansions Ready" to suit Frony or anybody else on the ridge. I have earned myself a new kind of reputation. "Man," folks say appreciatively, "Henry's woman kin shore play good," and their feet start tapping and their shoulders swinging. It's nearly always played very fast and swingy, of course. What a ten-piece jazz band couldn't do to some of those songs!

When the kettle boiled, I made tea that day Frony came. I got out my best blue plates and cups and opened a box of cookies. I poured the tea and offered Frony cream and sugar. She sipped and then made a face. "I wouldn't keer fer sich," she said, "but I'll try a coupla them cookies. They look real good."

I passed them to her. "Have you lived on the ridge very long, Frony?" I asked her.

That was when she told me how she felt when her man brought her from South Carolina. And when she had finished, she said, "You think you're goin' to like?" Ridge folks don't add the indefinite "it."

"I suppose so," I said.

"Oh, you'll like a heap better when you git you somethin' to tend," she said, "a cow an' some chickens an' a coupla pigs mebbe."

Passionately I made denial. "I'm not going to have anything to tend! I don't want any cow or chickens or pigs. I don't know anything about them and I don't want to know anything about them. Besides, I won't have time."

"What you aimin' to do with yer time?"

"I write . . . you know . . . books, things . . ."

"Oh. Yes, I heared you'd writ a book. An' yer aimin' to keep on?"

"I certainly am!"

"Does it pay purty good?"

"I don't know yet. My first book is just now being published."

Frony emptied the crumbs from her apron into her hand and politely got up to throw them out the door. "Well, if hit was *me,* I'd a heap ruther put *my* dependence in a good cow an' some chickens an' a coupla meat hawgs. I'd know fer shore I wasn't goin' hungry come winter then!"

"Oh, we'll manage."

"Mighty pore managin'. Hit'll cost you a sight."

I shut my mouth tight to keep from saying something rude. Just let it go, I thought. Just sit tight and let it go!

Then Frony rose. She smoothed her apron. "Well, I got to be gittin' on back. Agin I change my clothes hit'll be time to do up the night work. You shore they ain't nothin' I kin do to help?"

"Not a thing, Frony, but thank you anyway." Now that she was leaving, I could be gracious.

We stepped out in the yard. Across the road Henry was laying off the rows in our newly plowed garden patch. Frony eyed him for a moment. "Reckon you ain't none too stout."

I wasn't, but I have that peculiar kind of pride that never admits to illness. "Why, I'm perfectly healthy," I said.

"Reckon you ain't no good with a hoe, then."

"I can hoe . . . if I have to. Why?"

"Why's Henry doin' a woman's work, then? Makin' the garden!"

With that barb she raised a dust down the road, her bonnet tails flapping in the wind.

Frony and I have laughed about that first afternoon many a time since. "You were mean to me, Frony," I'll tell her, "just plain mean."

"I know it," she says in instant contrition, "but upon my word an' honor, Janice, you was so all-fired snotty!"

And then it's my turn to be contrite. For "all-fired snotty" is exactly what I was.

"But I got my come-uppance," Frony always adds; "had sich a sour stummick that night I couldn't sleep till I got up an' taken me a dost of sody. An' then I jist got right down on my knees an' ast the Lord to forgive me. I says to him I'd ort to of knowed jist how lonelyhearted you was feelin'. Me that knows how it is to go amon'st strangers. I told him I was jist a low-lifed, ornery critter to have spoke so sharply to a pore, furrin girl like that."

"Yes," I remind her, "but then you told him you'd sure been powerfully riled."

"Well, I wuz," Frony bridles, "I wuz jist plumb riled. You, aplayin' yore fancy music, an' amakin' tea, an' not goin' to have you nothin' to tend. Hit was enough to rile a saint hisself."

I don't suppose I need to add that Frony saw to it I had something to tend. It was the next year after we had moved to the ridge. *The Enduring Hills* had just been released and both Adair and Taylor County were inclined to make much over it. I was interviewed over the radio at Campbellsville. Frony knew about it, of course, and loyally she listened that afternoon. We hadn't much more than got home when she came fanning down the road, out of breath from hurrying, her apron strings and bonnet tails flying. "I heared you," she said, when she could get her breath, "I heared you jist as plain, an' hit went jist like you. All them words, an' oncet when you laughed I knowed jist how you wuz lookin'. But, Lordy mercy, I wuz so skeered you'd fergit yer piece an' git yerself all balled up I was in a cold sweat time hit was over with."

"I didn't learn any piece, Frony," I said, "I just answered the man's questions."

"Well, hit went jist like you knowed ever' word you was sayin'. Jist as natural."

"Well, I'm glad you like it."

"Oh, I never to say liked it. Never knowed what you was talkin' about fer the most part. But I thought you done good not to git skeered. I got to be goin'," and then, as if she hadn't come purposely to tell me, she turned and said rather shyly: "Oh, I like to fergot! I got you a present."

"Oh, a pie?"

"No."

"A sunbonnet?" I'd been begging her to make me one.

"No. Hit's a dozen leetle chickens! As I told 'em, Janice ain't never had nothin' to tend in all her life an' she jist don't know how a flock of leetle chickens'll pleasure her. I says I'll jist take her off a settin' of my Hampshire Reds an' give 'em to her. An' they've hatched out now, an' they're the purtiest things! I'll go git 'em fer you." And she took off before I could get my breath.

I had about as much use for a dozen little chickens as a hog has for a sidesaddle, but you may be everlastingly sure I all but sat up nights with them. I knew I'd have to account to Frony if I lost a single one of them. And I take great pride in the fact that I raised all twelve of them. They provide us, usually, with all the fresh eggs we need. But occasionally they go temperamental on us and quit laying. Frony says you can't expect a hen to lay three hundred and sixty-five days out of the year. But I can. And do. They certainly never quit eating. I have a very good idea that with chicken feed costing what it does today, we are paying considerably more than the market price for our eggs, and sometimes I am tempted to sell the whole dratted flock. But I know I won't, for if I sold them, Frony would just give me another bunch of little ones to tend, and that I'm not going through with again.

Her man brought a most reluctant Frony to the ridge forty-odd years ago. But she has taken root here and become a part of it. I doubt if she has been more than fifty miles away from the ridge in that forty years. Once she said to me: "You've been a sight of places, ain't you? An' seed a sight of things? "

"Well, yes." I am always a little cautious with Frony lest I be accused of acting prideful again.

"Have you seed the ocean? "

"Yes."

"I reckon hit's awful big? "

"It is . . . bigger than you could ever imagine."

"They say hit goes plumb out of sight! "

"It does."

Frony sighed. "Hit goes quare that any water could be so big. An' have you seed them tall mountains? "

"Yes."

"They're bigger'n the hills, I reckon."

"Oh, much bigger."

"How many days did you say hit takes you to go to Libby's?"

Libby, my daughter, lives in New Mexico. "Three days," I tell Frony.

"Three days an' nights?"

"Well, we don't travel at night, Frony."

"No," she ponders, "I don't reckon you could hold out to be on the go nights too." Her eyes look beyond the hills at sights she has never seen. And then she brings them back. "I'd love a heap to see all them furrin places. I'd love to go so good. I wouldn't never mind jist goin' an' goin' the whole day long," and then the blackness of her eyes lights up, "but I'd want to git home by night."

"Why, Frony, you couldn't."

"I know. But I couldn't noways rest anywheres but in my own bed, come night. An' besides, who'd do up the night work?"

Frony's man died a few years ago and she is alone now. Her son lives not far from her and he sees that her garden patch is plowed each spring, and that her woodpile is kept replenished, and one of the family goes each evening to sleep in Frony's house with her. Not that Frony wants them — she can make out very well by herself, she tells them. But her son does not like her to be alone at night. After all, Frony is nearly seventy-five.

But don't think anyone else works that garden patch for Frony. Not on your life! She plants it, and hoes it, and keeps it as clean as your front parlor. Then she picks her beans and tomatoes and corn and cans them all summer long. And she doesn't even like garden stuff herself. "Why do you do it, Frony?" I ask.

"Why, Lord love you, child," she says, "what would I do when some of 'em comes home 'thout a few cans to open!"

She keeps a cow too, and a flock of chickens and a pig. Her son's cow would provide all the milk and butter she could ever use, and his chickens would furnish her eggs and fryers when she wanted them. His hogs would give her more meat than she could possibly eat in a season. "You just *make* work for yourself," I fussed at her.

She laughed and smoothed her apron. "I do, don't I? But — " and again her eyes seek faraway things — "but somethin' to tend is a sight of comfort."

I have never said anything to Frony again about the things she tends making work for her. Of course they do. But she wants them to. They are a part of all those years when there was need for them. When she had a strong, hearty man by her side, and a house full of young'uns to do for. When it took a half-gallon can of beans to make a mess for her family, and they ate a side of meat in less than a week. When she stirred up a dozen eggs for breakfast and emptied a gallon crock of milk to fill the glasses around the table. She is keeping all that's left to her of the old ways and the old days. And if you took them away from her, Frony would wither and die.

She has a delightful sense of humor. Once she went with us to Campbellsville. When we went by for her, she was sitting on the porch, dignified in a navy-blue sheer dress, little white hat perching unfamiliarly on her thin knot of hair, new black shoes shining proudly under the tip of her dress. I thought of Hoagy Carmichael's little old lady dressed in blue. She looked so sweet and so neat and so prim.

We had a big day planned in town. Frony had shopping to do and I had shopping to do, so we separated and went our own ways. "I'll meet you at the coffee shop for lunch," I said, and she nodded, already busy with her own plans.

About the middle of the morning a hard wind and rain blew up and I worried a little about Frony, knowing she had neither an umbrella nor a wrap. Oh, well, I told myself, she'll just stay in some store until it slacks up. And I parked myself under an awning to wait, for it was a summer rain and I didn't think it was likely to last long. But I was mistaken. It turned into a steady drizzle, so that there was nothing to do but finish the shopping in the wet.

I got to the coffee shop first and found a table. By strategically hopping from one sheltered place to another I had avoided getting too wet, but I was shaking out my damp feathers when Frony came. Something was different about her. Her skirt was shorter and she was all bunched around the middle. When she got to the table, I whispered, "What happened?"

She plumped herself down in her chair and stacked her packages on the floor beside her. "This dad-ratted dress," she fumed, "I'd ort to of knowed hit was sleazy! Come that rain, you know what hit done? Hit jist commenced adrawin' up on me! Ever' time I looked down hit had got shorter an' shorter. Crept up two, three inches at a time. I says to myself the plague-taked thing is goin' plumb to my knees! Never was so mortified in my life."

"But what have you done to it? That's not your dress!"

"No! Hit's my petticoat. Allus did like the petticoat better'n the dress anyhow. Hit's real good satin. I jist ducked in one of them rest rooms an' tucked the skirt up around my waist, an' let the petticoat show. They was jist one thing that worried me. Without no petticoat, kin you see through me agin the light?"

I shook my head. No, you couldn't see through her against the light. She heaved a big sigh of relief. "Well, that's a load offen my mind. What you goin' to eat?"

Once she went with us to the county fair, and Libby's little two-year-old couldn't have been any more excited. She ate hot dogs and peanuts and popcorn and cotton candy, and then nothing would do but she must ride the Ferris wheel. The first time over Frony clutched her stomach. She slued her eyes at me. "Tell him to stop," she said.

"Why, we've just started!"

"You better tell him to stop, Janice! I'm fixin' to be sick all over this here merry-go-round."

But of course there was no way to signal the starter until we came down again. I don't know whether anyone else has ever been sick from the top of a Ferris wheel before, but Frony was. When she got through, she leaned back and sort of shuddered. Then she braced up. "What time did you say the horse races commence?"

There's just one thing we can't get Frony to do with us. And that's go to a movie. She went to one once, 'way back in the days of silent pictures. "Jim takened me," she told me, "over at Campbellsville, oh, hit's been a time an' a time."

"Did you enjoy it?"

"I never looked. Not after I takened one glimpse. Them horses was acomin' right at me, jist gallopin' an' the men was fallin' off of 'em, an' they was a train acomin', an' I knowed in reason the whole shootin' match was jist goin' to mash me six ways to thunder. I jist shet my eyes, an' I says to Jim, I says, le's go, an' I got out of there in a hurry."

"Why, Frony, it was just a picture! They weren't real. They were just on the screen."

Frony humphed. "That's what Jim said, but I wasn't takin' no chances. No, sir. I ain't goin' to no movies. Much as yer life's worth. Not me. They ain't goin' to tromple me that-a-way."

That's Frony.

Chapter

5 ✒ ✒

When Henry and I had recovered sufficiently from my attack of hysterics, we pitched in to work with such vigor that at the end of June we made a really remarkable showing.

But the first thing we did was to sit down and balance the budget. Thank goodness, it balanced, although there was very little left over. When we took stock and made a final accounting of our assets, they were, to wit: one forty-acre farm in doubtful condition for farming; one house, more or less; one 1939 model Oldsmobile coupé which needed a new water pump, a new battery, and a new generator; four rooms of furniture, the wrong kind for the country (When were we ever going to need a gas range and an electric refrigerator again?); one dog, of doubtful ancestry but very lovable disposition; and $289 in cash.

Our liabilities far outweighed the assets. The few acres across the road from the house, which had once been cleared and under cultivation, had grown up in sprouts and weeds

71

which must be cleared again. We had no tools with which even to make a beginning, not even a hoe. The house *had* to have a few repairs. Something had to be done about the floors and the walls, and the upstairs room had to be finished with at least a floor and ceiling. We *had* to have water, and we had to have an outhouse. So we knew that most of our cash must be spent immediately. And where the next was to come from, we had no idea. "We'll worry about that when the time comes," Henry said loftily.

Well, we worried about it before the time came, of course, but for the moment there was nothing to do but put first things first. And the absolutely first thing was to get a garden planted and the tobacco crop in. The season was already late, but not hopelessly so. Gardens are usually planted in May on the ridge, and tobacco is usually set between May 15 and June 1. So we had no time to lose. We bought a few tools — a hoe, rake, ax, spading fork, scythe, and so forth — and Henry set to work grubbing out the sprouts on our acreage. Since the Government controls the planting of tobacco, each farm is allotted a base. On the ridge most farms are allowed one acre. I have never been able to figure out the basis on which the allotments are made, for a man with 25 acres will have as large a base frequently as a man with 150 acres of land. An acre doesn't look like much land — until you start grubbing out sprouts. Then it can cover an awful lot of territory.

But it was very important to get the tobacco crop in, for that is the big cash crop in this section of the country. We had to count on that for most of our income. I don't know what a good valley farm yields in the way of an average crop, but here on the ridge tobacco is expected to yield from fifteen hundred to two thousand pounds per acre. With present prices, the income runs to between $700 and $1,000 per acre. And on the ridge that much money is wealth.

From one of Henry's cousins we borrowed a team of mules and a plow. We brought the plow over to our place in the back end of the car, and then Henry walked back to drive the mules over. He hitched them up and took off. It had been quite a time since Henry had done any plowing, and it may be that he was a little nervous and awkward at it. It is certainly true that the mules were young, frisky, and skittish. At any rate they took off like a house afire, and before my astonished eyes three things happened in rapid-fire order. First, Henry's hat flew off his head; second, Henry himself flew off his feet; and third, the mules flew off down the road! To this day we can't account for the fact that he managed to get himself untangled from the reins and wasn't dragged along with the plow. Down the road those mules went, running like mad, the plow bouncing and dragging all over the road at their heels, making a noise like Judgment Day. Henry took off after them, yelling at the top of his voice, which I thought merely added to the confusion. In moments of crisis like that Henry's vocabulary can be counted on to rise to the occasion. I wondered if Sereny, up the road, was learning any new ways to cuss. If she wasn't, it occurred to me she was missing a mighty good opportunity, one she very likely wouldn't have again in a lifetime.

I just sat down on a big rock in the shade of a tree and began to add up what a team of mules and a new plow would cost. I thought that was about the extent of my helpfulness.

In half an hour or so Henry came leading the dratted mules back. "No damage done," he reported, "but I'm taking them back. Next time they'll either kill *me* or I'll kill them!"

The plow had been banged up considerably, but all the dents could be ironed out at the blacksmith shop. And the hard run down the road hadn't even lathered the mules. When Henry took them home and explained to his cousin what had happened, Elby laughed. "They're sort of mean to run," he said, "likely a piece of paper skeered 'em."

Likely.

Next we borrowed a horse. She was about half blind, but the man who owned her told us she was awfully slow but she was dependable. That's just exactly what we wanted. A good, slow, dependable horse. Sallie was willing — I'll say that for her — but she was terribly handicapped. The garden site slopes gently to the south, and of course Henry was plowing across the slope to prevent washing. He would head Sallie straight across, but within ten feet she would be angling up the slope. The resulting furrow was as beautifully scalloped as if Henry had drawn a pattern. Just in case Sallie too should be allergic to a piece of wind-blown paper, I went in the house when Henry hitched her up. The thing he minded most about the mules running away was his ignominy in front of me, I think, and it was my idea to spare him anything further along that line. I peeked out the door once in a while to see how he was getting along and, inexperienced as I am in the matter, I could tell the plowing was not progessing very satisfactorily. Henry shouted " gee " and " haw " vociferously and Sallie wavered indefinitely as if she never knew just what he meant. His face, which is normally ruddy anyhow, got redder and redder as time wore on, and the back of his shirt was soaked through with sweat in no time. Finally he came to the house. " You'll have to come lead her," he said.

" Why? "

" She's not only blind — she's left-handed or something. She's got ' gee ' and ' haw ' mixed up. She goes just the opposite from what I want! "

It was true. " Gee " means right and " haw " means left to any farmer, but whoever had taught Sallie gee and haw had taught her just backward. When Henry shouted " gee " at her, she obediently turned left, while he pulled her to the right. One of them would have developed a neurosis by nightfall. So we plowed the balance of the acreage with me leading Sallie back and forth, east to west, west to east, monotonously but profitably. Late in the evening, when my legs were about to fall off, it occurred to me I might have ridden her just as profitably. But I never think of practical things like that in time to do any good.

Within a week we had the garden planted. I loved that part of it. Dropping seeds, covering them, working with the soil. " Oughtn't we to mark the rows so we'll know what's planted where? " I asked Henry.

He laughed at me. " How can you mistake what's planted in them? "

He should ask!

We planted radishes, lettuce, squash, cucumbers, carrots,

beets, green beans, corn, and peas. And neighbors were generous with their young pepper, tomato, and cabbage plants. On the ridge we sow those things in the tobacco beds when we sow tobacco seed. The tobacco bed makes an almost perfect plant bed for the young vegetable seedlings. People from all around stopped to tell us, "They's aplenty of tomaters an' peppers over in my bed. Jist help yerself."

And we did.

We got our tobacco plants the same way. Everyone else was through setting and the plants that were left were now useless. Of course they weren't choice plants. But they were our only hope for having a tobacco crop that year. So, from this bed and that one, we gathered seedlings and eventually got our full base set out.

I remember the first time I ever saw a field of tobacco growing. My parents, Libby, and I had been to the World's Fair in Chicago, in 1934 I think it was, and we drove home a roundabout way through Kentucky. As a matter of fact we passed within a hundred miles of where I now live, but if anyone had told me that day that I would one day be living on a farm in Kentucky, setting out my own tobacco field, I would have told him he was crazy. Me in Kentucky? Me on a farm? And especially me setting out tobacco plants?

But here I am, and I sure did set out tobacco plants. Tobacco is set mechanically on large farms, but it is still set by hand here on the ridge. When the field had been plowed, disked, and harrowed, the fertilizer was drilled into rows, and the field was then ready for setting. We took tubs and went to the tobacco beds and carefully pulled up the young seedlings by the roots. We filled several tubs and brought them back to the field. We did have the use of a hand setter, which kept us from having to dig the holes by hand.

The setter is a clumsy, heavy apparatus which holds about a gallon of water in a small tank on one side. There is a sort of funnel on the other side, down which the plants are dropped, root first. The funnel and the tank join at the base in a sharp point. The point is set in the soil, twisted a time or two to dig a hole, a trap releases the plant and waters it, and then

75

the farmer moves on sixteen inches to repeat the operation.

It takes two to operate this gadget. It was my job to walk along with a basket of tobacco plants swinging from my arm, dropping them one at a time into the funnel. Henry was so adept at using the hand setter that with about four motions he was ready to move on. At first I held him up by not having a plant in the funnel in time. But after some dozen or so black looks from him I learned how to loosen the plants in the basket and always, always have one in my hand ready to drop the moment the trap closed.

In two weeks we had both the garden and the tobacco planted. We were proud of that. But it had taken sixteen work hours each day to get it done. And I was supposed to be resting six hours a day on the bed. I kept telling myself I *must* begin resting. I *must* not risk a perforated ulcer. "When we get the garden and tobacco out," I said, "I'll start resting." But I never did. There was so much to be done, and Henry couldn't possibly do it by himself.

After the garden and the tobacco the next thing was an outhouse. Until we got that built, the *pot de chambre* had come in very handy. For me, that is. Henry merely sought the jungle back of the house. There are so many ways in which it is convenient to be a man! But it was with a good bit of glee that I saw his sheltering thicket hacked down, and it was with no sympathy at all that I looked upon his final frustration when the last of the tangled vines and sprouts were gone. The back yard stretched clean and open to the boundary of our line. It would not have hidden a partridge, much less Henry. It was then I reminded him that he who laughs last laughs loudest.

We had torn down the old chicken house across the road to make room for the garden, so there was enough old lumber, perhaps a bit "mitey" but still sound, to build the structure. Nothing fancy, mind you. Not even the conventional crescent in the door. Just a square, blunt, businesslike box, with a two-holer inside. We hope eventually to put a trellis around it and train honeysuckle and roses over the trellis. But as yet the outhouse stands at the far back of the yard, forthrightly announcing its purpose and function to all who can see.

Then we began on the house. We tore all those layers of old wallpaper off, clear down to the sheathing. Looking at the bare boards that were left, we wondered what to do next. We figured the cost of resheathing the house. It was simply out of the question immediately, even with the cheapest lumber. And we had a dismal picture of ourselves hugging the stove all winter while the wind blew coldly around our heads. It was I who had the inspiration. I had been unpacking dishes one morning from a heavy cardboard carton. When I finished, Henry broke the carton down and took it out to burn. "Hey, wait a minute," I yelled. "Why wouldn't these heavy cartons make good temporary sheathing for the house?"

Henry blinked at me. "By George," he said, "they would if we could get enough of them."

"What do the stores in town do with them?"

"We can soon find out."

So we jumped in the car and headed for Columbia, the county seat town. We propositioned all the grocery stores there and were told to help ourselves. We prowled around in back of them, jubilant over the big piles discarded for burning. We collapsed them as we found them and tied them in flat bundles. For several days all we did was drive back and forth to town, hunting and bringing home cardboard cartons.

When we had a good-sized stock pile on hand, I began cutting them. At first we tried making them all the same size, but we soon saw that this not only involved too much work but also wasted the cardboard. So then we concentrated on getting the most cardboard out of any one box. I soon learned that scissors wouldn't do for this kind of cutting. The cardboard was too heavy and the scissors weren't long enough. I abandoned them for a long butcher knife, and it wasn't long until I had developed a sawing technique that went rapidly and neatly.

Then we started tacking it up. We began at the top of the wall and tacked in strips to the floor. We tried thus to have a fairly straight edge on each strip. Over the crack where the cardboards came together we pasted strips of cloth. We did all four walls and the ceilings of both rooms downstairs. We literally boxed ourselves in with cardboard. And then we papered with a very cheap grade of wallpaper. I think it actually is a building paper, which comes in solid colors and a few patterns. It is fifty-four inches wide, and is very heavy and coarse. All the ridge folks paper with it. It costs only $2.50 per roll, and one roll will paper the average room. We avoided the patterned paper and chose a solid color.

Neither of us had ever papered before, but we started out blithely enough. Henry, being a perfectionist, measured to the sixteenth of an inch the exact length needed, and then he cut the strips while I mixed up the paste. Miss Bessie never bothered to buy paste. She makes her own, but that sounded awfully messy to me, and besides I didn't know how. So we bought ours.

We know now, of course, that we should have cut that fifty-four inch width in two, but at the time we didn't know, and we didn't ask, so we struggled with each heavy strip. Henry would hold it at the top, trying to keep it even, and I would smooth down the wall. In spite of Henry's perfectionism no two strips ever came out even. The walls weren't true, of course, and that provoked Henry mightily. Even so, we managed well enough on the walls.

It was when we started on the ceiling that we met our Waterloo. Now it's difficult enough to paper a ceiling with eighteen-inch paper, scaffolding, and the proper brushes. It calls for a neat, professional touch, which we definitely did not have. Neither did we have the scaffolding nor the brushes. We laid planks across chairs for scaffolding and we used rags for brushes. But the worst thing was the paper itself. Try making a strip of heavy building paper, fifteen feet long by fifty-four inches wide, stick to the ceiling, will you? It won't, I can tell you. It simply will not.

But we learned the hard way. We smeared the back side of the first strip and hopefully crawled up on our makeshift scaffolding. "Now I'll get it started up at the end," Henry said, "and you hold it up. Then start walking toward the other end and I'll follow and smooth it out."

So. It sounded simple enough. But as fast as Henry turned

loose of what he had already stuck up, it came unstuck and trailed along behind him. He would hold it in place and smooth it, then I would start walking along the scaffolding. He would turn loose and follow, smoothing frantically. But he was never fast enough. It always buckled, then sagged, then dropped. The law of gravity was in full operation. Time and again we tried it, getting paste and paper all over us, getting hotter and crosser by the minute, getting cricks in our necks and cramps in our arms.

We never did get a single strip up, for the end came when the whole thing fell and glued itself to Henry. I turned around just in time to see it settle itself over him. He looked like a ghost in a blue winding sheet. I giggled, which was, of course, the wrong thing to do. It was, in fact, the very worst thing I could have done, but I was more than a little hysterical by then and I couldn't help it. I heard a deep sigh, and then there was a violent upheaval within the folds of the paper. First Henry's head emerged, with what few hairs he has left on top of his head standing straight up, stiff with glue. His face was smeared with paste too, and underneath the paste it was dangerously red. He threw the paper off, tearing it loose from him. " Dammit," he yelled, " I'm through! I'm through with this, if the dad-blamed house *never* gets papered! " And he kicked the soggy, sticky mess high into the air. I stood and watched it curve gently up and through the door into the kitchen. Watched it make a slow arc and land, paste side down, of course, on the table. And then I watched Henry stalk majestically from the house. He meant it. He was really through. He didn't touch another strip of that paper, and to this day he has never so much as stuck his head inside the house when papering is being done.

I got the ceiling papered eventually by a method which may be unusual but which was certainly practical. It should have occurred to me sooner. I simply whacked the paper into small squares and stuck them up. And they stayed stuck. There were a lot of seams, of course, but the main thing was to get the paper up there to stay. I let the seams fall where they would, and when I got through, I looked blissfully around me and thought I had never seen two such lovely rooms as we now possessed.

And truly they didn't look bad. The paper was a soft, grayish blue, and its coarse, oatmealy texture added to its attractiveness. The walls had an almost professional look, for we had been able to keep the seams true. And I just didn't look at the ceiling. Who but a fly was ever going to notice the ceiling? And no wind could whistle through. That was for sure. That thick, heavy cardboard was between us and the north wind. The soft, gray-blue paper made an effective background for the furniture. The pink slip covers on the old couch and Henry's big chair looked soft and warm against it. An old sideboard which we had refinished in the city gleamed softly, and the piano fitted snugly into a corner, its gaunt old upright frame looking less awkward and more at home than I had ever seen it.

For the first time since we had moved I began to have a hopeful feeling about the house. I even began to have a few highfalutin notions about it. Such as giving the place a name . . . Pennyrile Farm, I thought. And I had visions of a rustic sign swinging from a post near the mailbox. I could see a coach lantern on top of the post, and maybe a whitewashed wagon wheel leaning against it. Pennyrile Farm! Hoosh! I forgot that in a hurry. It would take more courage than I've got to hang a rustic sign by our mailbox and take the ribbing we'd get as a consequence. I can hear the folks hooting at it now. We'd never in this world live it down. This here farm is " Henry's Place " — and Henry's Place it'll be, " forever and enduring." And it doesn't need a sign to say so.

The floors were another big problem. They were not the usual kind of floors at all. They were merely wide poplar planks, which had been laid down green and had subsequently shrunk and buckled until there were half-inch cracks between most of the boards, and a half-inch drop between some of them. I knew they would be beautiful if we could take them up and re-lay them, sand them, and polish them. And I still hope to do that someday. But in the meantime there was only one thing to do with them — cover them from wall to wall.

I despise linoleum except where it belongs: in halls, kitchens, and bathrooms. It's cold, slick, and repulsive-looking to me. I think there is nothing in this world uglier than the huge floral patterns designed in imitation of rugs. But I was already learning, from the amount of dirt we tracked in daily, that linoleum was the only practical floor covering in the country. So, recognizing the inevitable once again, I sat down to do some figuring. When I got through, I had that hopeless feeling that lack of money always gives you. We couldn't possibly afford good linoleum from wall to wall, and even if we could have afforded it, I knew it would be foolish to put it on those rough, buckled floors. They would have simply broken and cracked it all over.

Henry took me to town again and I began searching for the next-best thing. I found three very cheap linoleum rugs, two of them a plain gray and rose marble, and the third a red and black marble. As well as I can remember, they were $5.95 each. We bought all three and brought them home. We centered the two gray and rose ones in the downstairs rooms, and then cut up the third one and laid it around for a border. Believe it or not, we had two very distinguished-looking rooms when we had finished, although it shocked the entire settlement that we should cut up a perfectly good rug.

So with cardboard and building paper on the walls and linoleum on the floors we made our house about as tight and windproof as it could be made. It had cost us less than twenty-five dollars, and I mention that figure simply to show what you can drag up from the bottom of the barrel when necessity compels it. We didn't count our aching backs and tired tempers.

We tackled the upstairs next. Henry had merely laid some planks across the rafters to hold our bed and a couple of dressers, and the rest of our furniture, boxes and crates, and odds and ends, had been shoved to one end of the long room. These were things we didn't need, and might never need again. But we had them and they had to be given shelter. That upstairs posed a real problem. To begin with, it was the entire length and width of the house. We had to have flooring and sheathing of some kind. The cardboard wouldn't do here, for there was nothing to tack it to. Someway we had to get hold of some lumber, and Henry's figures proved that enough lumber to floor and sheathe that huge room would cost more than we had. But we knew we couldn't sleep up there when winter came, with only the clapboard siding between us and the elements, and a cold, tin roof over our heads. We saw no answer to this one, however. Cudgel our brains as we might, we couldn't make dollars out of thin air.

And then — and it was like a miracle — one day another cousin of Henry's came to him and asked if he could rent a small field over on the ridge next to him for corn. I don't think either of us even knew we had a field over there. He had some old lumber he thought maybe Henry might be able to use, and he'd like to make a trade. That's one trade that was made in record time. For the use of that field for a year, we got enough lumber to floor and ceil the upstairs room, and enough of some kind of queer, metallic building paper that Fred had got for free at an Army depot to paper it. If we'd inherited a small fortune, we couldn't have been any happier than we were over that trade. We set to work with great zeal. We decided to partition the room two thirds of the way down, so that we would have one large room for a bedroom, and a small one for a storeroom. The bedroom is fifteen feet wide and twenty feet long. The storeroom is ten by fifteen.

The bedroom is so large that we made it a bed-sitting-room. It really contains our most prized possessions. We are not crazy about antique furniture as such. But we do possess a bed and two dressers of which we are very proud. We salvaged the bed from an old barn here on the ridge several years ago and refinished it ourselves. When we had taken seven coats of varnish and paint off, the wood emerged mellow and beautiful, poplar and cherry. The posts are quarter turned, and when we took them to pieces, we found that the bed had been put together with wooden pegs. We sanded it clean, put one coat of white shellac on it, rubbed it down with steel wool, and then waxed it. It is really a handsome piece of furniture. One of the dressers we picked up in a junk shop in the city and refinished, but the other one was my grandmother's.

82

It too is golden poplar, with a marble top and small drawers built up on each side. I remember that my grandfather kept his collar buttons in one of those little drawers.

The only other thing we have that is of any value is an Oriental rug. This we laid in the sitting end of the bedroom. We have an old-fashioned Franklin stove right in the center of the room, for the flue was built directly in the middle of the house. And there are two comfortable chairs, the Hollywood bed, which makes a good studio couch, and my desk. This is the flat-topped mahogany desk that Dr. Sherrill gave me. It had been in my office all the years we worked together, and when I left, he insisted that it belonged to me. It is more than my writing desk: it is my study; for where that desk is set down, there I can write. The work habits of years have been formed at it, and I need only to open the typewriter to be completely and easily at home.

Sometimes when I am at work up here in the top of the house, I have the feeling I had as a child when I took a book and stole out to an old apple tree back of the house, crawled up to a crotch high above the world, and sat there, remote and insulated. It was a snug, alone feeling, high and away where I could read and dream. This upstairs study of mine is my treetop now. High and alone, as one must be to dream. And writing is but dreaming made articulate.

That was our house, finished for the time being. And except for adding a fireplace to the living room and paneling that end of the room with pine, we have done very little more to it. Occasionally when I look at the beautiful rooms in one of the home magazines I get a yen to fly in and redecorate. I think, now that kind of rug would be lovely in the living room, and it would be practical too. But I know that the old gray and rose linoleum with the braided rug in front of the hearth is, after all, best. With a long-haired dog spoiled to sleep in front of the fire, and with two pairs of muddy boots tracking in and out all day, any kind of rug would be a pain in the neck to keep clean.

I have had only one experience with a professionally decorated apartment. And it brought me no pleasure. Everything had to be just so, lamps, sofa pillows, books, even ash trays. Everything was placed to its best advantage. If it was moved, something was out of balance. We could never relax and throw the Sunday papers on the floor, leave the dust ruffle off the bed, push the curtains back. It was like living in a bandbox. Every comfortable, normal impulse to leave things around had to be curbed, for the apartment, to look its best, had to be in immaculate order. I never want that again, and I certainly don't have it.

I have just taken a quick look around the living room to see. Henry's guns stand in one corner by the fireplace, and his fishing tackle is scattered over the mantel. Here in the middle of the winter Henry is hopeful of a warm day and he has been oiling his reels. A pair of gloves and Henry's boots are drying on the hearth, and Honey lies there with her paws stretched to the fire. In another corner two bags of cement are stacked. The house is the only place where Henry can be sure they will stay dry. The bookshelves ranging around two walls are full to cramming, not only with books but with the few pieces of ironstone I possess, several house plants, and dozens of pictures of Libby, Nash, and the babies. On the table at the end of the couch is a stack of magazines, a dozen or so books, two reams of paper, three ash trays, a cup of coffee, and Henry's drawing instruments. He is at present working on plans for the barn.

But that's home. That's what makes it home, and when you evaluate happiness in terms of comfortable living, it takes remarkably few gadgets. For us it seems to take a chestnut log crackling on the fire, the popcorn popper handy nearby. It takes the wall of books, and the piano. It takes Henry on one side of the fire and me on the other and Honey in between. We've got a stout roof over our heads, tin though it be, and tight walls between us and the winter winds. We've got forty acres of wood to burn if we need it, and food in the pantry. We talk idly about building a new house someday. We may. But I wouldn't bet on it. We've lived ourselves into this little house now, and it gives us just about everything we want or need. What more could a new home do?

Chapter

6 ✒ ✒

You realize, of course, that the crab grass, careless weeds, and cockleburs were not patiently waiting for us to get through with the work on the house to begin growing and taking over the garden and tobacco. Of course they weren't. It would have simplified matters if they had. We accomplished the work on the house, as Frony says, "sort of in-betweenst."

We stir early on the ridge, so that first summer daylight usually saw us up and about. And daylight comes around four thirty during the summer months. By sunup breakfast was usually ready. And breakfast, with ridge folks, is a hefty meal. I don't get by with fruit juice, toast, and coffee any more. We begin with fruit juice, but we go on to hot biscuits, ham and eggs or bacon and eggs, sometimes fried chicken or squirrel and cream gravy, and then we top off the meal with more hot biscuits and homemade jelly or preserves. In an emergency I can put breakfast on the table in thirty minutes. But given plenty of time I usually take an hour. Shades of the days when I served what passed for breakfast in ten easy motions! In those days I didn't like breakfast. Never had a breakfast appetite. A sliver of toast, two cups of coffee — that was it. I eat like a field hand nowadays. I polish off four hot biscuits, two eggs, and my half of the ham or bacon, and frequently snitch a couple of bites from Henry's plate. One thing you can count on having in the country — that's a healthy appetite. Breakfast is really our favorite meal and we never rush it. We take plenty of time to cook it and enjoy it. Nothing is hurrying us so that we must swallow it whole and dash out. I think taking the hurry out of it is what has made it such a pleasant meal for us. And it's the best way I know to start the day right.

Breakfast over and a smidgen of housework done, I was ready to tackle the crab grass and weeds alongside Henry. After Frony batted me down with that caustic remark about the garden being a woman's work, I was a very zealous gardener. "I'll do the garden," I told Henry, "and you can get on with the tobacco."

In justification of what happened I should like to say that I had never before had intimate contact with a garden. My father always had a small vegetable garden, but he would never allow any of us inside the fence. He probably knew what would inevitably happen. Occasionally we gathered peas or beans under his direction, but normally he even harvested the crop. So this was my first garden experience.

My, what a lot of little weeds there were! Happily I hoed down the row of onions and back up the row of radishes. Next came a row in which there seemed to be nothing but weeds. Queen Anne's lace, I decided, kneeling to get a better look at the tiny, delicate little fronds curling up from the earth. I had forgotten what we planted in that row, but whatever it was, Queen Anne's lace wouldn't do it any good, so I slashed the whole row clean. There wasn't a sprig left when I finished. It was as clean as the palm of your hand.

The next row had lettuce coming up, which I recognized, and careless weeds getting a good start at the other end. I clipped viciously at them. The next row was peas just beginning to push through the top crust of earth. I didn't try to hoe the peas. I got down on my hands and knees and pulled the weeds out. In the next row there was nothing but some tall, slender spikes of grass shooting up. This must be crab grass, I thought, and I carefully slashed every blade and left another row clean. A funny little sprangling vine crawled along the next row. Ha, wild morning-glories! I snipped them off at the roots.

By that time the sun was overhead and I had dinner to cook. But I had done a good morning's work. Blissfully I went into the house and I just wished Frony could have happened by to see me at my gardening. It was a lucky thing she didn't. When Henry came in for dinner, his face wore a peculiar expression. I couldn't tell whether something was hurting him, or whether he had swallowed his tobacco. He looked kind of sick.

"What's the matter?" I asked.

"Nothing," he said.

I dished up dinner and he washed and sat down at the table.

"How did your morning go?" I asked. "Lot of weeds in the tobacco?"

"Considerable," he replied.

I have grown more or less accustomed to the taciturnity of a ridge man, learning by experience that his silence is not always golden. When he has nothing to say, he says nothing. But occasionally when he has nothing to say he is pondering the best way to say a lot. With Henry I am sometimes quiet, waiting for whatever he is pondering. Sometimes I chatter on, knowing he will interrupt when he is ready. This was a time when I chattered. "I don't think I'm going to mind taking care of the garden at all," I said. "It doesn't seem to be much of a chore. I didn't have a bit of trouble this morning."

Henry grunted.

"But a lot of that stuff we planted hasn't come up yet, Henry. The corn, and the squash and cucumbers, and I didn't see any carrots. And I thought you set out some peppers. But," I went on happily, "maybe they'll be up in another day or so."

"Not very likely," Henry said, over a mouthful of potatoes.

"Oh? Weren't the seeds any good?"

"Seeds were O.K."

"Well, why won't they come up then?"

"They *were* up."

There was a long silence while this sank in. I had a premonitory flutter in my stomach. "They were? Where?"

"Right where they were planted. You've cut them all down."

"I don't believe it!"

"O.K. Come along and I'll show you."

Sadly I followed him to the garden, for even though I was having to be shown I knew he was right. "Here," he said, pointing to my first clean row, "is where the carrots were."

"I thought that was Queen Anne's lace."

"Well, they do look somewhat alike," Henry admitted.

He went on to the next row, at one end of which was the

lettuce I had recognized and the careless weeds at the other
end which I had chopped down. "Those were peppers at this
end," he said, "all living and doing fine." There they lay now,
wilted and dying in the noon sun.

He crossed the row of peas which I had also recognized and
came to the next clean row. "What did you think this was?"
he asked, pointing to the slender sprigs and blades I had
slashed down so vigorously.

"Crab grass," I answered slowly.

"That was corn. Good stand too. And what in heaven's name
did you think this vine was?"

"Wild morning-glories, and you told me they were a nui-
sance!"

"Wild morning-glories, for heaven's sake! Those were cucumbers at the far end, and squash up here!"

Without another word he turned around and went back to
the house. And without another word I followed him and wept
into the dishwater as I did the dishes. I heard him hammering
away at something before he went back to the tobacco field, but
it wasn't until the middle of the afternoon that I discovered
what he had been doing. Thinking to make peace with him, I
made a big pitcher of lemonade and went to the door to call
him. Then I saw it. There, at the edge of the garden, staring me
in the face, almost as big as life itself and for all the world to
see was a sign:

OFF LIMITS
to
JAN

I was so mad that I poured the lemonade out and sulked all
afternoon. But late that evening, more humble than I knew I
could be, I helped him replant all the denuded rows. It took
quite a time for me to live that down. As a matter of fact I
haven't. People ask me yet if the garden is still off limits to
me. Of course it's not. I know a weed when I see one now.
And if I am in doubt I just let it alone. I'd rather see the whole
garden become a mass of wild morning-glories than to risk
chopping down the smallest sprig of cucumber vine. And as
for crab grass, everyone knows you can't get rid of it anyhow.

88

I think the thing I minded most of the new chores I had to learn was the washing. When we told people we were moving to the ridge, they all said to me: " Oh, how will you ever manage without electricity and plumbing and water! You'll simply be lost without modern conveniences."

Well, I wasn't. If it seems very farfetched that I should be able to change practically every habit of my life without a great deal of trouble, I'm sorry. But it is true. Except for the lack of an electric iron and a refrigerator I didn't mind not having electricity at all. But I must admit that I never did get accustomed to doing without refrigeration. Not having a spring handy in which to keep milk and butter, I had to keep it in buckets of cold water. And leftover food simply had to be thrown away during hot weather. Nothing would keep even until the next day. Honey fattened considerably that first summer and winter before we got electricity.

As for lamps, I loved the kerosene lamps. We had two good Aladdin lamps, the kind that use a mantle and give a very bright light, but even when compelled by the circumstance of all the mantles being crumbled to use a common small lamp, I didn't mind. The light was soft and yellow, and it had a cozy, warm glow. I didn't even mind cleaning and filling the lamps daily. It was a sort of satisfactory chore. I usually washed the lamp chimneys when I did the breakfast dishes, but I always filled the lamps in the evening. Bringing in the wood, filling the lamps, drawing up the night water, those were part of winding up the day. They became routine chores, and I remember thinking once as I brought in an armful of wood: How did I end the day in the city? With this feeling of content? With this simplicity of making ready for the night? With this knowledge of a day lived fully and richly? There is a significance to me in the evening chores. They settle my account for the day. They sum up, add, and total another turning of the earth, and generally I come to the end of the day replete with happiness. Even at first, when I was only beginning to sense these things, I knew a peace and a contentment I had never known before. And that may have had something to do with the ease of the adjustment I made.

I never minded, and I don't yet mind, not having a bathroom. People from the city say to me, " It will be so nice when you can have water in the house and plumbing." I've got news for them. I don't think we ever will have water in the house and plumbing. It doesn't seem the least bit important to us. We take our baths in the biggest washtub, on the hearth in winter, on the back porch after dark in summer. We may not take as many allover baths as we used to do in the city. In the winter we only take one tub bath a week. But in the summer we frequently sponge off and change twice a day, and always wind up with the tub bath at night.

In the winter we take our tub baths on Saturday night, and it's quite an occasion. We fill the reservoir to the big, black kitchen stove (which holds fifteen gallons) early in the morning. By night, what with a cooking fire going most of the day, it is boiling hot, and we simply add what we need to heat our tubs of cold water. And I have to ask you to believe that I like, I actually like, folding myself up in a washtub in front of a roaring fire and parboiling myself. Even cleanliness becomes aesthetic under those conditions. It is a physical and spiritual pleasure, for I watch the flames of the fire dreamily and contentedly, and soak and sing and surrender myself to its spell. A bath becomes a rite performed before the altar of the fire. Unless, that is, Henry opens the door and lets the " cauld blast " in on my back. Then I howl bloody murder and finish in a hurry. He has a way of doing that when I have been dawdling too long.

As for central heating, that is simply a thing of the past, and I have accepted it. There is no way, on a shoestring, to have an entirely comfortable house in the country during cold weather. We just keep roaring fires going and pile on more clothing. In the city, weather doesn't make much difference. You are in warm buildings most of the time and can be comfortable in a minimum of clothing. When you go out, it is only for a brief scurry to the car or down the street, and you merely add a coat, hat, and gloves, and scurry. In the country you certainly can't do that. You live with the weather in the country. There are always cold corners in your house, or even cold rooms. It would take a mort of wood to keep an entire house thoroughly warm all over, so you leave certain rooms that are not constantly used cold. And then there are always the outside chores to be done. You dash in and out of the house all day long. We are glad to don red flannels, come winter, and more than once I have cooked breakfast in three shirts and a sweater. If I waited for the kitchen to get completely warm, we'd have breakfast somewhere around noon.

Clothing in the country is different anyhow. I had accumulated in the years of working in an office in the city a rather complete wardrobe of dresses, suits, blouses, shoes, hats, coats, and so forth. I packed them, of course, and brought them with me when we moved. But it took me only about six weeks to realize that I would never wear most of them again. I kept one good black dress, with accessories to match, a dress suit and a gray flannel for ordinary wear, one topcoat and hat, and shipped the rest of the things to Libby. Since then I have given her most of the things I kept, for a black dress, black suit, black coat are almost entirely useless to me. Honey is a long-haired dog and she rides everywhere with us in the car. She also has free use of the sofa and chairs in the living room. You can imagine what a soft black topcoat looked like by the time I got to town. I now have both a tweed suit and a tweed coat, and if I could find it I'd have a tweed hat. Tweed is the thing for dust and mud and dog hairs.

I have always liked to work around the house in blue jeans so I possessed no house dresses when we moved. I needn't add, surely, that I have not acquired any. I just laid in a more adequate supply of jeans. And about that time my family started sending them to me also, so that I have enough on hand now to last me a normal life span. I wear them constantly. They are sturdy, protective, and, for me, comfortable. In the garden they protect my legs from briers, sweat bees, and the acid fuzz of vines. In the yard I can get down on my knees to work in the flower beds with freedom and without concern for my skin or my clothes. In the house — well, in the winter they are warm, and in the summer I just let them soak up the sweat. About the only vanity I have left in clothes is in shirts. I do love beautiful plaid shirts. I particularly like the Western styles in soft gingham or flannel, and I don't think I could ever have too many of them. The brighter the colors, the better I like them.

And shoes. I have one pair of dress shoes: the others are strictly practical. Around the place I wear moccasins or strollers. Not Oxfords — they are too heavy. Just the plain slide-into strollers that high school girls love, or the beautiful, soft, handmade moccasins of the West. On one of our trips to Santa Fe I discovered the Tesuque moccasin through Libby. I never intend to be without a pair of them again. They are perfect for wearing in the house, and outside if the weather is nice. They are made of some sort of soft skin, undressed, and they are as near to going barefoot as you can get. They tie close around the ankle so that there is no difficulty with slipping as there is with most moccasins. Libby and I buy the very plainest kind, although you can get them beaded or dressed up with other fancy doodads. The plain ones are, naturally, the cheapest, and suit our purpose just as well. But they're no good in wet weather, for, like doeskin gloves, they soak through in no time and are slick and slippery. However, they will slip into rubber boots or arctics very nicely and make warmer protection for the feet than boot socks. And about boots. I have leather boots for bad weather or for walking in the woods. And arctics for snow and slush and deep mud. Not rubbers — they're much too light — plain, big, heavy, old-fashioned arctics.

I wear wool or nylon socks the year round. My mother knits them for me, and keeps me supplied with more than I need. I think she must always keep a pair of socks for me on the needles. She uses the scraps of yarn left over from her other knitting, which is why I have so many pretty pairs of nylons. She knits Joan and Penni, my nieces, twin nylon sweaters, and forthwith I get a couple of pairs of beautiful soft yellow socks. She knits my brother a heavy gray pull-over, and I get three or four pairs of gray wool socks, banded in red, green, or blue, according to the scraps she has on hand. Sometimes she is so low on scraps that she uses four or five different colors to eke out; then I get a pair that are very fancy indeed. Red, green, yellow, and gray, and sometimes a pair look as if they have been mismated, for maybe she ran out of red on one sock. But I have told her never to worry about that. Who's going to count the stripes on my socks, anyhow?

Our clothes do not present any great laundry problem, but even so, the washing was one thing that almost made me move back to town. Every week there was that huge pile of dirty clothes. It had been my good fortune never to have to do my own laundry. And I didn't even know how to start. Vaguely I knew that white clothes and colored clothes had to be separated, and from Miss Bessie I learned that things come clean faster if you soak them overnight in bleaching solution. From her too I learned that white things had to be boiled. So each Sunday night we put a tubful of clothes to soak. Monday morning bright and early they were transferred to a wash boiler of suds and put on the back of the stove to simmer during breakfast. Once breakfast and the dishes were out of the way, they were usually ready to scrub. That meant transferring them from the boiler to a tub of clear hot water, over which I broke my back while scrubbing away with a bar of soap on a washboard. Then they must be wrung out and put through two rinse waters. All that wringing and sloshing around. And our clothes were very dirty. You can't grub weeds out of a garden and tobacco patch without getting a lot of soil and sweat on your clothes. Henry's jeans and shirts were always caked with dirt and mine was almost as bad. And towels. I don't recall ever seeing a really soiled towel in the bathroom in the city. But down here they looked as if a coal heaver had been using them, so there was nothing to do but scrub.

I tackled one or two washings by myself, calling on Henry only to help with drawing the water and emptying the tubs. But there are limits to physical strength, and while I am not a weakling by any manner of means, I simply cannot do a washing and remain human. Henry saw that, and after the first time or two he dedicated Monday to helping with the laundry. It was never a happy day for either one of us, and we did it only because there was no laundry in either of the two neighboring towns at that time, and because we didn't have the money to have it done at a laundry if there had been one. There was nothing to do but sweat over it and get it done. I always felt raddled and haggard by the time it was over.

Thank goodness, by the time the tobacco crop was sold and we were in funds again a laundry had opened at Campbellsville. It was the most sublime moment of my life when I took the first bundle of clothes to that beautiful modern laundry and left them, knowing that when I went back for them they would be clean, ironed, and folded, and my only contact with them would be putting them away in the dresser drawers.

A lot of foolish fancy has been written about the beauty of clothes hanging on a line (stretched, perhaps, between apple trees in bloom), blowing free in the breeze, soaking up the sunshine and the fresh, clean air, smelling so fragrant when you take them off the line. The average family wash is not beautiful hanging on a line stretched anywhere! Papa's long underwear is just long underwear, whether it's stretched between apple trees, fig trees, or just plain persimmon trees like ours. It flaps forlornly wherever it's stretched. If he doesn't wear long underwear (and he'd better during a ridge winter unless he wants frozen shanks to say nothing of a frozen fanny), his shorts and T shirts aren't much more graceful. Mamma's petticoats, brassières, and panties hang limply alongside, and the whole world can see that she's pinned the straps of her brassières, and that the elastic in her panties has lost all its stretch. And if you hang more than two sheets in the wind, the whole ridge will nod knowingly and say: " H'm! Henry's commenced sleepin' by hisself! "

Clothes dried in the sun and air *do* smell sweet. That I'll grant. But I never had strength enough left to pull in a good, deep whiff, so even that virtue was lost on me. Besides, I can't find anything wrong with the clean, fresh smell of clothes done at the laundry.

The next day after the washing there was the ironing. I kept that down to a minimum by folding the sheets, pillowcases, towels, and dish towels as they came from the line. I even tried it with our shirts and blue jeans, but Henry had

such a hangdog look on his face when he had to wear unironed
clothes that I gave it up. He sort of slunk around, like Honey
when she has been scolded. Even knowing the work it saved
me, he couldn't take any pride in going out to the tobacco
field in uncreased breeches and a wind-wrinkled shirt. "It's
healthier," I told him. "Think of all the sunshine and fresh
air that haven't been pressed out of your clothes!"

"I get enough sunshine and fresh air," he grumbled, tugging
at his shirt sleeves and his pants legs. "I don't need it floating
around in my clothes. I feel like Little Orphan Annie."

So there was nothing to do but iron. At first I ironed only
his clothes. I didn't feel like Little Orphan Annie, so I skipped
mine. But the first time we went to town and he let me out
at the corner so that he wouldn't be seen with me, I realized
I was defeated. After all, you can't have your husband taking
the high road, leaving you to the low, just over a matter of
unironed clothes. For the next six months, then, I ironed on
Tuesday. And that meant a sweltering fire all morning, and
profanity as I tried to keep the irons at the proper temperature. Whoever first called them "sad irons" was an imaginative
soul to say the least. Sad they certainly are. Sad to heat, sad
to keep hot, sad to iron with, and sad the day they were ever
invented. It was with a whoop of joy that I threw them into
the rubbish heap the day the electricity was turned on.

When we had electricity installed, everyone supposed the
first appliance we would buy would be a washing machine.
It usually is around these parts. But not me. We couldn't have
an automatic out here on the ridge, for that requires running
water. But even if we could have one, I'm still not sold on
them. They haven't yet been perfected to the point where I'd
like one. When they get them to the place where you can pile
a tubful of clothes into them, push a button, go back about
an hour later and take out the clothes, starched, ironed, and
folded, then I'll be interested. Until then, and as long as I
have two brains which for some reason rub together and produce words that will sell, I'll just keep on paying the Campbellsville Steam Laundry to take care of my clothes. And consider it a privilege.

Chapter

7 ↙↙

We come, now, to the middle of July and to the spring-poling of the well!

For six weeks we had been as busy as a hive of bees with the garden, the tobacco, and the house. All that time we were carrying every drop of water we used from a neighbor's well. I wasn't about to start carrying it from that spring a quarter of a mile away. The neighbor lived about, oh, say, roughly, three city blocks down the road, and it was bad enough to pack two buckets of water a dozen times a day *that* distance. We knew we had to have a well, but it had to wait for a few other things.

But one morning at breakfast Henry announced, "Elmer's coming today to witch the well."

Here on the ridge we don't dig a well until we have it witched. Of course we know there's water anywhere if you dig deep enough. But when you're going to spring-pole a well, by hand, you certainly don't want to have to spring-pole half-way to China to get water. It's much simpler to have a water witch come and locate the stream and tell you exactly where to put your well.

We do a lot of things that sound superstitious to others. For instance, we plant by the moon. We plant peas, beans, corn, and things that ripen on the vine above the earth, in the *light* of the moon. And we plant potatoes, carrots, beets, turnips, things which mature beneath the earth, in the *dark* of the moon. The theory is that in the light of the moon the pull is up, so things that ripen above the earth must be planted in the light of the moon to do well. In the dark of the moon the pull is down, so things that mature beneath the earth must be planted in the dark of the moon. It applies also to other things. You lay a shingle roof in the *dark* of the moon, so the shingles will lie flat and not curl. If you forget and lay them in the light of the moon, the upward pull will make them curl every time. And you lay a split rail fence in the *light* of the moon. If you don't, the downward pull will sink the bottom rail into the ground.

I don't question this wisdom at all. I don't pretend to understand it, but I don't doubt it. If, being a woman, the rhythm of my own life is controlled by the monthly rising and waning of the moon, and if tides ebb and flow under its influence, I don't see any reason at all to question its effect upon other things. If, at this late date, we have learned how to split an atom, it seems entirely reasonable to me to suppose that there are many natural influences at work in the universe about which we have long been skeptical and which we may not understand. After all, God doesn't make much sense when you try to reason about him.

I hurried with the housework that morning so as to be free to watch Elmer witch the well. He arrived, flanked by his two sons. One of them, I understand, is also a water witch. The other is not. The ability, or talent, or whatever it is, is handed down from father to son, but only to one son. Elmer's father was a water witch, but Elmer is the only one of five sons who came into the inheritance.

Elmer is a small, thin man with a hesitant speech and a constantly apologetic air. " I'll do the best I kin fer you, Henry," he said. " Now I ain't to say as good as my pa was. But I've witched several wells in my time an' ain't never missed. I *might*," he went on to say, " I might miss a foot or two on the depth, but I've not never missed out totally on hittin' water."

" That's good enough for me," Henry assured him; " just you say where the stream is, and that's where we'll dig."

I stood to one side and watched. Elmer took out his pocket-knife and walked over to the dogwood tree at the back of the yard. He looked it over carefully and then reached up and cut a small limb that was forked. He trimmed it and came back toward us. I noticed that the branches of the fork were left about sixteen or eighteen inches long, while the trunk of the limb was cut down to about six inches.

He walked to the corner of the yard and grasped the ends

of the forked branches. His hands were turned so that his thumbs covered the ends of the forks. The well was to be in the back yard of course. Grasping the green dogwood branch firmly in his hands, Elmer started walking slowly from the corner of the house out into the yard. Not more than twenty feet from the house I saw the trunk end of the branch, which Elmer was holding straight out in front of him, bend sharply toward the ground. He stopped and Henry marked the spot. Elmer then walked on, and in less than three feet the branch rose upright again. Systematically, from every corner of the yard, from every angle, he worked with that now-bending, now-straightening, branch, until he had the course of the stream laid out. Henry marked it each time the branch bent. It ran in a diagonal straight line clear across the yard, twenty feet from the corner of the house at one end, and about forty feet at the other. Elmer stopped finally when Henry had charted the stream entirely across the yard. "Well, there's yer stream," he said. "Anywhere's along that line you'll hit water. Now, you want I should try to figger how deep you'll have to go?"

"Yes," Henry told him.

He walked away from the line of the stream and gripped the branch again. He began counting to himself when the first movement downward began. And he counted until the branch tipped directly toward the earth over the stream bed. "I make it forty foot," he said then. He missed it three feet as we found out later! and he was very apologetic about it. "My pa wouldn't of missed it three inches," he said. "But I can't figger as good as my pa."

There is a feel in the branch. I know, for when he had finished I asked Elmer to let me put my hands on the branch close to his and try it. I don't pretend to understand it, and I have no explanation to offer, but the branch pulls downward so strongly that there is no power that can hold it straight. I watched Elmer's hands grip the ends of the fork so tightly his knuckles whitened, and I saw the bark twist free from the limb, and under my own hands I felt it pull and turn and slowly and inevitably bend toward the stream of water underground. Alone, in my own hands, the branch was lifeless. But when Elmer's hands gripped it, it was alive and knowing.

"What do I owe you?" Henry asked, when it was finished.

"Nary a thing," Elmer said. "Jist a drink of cold water in passin'."

"Any time," Henry told him, "any time."

In my ignorance I supposed that Henry and his father would dig a deep, round hole in the ground until they hit water. But even I thought forty feet was going to be a lot of digging. That was when I learned about spring-poling. "No," Henry said, laughing at me, "we'll dig down to the solid rock, then we'll drill."

They dug, with pick and shovel, an oblong hole, not a round one, about four feet by six feet, and it was nearly eight feet deep before they struck rock. Then they went to the woods and cut a long, green sapling. At its base it was about nine inches in diameter, and at its top it was about four, and, being green, it was, of course, very springy. They cut the limbs away and dragged it to the house. Then they cut a smaller sapling which was forked a few feet from the ground. They stuck it upright in the ground a few feet from the opening of the hole. Then they braced the long sapling in the fork of the upright, weighting the far end of it well with heavy rocks. Directly over the center of the hole in the ground they then hung a thick cable rope on which a two-hundred-pound bit was tied. You see why it's called a spring pole? The end of the green sapling is springy, and by hand you push it up and down, and the motion drills the bit through the ground on the same principle a power engine does. But by hand, mind you!

The bit drills a hole about six inches in diameter, but of course it must be turned and guided by hand. Mr. Frank took a stool and crawled down into the oblong hole, and there he sat day after day, guiding and turning the bit. Henry did the springing, up on top. It was a long, heartbreaking job. I timed Henry once, and ninety seconds was absolutely the limit of his endurance to spring that heavy pole and bit up and down. And more than once I saw him lean, gasping, over the end of the pole until he had breath enough to move away. It made me ill to watch him, and I tried to help all I could. But I could never last longer than thirty or forty seconds. Even so, Henry never refused even that little bit of help. For four hands pulling down on the pole were much stronger than two, and added just that much more power.

I could have cried because we didn't have any money then. A well-drill outfit could have done the job in three days. But they would have charged $2.75 per foot. Figure forty feet at that price, and remember what we started with, more than half of which had already been spent, and you'll understand why we didn't even consider having the well drilled mechanically. I rather timidly suggested a cistern, when they got that nice oblong hole dug. But as far as I remember Henry didn't even answer me. No one on the ridge has a cistern, although for the life of me I don't see why not. But ridge folks like a well, and generally they drill it with a spring pole. So, of course, that's the way we drilled ours.

In three weeks Henry, with my feeble help, had drilled thirty-two feet. Then came that black day when we hit rock so solid that in an entire day we drilled only one inch. At the end of the day we were disconsolate. "How thick do you suppose that rock is?" I asked Mr. Frank.

"Hard to tell," he said. "May be six inches, may be six feet."

"And eight more feet to water!" I wailed, for I believed firmly in Elmer's prognostication.

"Nothing to do but keep at it," Henry said.

So the next day we kept at it. That day we could not tell that we drilled even a quarter of an inch! Once more we held council at the end of the day. "What can we do?" I asked.

"Might help if we had four or five men on the spring pole," Mr. Frank said.

"Then for goodness' sake, let's get four or five men," I said.

"Have to pay 'em," Henry warned.

"Then pay them." I didn't care if it took our last dollar. I was sick of seeing Henry pull his insides out at that awful pole. Literally that was what he was doing. He lost forty pounds digging that well.

He rounded up the men, and, considering the kind of work it is, they were angels to promise to come. Not one of them but had to stop his own work to help. They came a little after sunup the next morning and I was never so glad to see people in my life. You can talk all you please about the beauties of nature, about the sweetness of purple twilights, about the lovely, rounding curve of the hills, about tall trees etched against the sky . . . talk about them, rhapsodize over them, and enjoy them. I do too. But in the last analysis they don't count. Nature is completely indifferent. Purple twilights, gaunt old trees, graciously curving hills don't give a tinker's damn whether you live or die. Aesthetically I appreciate them. I find a certain amount of peace in looking at the hills, a certain quietude of spirit. They provide me with a stillness of soul that enables me to gather my forces. But I don't fool myself that they can offer me help or comfort. It's *people* who have goodness in their souls, not twilights! It's *people* who have hearts inside them, not hills. It's *people* who care when you're sick, or in trouble, or when you're spring-poling a well. No one likes that work. No one wants to help spring-pole a well. But five husky, brawny men showed up that morning and they looked like angels straight from heaven to me.

Even so, and grateful as I was, I should probably have violated the one inviolable rule of the ridge the next day had Henry not warned me. The rule of obligation. We were just finishing breakfast when the first of the men came. Henry pushed his chair back from the table. "You going to have enough for dinner today?"

There never had been any question before about whether there was enough for dinner. I had usually managed to scrape something together. "Yes," I said, "why?"

"Well, it doesn't make much difference what you have," he went on, "just be sure there's plenty. Seven men can eat a right smart."

He was going out the door. "*Seven!*" I grabbed him by the shirttail. "What do you mean, seven?"

Impatiently he motioned outside. "We got to feed these men. And you better have it ready about eleven."

Well, how was I to know? You don't pay a plumber or an electrician in the city and then feed him too. But then, neither has that plumber or electrician dropped his own work to come help you out. As a matter of fact, what he charges you by the hour is his guarantee of being able to provide his own food. There is no obligation beyond paying him.

I suppose the habit of feeding workers began back in the old days when men traded work and there was no money involved. It was a further extension of hospitality and gratitude. Doubtless it also saved time. For in the days when farms were miles apart, a man coming to help in your hay could hardly take time to go home for his dinner. But it is a nice custom which still abides on the ridge. Any man who is good enough to come to your aid is fed gladly and abundantly. It is a tangible expression of gratitude.

But I had not yet learned, and I was aghast at the idea. I think it was the first time in my life I was ever faced with the necessity of cooking for a crew of laboring men. How much was plenty? Mentally I measured what I knew Henry normally put away at the noon meal and multiplied it by seven. Then I set to work. Our garden was bearing lettuce, green onions, radishes, and a few small cucumbers. But green beans, tomatoes, and so forth were not quite ready. Miss Bessie's garden was rich with those treasures, however, so I dashed over there and she helped me pick a peck of green beans, two dozen ears of corn, half a dozen squash, and, for good measure, three or four cucumbers to go with mine. Blackberries were in season and I had nearly a gallon on hand. They made a luscious, juicy cobbler.

The table groaned with the quantity of food that day when the men sat down, and, if I do say so myself, the quality wasn't bad. I had been coming to the ridge and eating Miss Bessie's cooking long enough, and had been married to Henry long enough, to know what good ridge cooking is. With green beans it is boiling them all morning with a piece of smoked meat. You put them on in plenty of water, with the meat, and let them simmer slowly three or four hours. You never add water, for to be completely delectable they must cook down dry. It is a matter for shame if, when you serve them, there is liquid either in the beans or in the bowl. The meat should have cooked to pieces so that it has come apart and spread through them. I don't suppose there is a vitamin left in them, but they're mighty good just the same.

Corn is cooked on the cob, very similar to the way it is cooked anywhere. We add salt to the water, heat it to a rapid boil, plunge the fresh-shucked ears in just long enough to take the rawness out. About twelve minutes is right. It is still crisp, juicy, and sweet. We all raise a yellow sweet corn in our gardens, and we never think of cooking less than a dozen ears at a time.

Squash is scrubbed, sliced unpeeled, and parboiled about five minutes. Then it is turned into a frying pan, bacon drippings are added, and a liberal sprinkling of pepper. Then it is slowly fried dry. Salads are not served with dressing. We pile a bowl full of lettuce, sliced tomatoes, cucumbers, and green onions and set it on the table. No one ever adds anything but salt. A dressing would merely ruin the flavor.

And of course a cobbler is a cobbler anywhere in the United States. Some people make it with rich biscuit dough. But I stick to pastry. I serve it hot, with a half cup of butter sloshed over each helping. It should be juicy, but not soggy. It should, and does if made with a light hand, melt in your mouth.

Bread is corn bread to ridge folks. Biscuits are biscuits, loaf bread from the store is light bread or boughten bread, but when you say bread, you mean corn bread. I don't make it like the other ridge women, for I have never learned to like it that way. Miss Bessie, for instance, beats up a sifter full of meal with salt, soda, baking powder, adds buttermilk and a dash of melted lard, and turns it into a pan. She uses no egg, and when she doesn't have milk, she uses water. That is the usual method of making corn bread. But I make egg bread. It is lighter and fluffier. But ridge folks don't like it with egg. We have our meal ground from our own corn at the mill, so that it isn't necessary to add flour to it when making bread as you have to do with bought meal. It is glutinous enough without flour. You make biscuits too, when you serve a meal to ridge folks, but the mainstay is corn bread.

Meat is always pork, either fresh or cured. You may serve beef, but you won't call it meat. It's beef, just as chicken is chicken and squirrel is squirrel. But because everyone raises one or two "meat hawgs" each year, very little meat is bought, so naturally *meat* is pork. In the winter, just after hogs are killed, fresh pork is plentiful. During the summer there is side meat, jowls, and what we call fat back. Fat back is the fat, white, salted meat that is usually used for cooking. It is very good fried, if you pour boiling water over it to take the salt out, dry it, dredge it with flour and then brown it. And it makes delicious gravy. But you're down to the bottom of the barrel when you start frying fat back. A common way of expressing extreme poverty is to say, "They're fryin' fat back." And the traditional way of saying people are pretty well off is to say, "They eat fur back on the hawg." But this term may also describe extravagance.

You offer ridge folks sweet milk, buttermilk, or coffee to drink with a meal. All of them, if you have them. But you never offer them tea. We ourselves have got out of the habit of drinking tea since we have been here. And there was a time when iced tea was an imperative to us in the summer. There is a joke about tea here on the ridge which is told every time tea is mentioned. It happened to a distant cousin of Henry's who had gone to Indiana to pick tomatoes for the cannery during the season. He was staying at a boardinghouse I suppose. His first meal there was supper. But he tells it better himself.

"I set down," he says, "an' hit looked like they set a right good table there. Had a plenty fer all, an' hit looked good an' tasty. The woman, she poured somethin' in a big, tall glass fer me an' set it down alongside my plate. I never ast what hit was, jist takened a sip of it. Upon my word an' honor, hit like to of gagged me! I'd ruther of took a dost of salts. But, not wishin' to appear impolite, I drunk it down to git shet of it. Then I set out to make out my supper. D'reckly she come around agin, an' blest if she didn't fill my glass up with some more of the stuff. I was shore in a spot. Hit was worse'n medicine to git down, but I drunk it down, not wantin' her to think me unmannerly. I eat awhile, an' the vittles was real good, then dogged if she never filled that glass up agin. I swallered it down, but hit was a bitter dost, an' I says to myself, if she fills it up agin they ain't nothin' I kin do but leave her think what she will. I cain't go no more of it! She filled it up, an' I jist left it stand. Leastways, I says, hit'll keep her from fillin' it up agin. I jist left it, but I knowed in reason she was thinkin' I hadn't had no kind of bringin' up. An' I couldn't face her no more, so I changed my boardin' place next day."

No, you certainly do not offer tea to ridge folks.

And a ridge hostess does not sit down at the table with her guests. She stands alertly, watching to see that no man's glass runs dry, that the bread plates are never empty, that the vegetable bowls never get low. Food must flow constantly from the stove to the table, from the milk pitchers to the glasses, and the hostess must urge more and more on the guests. It is a point of honor not to run short. "There's aplenty," you must keep assuring them, and to prove it you keep on bringing more to the table. When the men, for if there are women guests they help the hostess, have finished, then the women may eat. Snacking a little here and there usually as they redd up the dishes.

So I stood and served seven men, and don't think it didn't keep me busy. I would have died rather than let Henry be embarrassed by me or the dinner before his neighbors and relatives. A good hostess sees every need of the table, just as a good waitress in the city hovers near to fill your glass and refill the bread basket. Anxiously I kept an eye on the bean pot and the bread pan. I think I would have simply faded away had they run short. The men would have laughed good-naturedly had they done so, but they would have told their wives and it would have been whispered all over the ridge, "Henry's woman never cooked enough fer the men the day they worked on the well." Scandalous!

But they didn't. And the next day it was just a matter of doing the same thing over again. For when the garden is in season, you don't have a variety of foods except as it provides them. You have the same things day after day. While green beans are bearing, you have green beans every day. The same is true of corn, tomatoes, squash, and so forth. It doesn't do any good to get tired of them. There they are and they have to be eaten. I had another peck of green beans, another two dozen ears of corn, another bowl of salad greens. The only thing that varied was the cobbler. It was apple instead of blackberry.

It was about five o'clock the evening of the third day when they struck water. I shall never forget the thrill of it as long as I live. If it had been oil, it couldn't have made me any happier. They had drilled through the first layer of hard rock, hit a soft streak of blue clay, then another layer of rock. And all day that third day they had been chugging away at that rock. They were almost ready to stop for the day when suddenly the bit sank easily into sandy gravel. Mr. Frank, down in the hole, held up his hand and everyone was quiet. Unmistakably we could hear the gurgle of water. "That's it!" he yelled, and we all whooped with joy. Water. Finally. On the tenth day of August, 1949, anno Domini. Henry had turned the first shovelful of dirt on July 15. We had water, at a cost of thirty-five dollars in cash, and untold hours of sweat, toil, and aching backs. But we had water!

There was nothing to do now but tile the top of the well and wait a day or two for the stream to clear. Ridge folks do not case their wells. They don't like the taste the metal casing gives to the water. Of course you may get a little sand or gravel with each bucket of water you draw, but who's going to mind a little sand or gravel? The water is clear, icy cold, and as soft as rain water.

Sometimes when I am in a hurry, or it's raining, or the well rope is frozen solid, I complain about having to draw water. But that's only on the surface, and it's only to Henry. Deep down inside I have never got over being proud of our well. Each bucket I draw is something of a miracle yet, and I never fail to marvel at that unfailing stream of clear, cold water which remains constant and level down there in the dark below us. We have an eight-foot stand of water, which means that no matter how much we draw out, the water rises immediately to the eight-foot level in the bottom of the well. That's good enough for us.

Elmer is the only one who ever expresses dissatisfaction with the well. "I knowed in reason I could hit the stream fer you," he tells us each time he passes by, "but I hate missin' out on the depth thataway. Hit was plumb misleadin'."

We don't think so. What's three feet between water witches!

Chapter

8 ✔ ✔

Elmer and Sereny come very close to breaking my heart. They are so good, so very, very good, and life has been so cruel to them.

Sereny is one of eight children, three of whom are mentally subnormal. Elmer is one of six children, two of whom are mentally subnormal, and one, Barney, is so feeble-minded as to be adjudged an idiot. No one in his right mind would agree that these two people should have married. There was no future in it, none at all. But they loved one another and it never occurred to them not to marry.

Sereny has had to work hard all her life. As a girl she was expected to work in the fields right alongside her brothers and did so, even to helping with the plowing. At that time she was stout and strong, able and willing. And she never skimped her part of the work. Her mother has told me how Sereny worked.

When she was twenty, and Elmer was nineteen (for she is a year older), they decided to get married. But, Sereny said, not until they had something put by. Her way of putting something by was to work out, in other people's kitchens, for five long years at $1.50 per week, saving almost literally every penny she made. With the money she bought, one thing at a time, all the furniture with which to furnish their home. All of it. And it is, after sixteen years, still all the furniture in their home. She bought dishes, pots and pans, silver, and kitchen utensils. She made quilts and bought sheets and blankets. Then the summer she finally decided they had accumulated enough (I always wonder what Elmer contributed) she quit her job and made a big garden all of her own, so that she could can vegetables to have a store with which to begin their marriage. She was twenty-five then.

Elmer has never managed to make much of a living. He has rented and moved around and lived with his parents and rented from Sereny's brother and from her father. He just isn't a managing man, they say. Willing, oh, yes. So willing. He makes a little tobacco crop each year, plants a little corn. Altogether he manages to scrape up about $400 in cash each year. Sereny has a cow and a flock of chickens, and she always has a fine garden. From her cow, from the egg money, and from the garden, they make most of their living.

Sixteen years they have been married now, and Sereny has had ten children. Two of them have lived. Eight little dead babies are buried in a row up in the churchyard. And Sereny grieves with all her heart each time there is another one to lay there.

The two that have lived were among the first ones born. The older one quit school last year, at, I think, the sixth grade. He had trouble learning that far. The younger one has never got beyond the fourth grade. He only goes about half the time, and Sereny and Elmer don't insist. He "don't like," they say.

Just the other day we took Sereny and Elmer to town to the hospital for the eighth little dead baby to be born. Sereny knew it was dead. She hadn't felt life in nearly two weeks. She had a hopeless, despairing look on her face as we went. "I had sich hopes of this un," she said. "I done ever' least thing the doctor said. The boys an' Elmer's done all the work an' I've jist wallered the bed. But I know in reason hit's dead too."

"Maybe not," I comforted, knowing it was cold comfort. She'd had too many. She knew the symptoms.

Ordinarily Sereny does not go to the hospital, but this time the doctor had insisted, and Elmer had alerted us shortly before breakfast. While I went with Sereny to help her get settled in her room, Elmer and Henry waited.

The baby was dead. It had been dead ten days, and sadly we brought it home in its tiny wooden box, with the word "Head" stamped on one end of it. For some reason I felt as if the back of our old Oldsmobile wasn't a very good hearse for it. It seemed so careless just to put the little box in the back end of the car, close the top, and drive home with it. But rather matter of factly that's what Elmer and Henry did, and then, also matter of factly, the men of the settlement dug another small grave, and without ceremony laid the little box away in the long line holding the other little boxes. "I reckon," Elmer said, at the last, "I reckon I've had about as big a family as ary man in the settlement, not to have no better luck than I've had. Hit's jist beyond my understandin'."

After Sereny's fourth child, Elmer was offered medical advice regarding the use of a contraceptive. He told Henry about it as they waited for Sereny and me at the hospital the other day. "I appreciated the thought," he said, "fer I knowed it was meant well, but I jist never could git my consent to use it. Jist never could. Hit would of ha'nted my soul to of sinned so."

Oh, but I was furious for a minute! "I suppose it doesn't ha'nt his soul to drag poor Sereny down year after year with these little dead babies!" I stormed.

"Now you know as well as I do, Jan," Henry replied calmly, "that Sereny would not give her consent either."

And I know he's right. She wouldn't. The Lord sends the babies. It's the Lord's will that they die. Neither Elmer nor Sereny understand why it is so. It would never occur to them to think of their weakened, tainted, inbred blood stream. "It's the Lord's will," they say. "Praise the name of the Lord."

Eugenically speaking, these two people should never have been allowed to marry. But they love each other. I have seen it between them. They love each other tenderly and devotedly and wholly. It's a very beautiful love, and one you rarely see. Sereny would walk across hot coals to reach Elmer if need be, and she loves him so deeply that she cannot even speak his name without her face going soft and shiny with love. She was visiting me one afternoon in the summer and we were sitting out under the trees. "There's Elmer," I said, as he drove down the road from the far field.

She turned in her chair and watched him coming, and her mouth gentled at the corners, just from seeing him, and her eyes were sweet as they rested on him. "He's been aworkin' too hard agin," she said, "his shirt's plumb soaked through with sweat."

And Elmer loves her the same way. At the hospital that afternoon he was sick, blind sick, with nausea and a fearful headache. "I allus think," he told us, "that mebbe something'll happen to Sereny. I wouldn't want to go on livin' if it did."

Sereny tells me they have never quarreled, and I'm sure it's true. As a matter of fact, I doubt if either of them has ever had so much as one critical thought of the other. "Elmer says," and Sereny tells us proudly Elmer's opinion, never questioning its rightness, never once thinking he could be wrong.

And, having lost so many, they love the two that have lived with such a yearning, protective love that it makes you wince to see it. And you pray that nothing will happen to either of those two boys. I don't believe Sereny and Elmer could live through the loss of either of them. They are frantic with fear if they are gone from sight too long. They worry constantly over the least little things. A scratch on the arm, a cut foot, a rash, and a small temperature will bring Sereny flying down the road, her hands trembling and her voice caught in her throat. "Janice, come quick! Bring yer fever thing an' see. The least un's got a pain in his stummick an' he's so hot it parches yer hand to tetch him!"

And I fly with the thermometer. It reads 101, and I have to tell Sereny.

"O my God!" and she collapses on the side of the bed.

"Sereny, we'll get him to the doctor just as fast as we can. Hurry and dress!"

And Henry makes the Oldsmobile stir up a real dust getting to town.

Dr. Mike is used to these panicky fears. "You been eating any apples?" he asks the boy.

"Yessir."

Weakly we all grin at each other. Dr. Mike fixes a bottle of pink medicine and warns the youngster to stay away from green apples. But we never know, and we are willing, always, to go dashing to the doctor to ease the iron hand that clutches Sereny's heart.

What *is* the answer? Who is to say what they should have done? And who is to say what is right?

Chapter

9 ⚬⚬

Speaking of cooking (I wasn't, but I'm going to), I must confess that I do not always cook the ridge way for Henry and myself. I make biscuits, for instance, much shorter than is common on the ridge. We like very crisp, very short, golden-brown biscuits. And I accomplish them better with sweet milk and baking powder. But we are alone in our liking for this kind of biscuits. Ridge biscuits are made with buttermilk and soda, and as a rule they are rather flat and what I call " pully " for want of a better word. A ridge cook would apologize for my short, browned biscuits. She would say she had had a heavy hand with her biscuits that day.

Of course I always use butter for shortening. Of course. We do not have a cow, but we have an arrangement with Henry's folks to help feed their cows in return for milk and butter. Miss Bessie is so afraid we won't have enough that she keeps us supplied with much more than we can use on the table. I shall never forget the look on my sister's face when I baked a cake one day while she and her family were visiting us. Nearly a pound of butter went into the cake proper, and then another quarter pound went into the icing. Her eyes widened. "Do you *always* use that much butter in your cakes?"

I had forgotten how extravagant it must look. "Of course."

She shook her head. "I've got to get my menfolks away from here," she said, "before they become so spoiled by all this good food they aren't satisfied at home any more. Why, we'd go broke in no time if I cooked the way you do!"

I remembered then. You can't cook the way I do in the city. Take creamed cauliflower, for instance. I make the sauce with pure thick, yellow cream, and even add a generous dab of butter to that. And for new little creamed potatoes, or chipped beef, or tuna fish. I wouldn't think of making a cream sauce out of milk. All puddings and custards are made of cream — and, naturally, ice cream. All pastries, dumplings, breads, cakes, are made with butter. There hasn't been a can of shortening in my kitchen since we moved to the ridge.

Unfortunately I am alone also in the practice of using so much cream and butter in my cooking. For some reason people who have to take care of cows and milk and butter frequently do not like them. I know few families on the ridge who will touch butter. The cream is sold to the cream truck and most of the milk is poured out to the hogs. Some buttermilk is saved out to make bread with, and that's about all. And ridge women like to bake with lard better than with butter.

I like pure lard too, in its place. I didn't think I would. I thought it had an offensive odor and flavor and was much too rich and greasy. But I have come to swear by it for frying. Try it with chicken sometime, or fish or steak. And doughnuts fried in pure lard are more than slightly out of this world. It adds something to fried things. Maybe it's a crisper, crunchier brown. Maybe it's a delicate hint of wood smoke. Maybe, too, it's just that since it is pure lard it adds a tiny, fatty flavor, like suet with a roast, or the rim of fat on a ham. Whatever it is, I like it, and I now buy it by the stand, a stand being a fifty-pound can. I wouldn't even try to cook without it.

We differ again at the point of the most staple food in the ridge diet. Soup beans. Folks buy them by the hundred-pound bag, and all winter long, day after day, they make their appearance. Whatever else there is to eat, the soup bean is always present. In the city we call them pinto beans, or brown beans, but any merchant in any of the small towns hereabouts knows what you mean when you call for soup beans. The ridge wife puts her pot of beans on to cook as she prepares breakfast, and they simmer slowly all morning. Then they are served floating in a big bowl of their own soup. The idea is to crumble a chunk of corn bread and pour the beans and soup over it. With buttermilk and an onion this makes a meal. All too many meals, as a matter of fact.

We have them occasionally, and when we do I cook them exactly as Henry's mother cooked them all his life. For he wouldn't eat them any other way. But he has grown away from any genuine fondness for them, thank goodness. I have often wondered why the entire ridge population doesn't blow up like a balloon and float away!

Rice is another thing we serve differently. It is a breakfast food here — cooked until it is soggy and has lost all its identity, then served in bowls with milk and sugar. I grew up in the Southwest, where rice is a vegetable, and where its preparation is an art. The first time I served Henry rice cooked my way, every grain fluffy, white, and free from moisture, he looked at it dubiously. "Try it," I told him. "Try it with gravy from the roast." He did, and his look of astonishment was rewarding. "Why, it's good!" he said. And it was. We have it that way in place of potatoes often. Introduced thus gently to rice as a vegetable, he has come to like its other forms, brown rice and wild rice.

Ridge women seem never to have discovered the art of roasting either. The oven is used for baking bread, pies, and cakes. Never for roasting meat. There are only two ways to cook meat: fry it or boil it. If a chicken is too big to fry, it is stewed with dumplings. To bake it, with dressing, seems to be unheard of. Beef, of course, is practically unused on the ridge, but when someone occasionally butchers a calf and peddles it down the road, the big, raw chunks that cannot be fried are simply thrown into a kettle of boiling water and stewed until they are either tender or too tough to be chewed. When hogs are killed, the shoulders, hams, and sides are cured with salt and pepper, for the art of smoking meat has long since been lost on the ridge. Sausage is made of the scraps, souse is made of the head, and the ribs, backbone, and so forth are eaten immediately. Boiled. Barbecued or roasted ribs or backbone are not even considered. Fry it or boil it.

For that matter, that's the ridge's answer to how to cook almost any kind of food. Apples? Fry them or stew them. Bake them? Who would bother with " sich " ! Corn? Boil it on the cob or cut it off and fry it. Who is going to cut it off and beat up an egg in it, add cream and butter, and bake it? Squash? Slice it and fry it. Who's going to cut it in half, sprinkle it with salt and pepper and a chunk of butter, and bake? Soup beans? Boil them. Who wants to add a cup of molasses, a smidgen of onion, a couple of tomatoes, and bake? Who wants " sich fancy doin's " anyhow? Not ridge folks!

Once, before Henry and I were married, I was visiting his folks. It was November, Thanksgiving, as I remember, and as cold as blitzen. We had oatmeal for breakfast. Now, oatmeal, on the ridge, is really cooked. To begin with, it is the old-fashioned, long-cooking kind, and to make sure it is thoroughly done, it is boiled and boiled and boiled. With sugar. When it is served it is a sticky, sweet mass of glucose. But this I did not know. I am one of those nonsugaring cereal eaters. I never put sugar on any kind of cereal, not even the dry summer ones. So my first mouthful of ridge oatmeal was almost more than I could swallow. In the city I should have left the bowl of cereal uneaten, my hostess would have ignored it, and that would have been the end of it. But I had already learned that it is impolite to leave food uneaten on the ridge. You eat it or die trying, for you do not want your hostess to think either of two things: first, that you have not been properly brought up; and secondly, that her cooking is not superb. So I was caught. But I do not have a dead-pan face, and Miss Bessie has an eagle eye. She watched me for a moment and then she said, kindly: " If you don't like oatmeal, Janice, you don't have to eat it. I'll not think hardly."

" It's the sugar," I confessed, and then I told her how we

cooked oatmeal outside. Quickly, so that it retained its nutty, grainy flavor, and how we left the sweetening to the discretion of the individual. Miss Bessie always listens to me when I tell her things are done differently outside. She believes me implicitly. She listens thoughtfully, politely, patiently. But when I finish she laughs in her soft, sweet way. "That goes the foolishest," she says.

You see, the joke is always on the outsiders. It is never the ridge way that is foolish, or different. Always it is the "furrin" way. Ridge folks understand that things are done differently outside. But it's because outsiders just don't know how to do it right! It's the outsider who varies from the norm. The ridge way is the right way. And there is no use trying, ever, to change it. I long ago quit trying. At first I worried dreadfully over the inadequate diet so prevalent here. Over the positive malnutrition which is so evident. I did a little preaching, oh, more than a little! It does no good. And then, like Miss Willie in the second of the Piney Ridge books, I came out at a more or less satisfactory acceptance of things the way they are. I still ache and hurt over a little thin-shanked fellow who obviously needs whole milk and butter and eggs. And I grieve when a baby dies unnecessarily, or when some woman is cut down in what should be the prime of her life because she hasn't the strength to fight a virulent infection. But I remember that such things happen the world over, not just here on the ridge. And I remember that by and large ridge folks live just about as long as anybody, and if they are happier with fried chunk meat, eggless corn bread, and boiled soup beans, then it is their right to be happy with them. My personal responsibility begins and ends with being as good a neighbor as I know how to be. Not in being a missionary. I have no talent for it, and very little zeal, for I like too well to be let alone myself. When, with pricked conscience, I visualize a healthier ridge, with higher living standards for all, I recall that those things have not seemed to add greatly to the happiness of people elsewhere. And if life is to be evaluated in terms of peace and happiness . . . and here I always become philosophical, and when you begin to probe the philosophy of happiness, there is neither beginning nor end to it. So I am no missionary.

But the ridge has provided me with some very good dishes indeed. Dry land creases, for instance. The first spring we were here, one of my neighbors came by with a sack and her little paring knife one day. "Where you going?" I yelled at her. "To hunt dry land creases!" she said; "come go along."

I dug out a sack and my own paring knife and went along. I had no idea what dry land creases were, but I was willing to learn. We crossed the hollow and came out in an old field long ago abandoned to sprouts and weeds. "Ort to be a few here," she said, and she started browsing around. I followed. "There," she said, and she pounced quickly with her knife. I looked. It was a small, flat plant growing close to the ground, with leaves very similar to our water cress. Creases? Cress, of course. Dry land cress.

We found enough to fill our sacks. "How do you cook it?" I asked Henry when I reached our house.

"Just like any other greens," he said.

So I washed it carefully, examined the texture of the stalk and leaf, and decided it would need more time than spinach but not quite as much as mustard or turnip greens, and put it on in a minimum amount of water. When the greens seemed tender, I turned them out into a frying pan with some bacon drippings, salted them, and then served them with crisp corn muffins. They were delicious, with almost exactly that little sour tang that water cress has. They are the first greens to appear in the spring. They come up far earlier than anything else, and I no longer have to cross the hollow to find them. I have learned that they usually grow rank in a tobacco field, so now, along about the middle of March, I start watching our own tobacco patch, and we have dry land creases sometimes when there is still snow on the north side of the house.

You know about poke sallet of course. We find it here around old stumps, in fence corners, or where the soil is especially rich. Poke is one of my favorite greens, but it has to be mixed with others. By itself it has a slick, oily taste. I usually mix it with wild mustard, lamb's-quarters, or dandelions. I avoid dock, for it has a coarse, rough texture and I don't like to spoil the delicacy of poke with it. I always parboil poke too before mixing it with the other greens. Only a few minutes, for it cooks quickly. Butter or bacon drippings may be added, hard-boiled eggs sliced on top, and you have a dish fit for a king.

We also have dry land fish. Mushrooms to you. But they are not the familiar mushroom of the city market. They are a big, oval, porous plant, brown on top and pearly pink beneath. Henry tells me their botanical name is the common morel. They spring up in shady, damp places in the woods, especially after a rain, and we gather them by the pecks. They may be dried and used for seasoning in soups and broths, but we prefer them fresh. We split them, soak them several hours in salt water, dip them in an egg mixture, roll them in flour, and then fry them in deep fat. They do have a slight fishy taste. I think it is actually more a fish texture than a taste. The crisp, brown outside may be flaked off, leaving a mealy white meat, but if you're wise you'll pop the whole thing in your mouth, chew twice, and then reach for another one!

And have you ever tried fried turtle? Do, if you can find the right kind of turtle. Ours are the old hard-shelled kind, huge old monsters, and I am told that when one has reached the size of a dinner plate he is usually fifty or seventy-five years old. This is about right for frying. We find them in the creeks, rivers, ponds, sloughs, almost anywhere where there's water. We even found one in the little stream over in our hollow. Henry cleans them, so I can't tell you how it's done, except that of course you remove the shell and head and feet somehow. When he brings it into the house it is cut up, and the only pieces I can recognize are the neck and the four legs. The rest comes from somewhere under the shell. I soak it in strong salt water for several hours, then dip it in flour without drying, and fry in deep fat. It takes just about as long as chicken, but you will forswear chicken if you ever taste fried turtle.

I took my first bite very gingerly. Actually I think I would have approached rattlesnake about as willingly. But I had only to take one bite. Oddly enough, it is the neck that is the *pièce de résistance* of a turtle. It is fat, white, and delicately flavored. The legs are dark meat, or comparatively dark, and taste very much like squirrel or rabbit. Then there is a little piece from just under the shell, the tenderloin Henry calls it, that is like fish.

And of course there are frog legs. But you know about them. In our opinion they are no great shakes alongside of turtles.

We have also the partridge. I suspect you call them quail. It takes five or six of these tiny birds to make enough for two people. Henry plucks them, draws them, but leaves them whole. I am an inveterate soaker in salt water to tenderize things. So I soak the partridge in salt water an hour or so, then dredge them in flour and brown in deep fat. When they are brown, I drain some of the fat off, add cooking sherry, set them to the back of the stove, and leave them to stew in their own juice for a couple of hours. You can do with five or six for two people, but personally I'd rather have a dozen.

Our own special favorite of ridge foods is the squirrel. Fried, of course. We like to have two squirrels. After soaking, I flour them and fry. When they are brown, I cover them and set them to the back of the stove while I make biscuits. By the time the biscuits are done, the squirrel is just right. With cream gravy, nothing is more delicious. You understand, of course, that I cook on a wood stove. With a slow, hickory fire. No self-respecting partridge, fish, or squirrel will cook nicely on any other kind of fire.

I have added only one cake recipe from the ridge to those I already had. Ridge cooks, as a rule, are not good with cakes and pies. I think it is because they do not use enough butter, eggs, and cream, and, too, they are rarely patient enough to mix a cake properly. Another reason is that they do not use a recipe. They simply dump flour, baking powder, lard, an egg or two, and sugar together and beat like mad. But there is a jelly cake Miss Bessie makes that we like very much. I use my own basic two-egg recipe for the cake part. It makes, usually, a medium-sized three-layer cake. But for jelly cake you bake six or seven very thin layers instead. Then put them together

118

with any kind of jelly you happen to have on hand. We like it best with blackberry jelly, for it is usually sweeter and blends with the cake mixture better. With a glass of cold milk for a bedtime snack it's pretty swell.

Ridge pies are usually fruit pies, apple or peach mostly, and frequently they are fried. You make up a rich biscuit dough, pinch it off in small bits, roll out, spread with the fruit mixture, fold over, prick a couple or three times with a fork, then fry in deep fat. They burn easily, so you have to be sure to keep plenty of fat in the pan. They come out brown, crisp, crunchy, and juicy with the fruit inside. If you can stop under three or four hot ones, you have a better disciplined appetite than I have. Oh, sure, you may have indigestion a couple of hours later from all that grease! But is there a better cause than fried pies for which to suffer indigestion? Who's going to let a little stomach-ache stand between him and heaven? Not I.

Henry's grandmother — she who was called Muh by the whole ridge, and who lived to be ninety-six — had a recipe for a chess pie which I now share with you:

A scoop of sugar
Several eggs
A pound of butter
A smidgen of flour
A small crock of cream
A dusting of nutmeg
Mix, and bake in a pie shell.

You understand, this recipe has not come down to us written out. Muh told it to Miss Bessie, and Miss Bessie told it to me. I have translated it thus:

2 cups of sugar
6 eggs
1 pound of butter
2 cups of cream
1 tablespoon flour
1 teaspoon vanilla
Sprinkling of nutmeg
(This makes about four pies.)

I mix the flour with the sugar and cream it with the butter. Then I add the eggs, one at a time, and beat furiously. Lastly I add the cream, to which I have added the vanilla, a little at a time, and pour the whole into an unbaked pie shell. Over it I sprinkle the nutmeg and drop in several last-minute chunks of butter. A rule of thumb with me is that you can't get too much butter. Nothing more can be added to your life, I promise you. When you have eaten of Muh's chess pie you will have experienced the ultimate in gastronomical delights. But don't try to substitute milk for cream, and don't skimp on the butter. It won't be the same. Another virtue this pie has — it " sets light on the stomach." You have Muh's word for that.

I never knew Muh and Pah, but I wish I might have. They lived to celebrate their sixty-fifth wedding anniversary, then, although Muh was ten years older than he, Pah died at the age of eighty-four. That was in 1938. Muh lived until 1940, and was ninety-six when she died. Pah was James Washington Giles, called " Wash " to distinguish him from his father who was also James Washington Giles, called " Jeems." Muh was Mary Sanders from over Casey Creek way. She was not a ridge girl.

Muh was seventeen years old at the beginning of the War Between the States. Her family were slaveowners and were Southern in their sympathies. She must have seen, with anxious eyes, the Federal troops come pouring through these hills, and she must have waited fearfully for the outcome of the battle fought on the other side of Columbia. And it must have been with a sinking heart she heard that General Zollicoffer had been killed and the battle lost. When Morgan's men stormed through Kentucky, sweeping everything before them, she must have been thrilled, as were all other Southern girls, at the daring of the bold, dashing General John Hunt Morgan. She, along with her family, must have felt loyalty to the provisional government of Kentucky, established in November of 1861, representing the State rights party, and admitted to the Confederate States of America in December of that year. There were two governors and two governments in Kentucky during the War Between the States. One seat of government was in Frankfort, with Beriah Magoffin as governor. And he tried hard to remain neutral during the conflict. The southern half of the state seceded from the northern half and elected its own governor, George W. Johnson, and sent regularly delegated representatives to the Confederate States Congress. What a time to be a girl in Kentucky!

Muh was fifty-four years old at the time of the Spanish-American War, and she was seventy-three when the United States entered the First World War. She lived almost long enough to witness a fourth holocaust. Wars and rumors of wars. Muh knew what they meant!

I have asked and asked about the romance between Mary Sanders and young Wash Giles. But no one who now lives thought to inquire, and Mary was not a chatterbox. She never said why she married him. And of course there is no one of her contemporaries now living. She was twenty-nine and he was nineteen, and I have wondered about their love many times.

They say my Henry is a lot like his grandfather. If that is true, then I think I know the answer. If, when young Wash Giles came ariding to the valley on his best black mule, he had a laughing twinkle in his blue eyes, as my Henry has; if he had the same deep, probing dimple in his chin; if he had a mischievous, sparkling gallantry; if he had a dry, pungent humor that overlaid his slow ridge drawl; if he had a sweetness of spirit that brought a lump to the throat; if he had a high, handsome sense of freedom, then she married him because she knew her life wouldn't be worth a plugged nickel unless she spent it by his side! What matter if it brought her from Negro servants to a log cabin on the ridge? What matter if she had lived ten years longer than he? What matter anything, except to crawl on the back of his best black mule and go with him where he went?

Henry's folks live now in the house to which Wash Giles brought her. It was two big rooms then. And for years Muh cooked at the fireplace. Eventually a kitchen and another bedroom were added to the house at the back, but always to Muh the fireplace room was "the house." She would say, "Let's go in the house," when a meal was finished in the new cookroom, and she would lead the way back to the chimney corner. Miss Bessie has shown me the elbow of rock that jutted out from the chimney, where Muh kept her pipe. For she smoked a little corncob pipe, and her aprons were always in holes from the coals that dropped from her pipe.

Henry remembers her as a tall, stooped woman, already old in his first memories. He said she wore the dark colors all older women wore in that day. A black skirt sweeping the ground, and either black or gray waists with it. Even her bonnets were black. He does not recall ever seeing her in colors. Once, when he was a little boy, he said to his mother, "I don't reckon Muh and Pah will ever die."

"Whyever not?" she said in astonishment.

"They're too old," came his amazing reply.

Henry was her favorite among Miss Bessie's children, and Miss Bessie laughs now and tells how angry it used to make her for Muh to favor him over the others. Miss Bessie followed the usual ridge custom of making an older child give up to a younger one, but Muh furiously refused to do so. "He shan't be made to give Irene his pretties," she said, "leastways not when he's around me!" You see, the young Henry already looked a lot like the young Wash had looked.

She was a prideful woman, Muh was. She kept a full storehouse and she never was known to borrow. She had little admiration for anyone else who did, either. "I," she said proudly, "allus keep a little extry on hand. It's past my understandin' why others cain't." Miss Bessie remembers the chest in which she kept her extra sugar, flour, lard, and coffee. She never ran short. There was always something in the chest.

They say she was the best cook on the ridge, in her time. I have no doubt of it. She came from a family that were accustomed, probably, to better foods than the ridge knew, and she brought her knowledge with her. She used cream and butter and eggs in her cooking, and she knew about sauces and roasted foods. She planted an asparagus bed, sparrowgrass she called it, and Mr. Frank remembers how she served it, drenched with butter. The asparagus bed is still there. We cut it and bring it home with us. But it's not a ridge food, and I doubt if anyone else has ever tasted it.

Muh had the first fruit jar on the ridge. It was a half-gallon mason jar, with the old, clamp-on lid. She was half afraid to use it for fear it would blow up. They knew nothing of canning and preserving in those days. Everything to be kept was dried. Even blackberries were boiled, patted into little sausage cakes, and dried. Sweetening was added when they were cooked again to make jam, fresh each time they wanted it. Green beans were strung, snapped, and dried. Miss Bessie still dries a few that way each year. She calls them snap beans. Fruits were dried apples and peaches. No one knew about canning.

But Muh had her a half-gallon fruit jar. Of course it had long since been broken by the time Henry was born, but as a little boy he heard Muh tell about it many times. He went to meetin' with his mother one night and the next day he told his grandmother, " Muh, I know where your fruit jar is."

" And do you now? " she said fondly to him. " Where might it be? "

" God's got it! They sang about it at meetin' last night. They sang, ' God holds the fruit jar in his hands! ' "

What they had sung was " God holds the future in His hands," but the little boy had put his own interpretation on the words.

Muh loved beauty too. It is evident in the flowers she planted in her yard, which still grow in Miss Bessie's yard now. There is a beautiful big bronze bush (japonica), and a rambling cinnamon vine at one end of the porch. There are several huge althea trees, and many snowball bushes. But what I love most among the things she planted is the yellow rambler rose that winds its way up the old chimney. It's very old now, and yet every year it blooms, spreading a gold blanket over the entire chimney.

We have a yellow rose in our chimney corner too. Taken, of course from Muh's ancient planting. It had one little bloom this spring. And, sentimentalist that I am, I felt as if something of Muh's spirit had bloomed to bless her grandson's household.

If time lasts, I'm going to write a book about Mary Sanders someday. And you will recognize it by the fruit jar. The yellow rose has already been used in nearly every book I've written.

Chapter

10 ✗ ✗

"The old man was tall, bony, and lean as a lath. He folded his legs under my dining table and forked himself a cob of corn."

These are the opening sentences of "The Sheriff Went to Cincinnati," Henry's first short mystery story. In that story was established the character of the old Kentucky hill sheriff, Sim Parker. These sentences sprang into my mind full-fledged as Sale Coffey sat down to eat dinner with us the day he came to survey our boundaries. And since everything either of us writes is written with the help of the other, they became the lead of Henry's story.

Sale Coffey is tall, bony, and lean as a lath. And as I watched him jackknife his long legs under the table a story was born. I knew it, and so did Henry, before he ever opened his mouth. Two hours later all there was to do to the story was to polish it up, give it a little humorous twist, deposit a corpse in a church pew, and type it. What a storyteller Sale Coffey is! He knows he is the inspiration for old Sim Parker and he gets a kick out of it. When we go to the county seat and run into him he always asks: "Run out of stories yet? If you have, let's go out to the house and have a cup of coffee, and I'll tell you a few more." And he's just the man who can do it.

It was August now, and we had finished spring-poling the well. By rights we were entitled to a breathing spell. Only, breathing spells come few and far between in the summertime in the country. Everything in the garden ripened now and at once, and we were deluged with green beans, corn, lima beans, squash, tomatoes, peppers, and cucumbers. I was determined to waste nothing, knowing full well that a lean winter was staring us in the face. So I set to canning, and that first summer I literally canned everything in the garden except the stalks and vines themselves. I had a passion for saving it all, and early and late I was packing stuff into jars. I still have vegetables I canned that year.

With a pressure cooker and a kerosene stove it wasn't too bad, but you don't get those rows and rows of beautiful vegetables and fruits in your cellar or storeroom by wishing. You get them by gathering from the garden day after day, washing, husking, stringing, snapping, then packing and cooking. It's work. Hard work. The reward comes the next winter when you reach complacently for a jar of corn, or beans, or pickles, or catsup. Or when you put blackberry, or apple, or grape, or plum jelly on the breakfast table. During the summer you just sweat it out. But the next winter you eat well.

I was canning corn the day Henry came in in such a dither, yelling: "Where's my hat? Where're the car keys? Where's the checkbook?" Henry is the most "where's the" man I ever saw. And, like Dagwood, when he is vastly confused, he stands in the middle of the room and bellows. Like Blondie, I come on the double.

Now it's quite a chore to can corn. First it has to be gathered, and a bushel of corn is not any light load to carry in from the garden. By the time you have stripped three or four rows you are likely to have hauled eight or nine bushels to the house. Then it must be shucked and silked. I have a workbench out under the trees in the back yard, and I was out there, swimming in sweat and corn shucks, when I heard the first bellow. For once I stood on my rights, whatever they are, and yelled at him. "You'll have to come here and tell me what you want! I'm busy!"

"Where's my hat?" as he came through the kitchen door.

"Where're the car keys?" as he came down the steps.

And as he reached the workbench, "Where's the checkbook?"

Now I'm just lucky when I know where to find what he's looking for. It's an old bone of contention between us that things should have a place and be kept there. I maintain that life is much simpler if you put things where they belong as soon as you are through with them. Henry goes along on the theory that things always turn up anyhow, and what's the use of bothering? Where's the hammer? It's out in the crotch of the tree where he nailed up a bird-feeding station. Where's the saw? It's on the couch in the living room where he made the feeding station last night. Where's the brace and bit? Now, *where* is the brace and bit? Oh, yes. I moved it from the kitchen stove to the top of the refrigerator this morning when I started breakfast. That's the way things are in our house. But I suppose if something should happen to Henry the first thing I should miss, and the thing I should miss most often, would be picking up after him. I get frustrated and I scold. But I honestly don't mind too much.

Well, I know where his hat is, anyhow. Upstairs where it belongs. I said so. "*Why* does it belong upstairs?" he yells. "Why doesn't it belong downstairs?" I have no answer, except that to my unimaginative mind a hat is part of wearing apparel, and wearing apparel is put away in a bedroom. "Why don't you just let it alone? Why don't you just let it stay where I put it down? I'm going to put a nail right by the door so I'll always know where to find it!" Storm, storm. And well do we both know that if he put a hundred nails right by the door he would never hang his hat on one of them.

The car keys? "Have you looked in your blue jeans? The ones you pulled off last night?"

"No . . . by golly!" And off he goes to look.

Success! But I can't take any credit for it. Experience has taught me that's where they usually are. In the pocket of the last pair of pants he had on.

The checkbook? "Did you look in the middle drawer of the desk?"

"Yes, it's not there."

"When did you have it last?"

He thinks. "When I wrote that check for cash at the bank . . ." His voice trails off and he wilts. He has left nine checkbooks on the counter at the bank. Now he has left the tenth one. Like a small, guilty boy he slants a look at me out of the corner of his eyes, and I laugh, of course. There's nothing else to do. "Maybe they found it at the bank. Ask before you get a new one."

And then it occurs to me that there is a lot of excitement going on here at nine o'clock in the morning. "What's all the stew?"

"The widow Gibbs has sold her timber and they've started cutting. I don't know where the boundary is on her line, and I'm afraid they'll cut on us. Some of our best timber stands near that line. I'm going to Columbia and get the county surveyor to come out and run the line."

Henry is not a bad surveyor himself, and he had satisfactorily run our lines except for the one next to the widow Gibbs's. He could never get an angle on that one. Not the way the deed read, anyhow. You have to read one of these old deeds to realize the problem involved in surveying out here in the hills. Listen:

"Beginning at a double Black Oak; thence S31/20 W48 poles to a White Oak; thence S25½ E24 poles to a Chestnut Oak and Maple; thence S2½ W8 poles to a Beech, corner to the Campbell heirs in Stayton's line; thence S73 ″45 poles to a Beech tree on the Bayer's Branch, corner to Stayton; thence with another line thereof N81¼ W48 poles to a Chestnut Oak and Redbud, in said line on a point; thence N9 W50 poles to a Black Oak, Gum, and Hickory in Lucinda White's line; thence with her line N76 E86 poles to a small Hickory, corner to said White; thence with same N17 E86 poles to the beginning."

A pole, I learned, is a measure used in surveying. It is the equivalent of about 16½ feet. Most of these old deeds are copied from the original patent. And when you remember that some of the patents date back to 1800, you can see how confusing it becomes trying to run a boundary line today. The trees mentioned have long since disappeared. We found not even a stump to mark the double Black Oak to begin a survey. But with the help of a neighbor whose land borders ours we established a satisfactory point of beginning. We let Sale Coffey take over from there.

He found that the deed had been copied wrong. The second angle, reading S25½ E24 poles, should have read S25½ W24 poles. Every time Henry had run it, he wound up in the widow Gibbs's cornfield, which, understandably, distressed her no end.

They didn't come into the house, Henry and Sale Coffey, when they first drove up. They struck out across the back lot to begin the survey. I got a glimpse of a long, tall, Ichabod-Crane-ish figure. But I was busy watching the pressure on the first cookerful of corn. The rest I had put aside, for dinner would be the next item on the agenda. Fried chicken, green beans, corn, tomatoes, and I decided on apple dumplings for dessert. That last was an inspiration, for Sale Coffey loves apple dumplings next to nothing on this earth. I made a friend for life when I served him light, fluffy apple dumplings that day. But he approved the whole dinner. "You got a good cook," he told Henry when he had finished eating. "Beans are just dry enough and not too greasy. Corn is milky and tender, and man, oh, man, those apple dumplings! Were you raised in Kentucky, ma'am?"

"No. I was raised in Oklahoma."

"Oklahoma! Now there's a coincidence! I used to live in Oklahoma myself!"

"Oh?" I was interested immediately.

"What part you from?"

"Near McAlester. The eastern part."

He nodded. "Know right where you were. Been to Mc-Alester many's the time. Mighty fine state, Oklahoma."

"Are you from Oklahoma originally?" I asked.

"Oh, no. Born and raised right here in the hills. Went out there when I was a young man for a few years. Met and married my wife out there, though," and he chuckled.

"She was an Oklahoma girl?"

"No. She was born and raised in Columbia. Right around the corner, you might say. But, like I said, I'd gone out to Oklahoma to try my hand at making a living out there, and she came to the same town on a visit." He laughed again. "Reckon it was because we were both from Kentucky that first drew us together. But things got serious mighty fast, and first thing we knew she was writing her dad for money to buy her trousseau and we were aiming to get married right away. Now I'm a Republican and her folks have always been Democrats. Her dad knew me and all my folks. He sent her the money all right, but I never will forget what he wrote her along with it. He says, 'Here's your money, but it looks to me like you went a hell of a long way to find yourself a Republican that was born and raised right here in the same county!'" He eased himself in his chair and took another helping of dumplings. "We came on back to Columbia in a year or two, and been there ever since. Hard to beat this country for a place to live. How'd you happen to come to Kentucky, ma'am?"

So I told him I had come to work at the Presbyterian seminary in Louisville. He chortled. "So you're a Presbyterian too! Well, now, that makes us almost kinfolks. We're Presbyterians from 'way back!" and he reached across the table to shake my hand. The fact that he knew the Southwest and that he was also a Presbyterian did seem to make a bond between us, and we felt like old friends from that moment on.

He was never actually the sheriff of the county, but he was a deputy for years, and he can tell a lot of lurid tales. There are some that have been told on him too. Ask him about the time he got shot in the stomach. He'll laugh as hearty as the next man about that story. And he'll even tell it on himself without chagrin. Seems a posse was out raiding a still. The still was back up a hollow in a cave and the sheriff and his men had it pretty well covered. The sheriff yelled for the man to come out. Said they had him surrounded. The man's answer was a shot, and then a fusillade of shots. Sale was dug in, as were the others, but just as the fellow started firing, Sale grabbed his stomach and yelled: "My God, I'm hit! Boys, I'm hit in the belly!" and he lay down ready to die.

Men came to his rescue, but there wasn't any blood and the pain ceased. Sale cautiously examined himself. Not a sign of a wound did he have. The men guffawed. The moonshiner had fired into the hillside and raised a cloud of flying dust and pebbles. One of these pebbles, ricocheting, had hit Sale in the stomach. It had force enough to knock the breath out of him, but it was far from a mortal wound.

That day he leaned back in his chair and started telling about the moonshiner who was always gone to Cincinnati. The officers knew he had a still hidden somewhere back in the hills, and they knew he was selling moonshine, but they could never catch him. Any time they came browsing into the hills asking about Jim they were met with a doubtful shake of the head: "Believe he's went to Cincinnati." The whole countryside took a deal of joy in thus telling the officers exactly where Jim was, for they knew that he called the location of his still "Cincinnati." The officers caught on eventually too, but they were no better off than before, for they couldn't find Cincinnati.

"Jim was a slick one all right," Sale told us that day. "Hard man to catch. I was tailing him one day and I saw him go into his house. The dog gave me away when I went through the gate, and as I stepped up on the porch, I heard the back door slam. I cut around the corner of the house and saw him taking off through the woods. Now, I'm built like a greyhound and I've always thought I could run. But when I took after that little guy, he put on speed like a train going downhill. I windmilled right after him, thinking I could catch him easy enough. But I never even got close to him! I chased him, I reckon, three miles before I was too winded to run another step. Clean over the ridge to Barnett's Creek. The last I saw of him he was still going strong. But we caught him finally."

"How?" I was all ears.

"We found the still. Of course we could have raided it and destroyed it, but we had to catch him red-handed to make it stick. It was up a deep hollow, 'way to hell and gone from anywheres, and it was in an old abandoned cabin. When we came up to it, the cabin door was padlocked and the place appeared to be deserted. Not a sign of life anywhere around. But we knew in reason we'd found it, so we just camped there. We figured Jim'd show up eventually. We scattered in the woods and made ourselves easy to wait it out. It wasn't to say comfortable sleeping on the ground and going without food, but we didn't dare leave. Finally, 'long about the end of the second or third day — I forget which — I heard a thin, quivery voice calling my name. 'Sale? Sale Coffey! That you?' I looked around. Couldn't see a soul. 'I'm comin' out, Sale,' he says, 'don't shoot!' And by gum, if he didn't walk out of that padlocked door! 'You've starved me out,' he says, reaching as he come through the door. Well, we caught him, and we sent him up for a stretch, but it wouldn't surprise me any if old Jim's not got a still hid out in these hills yet!"

Henry laughed, and I guessed that he knew full well that old Jim had a still "hid out in these hills yet." Someone definitely has, and not too far from here. Every Saturday the men and boys who are his customers make tracks down the road in front of our house. "Going to get their moonshine," Henry says. He will never tell me where they're going, but I'll bet he knows just the same.

"What about that padlocked door?" I asked Sale Coffey.

"That, ma'am," he said, "was about the cleverest device you ever saw. It was padlocked all right, but from the inside, not the outside. He just put a padlock on a chain, pulled the chain through a knothole and put his real padlock on the inside. Simple. But it fooled all of us. If he'd stuck it out a few days, we'd have been so hungry ourselves we might have given up, never guessing he was inside. If he'd been real smart, though, he'd have provisioned that cabin against just such an emergency. There's always some little thing a lawbreaker don't think of. And it's generally that little thing that gives him away."

The sheriff went to Cincinnati. Henry took the story, added a love triangle, a murder, and a surprise ending, and *Ellery Queen's Mystery Magazine* bought it. He did the same thing with the Rat Cabin Creek killings. Only I am sorry to say that to this day the law has never learned who killed the first man. His team brought his bloody and very dead body home late one evening. It was whispered about that his wife had been having an affair with another man, and that he had killed the husband because he was on the verge of finding out. But it could never be proved. About six months later the lover, at whom the finger of rumor had pointed, was killed in a drunken brawl. And a few months after that the man who killed him in a drunken brawl was himself found draped over a barbed-wire fence with a .22 bullet hole between his eyes. No one knows who killed whom. But the ridge shakes its head and says sagely, "He who lives by violence shall die in violence."

There's always a foxhound or two in Sale Coffey's stories, for he's a great fox hunter. The long nights of following the hounds, the sweet, mellow music of the horn, the deep belling of the dogs, the frosty, moony deepness of the hills are a haunted, nostalgic refrain upon his lips. He doesn't do much fox hunting any more. But he remembers — aye, he remembers — and what he remembers he tells with a master touch. "Never will forget the time . . ." and he squints his eyes and begins the tale of Judy, the queen of all fox dogs, and the wise old gray fox who was never caught.

Sale was seventy-one just a few days before he came to survey our place, and he laughed as he told about it. "I hate to get old," he said, "hate it like poison. So many things I have to quit doing. But there was one nice thing about this birthday. Went to the post office that morning to get the mail and there was a birthday card. And inside the birthday card was seventy-one dollar bills! Now I can take a birthday present like that and not mind adding another year!"

"What are you going to do with it?" I asked.

"Put it with a little more I've got on hand and take my wife to Florida this winter for a little vacation. Always wanted to go to Florida. Figure I'll never do it any younger." And his keen blue eyes twinkled. "Well," he says, unwinding his long legs, "this is not surveying that line, Henry. Better get on back to that beech corner. Mighty good dinner, ma'am. Mighty good. When you're in Columbia, come see us. Just ask anybody on the square where Sale Coffey lives. They can tell you. Just my wife and me nowadays, and she'll be glad to see you too."

He ends a conversation abruptly thus. As if he knew he had tarried and talked too long. As if, suddenly, he couldn't afford to waste another minute. We see him occasionally when we go to Columbia. And we are always glad to see him. I think he's always glad to see us. It gives him a good excuse to stop work and tell stories.

Well, the sawmill crew was well on the widow Gibbs's side of the boundary, and we all heaved a sigh of relief. It was an anxious time when she thought perhaps a corner of her cornfield belonged to us, and we thought some of our best timber was going under the ax. But now we had it straight. To mark the angle Henry blazed a persimmon tree at the corner. The deed has been changed to read " S25½ W24 poles to a Persimmon tree "! A hundred years from now someone will puzzle over a persimmon tree that no longer exists, no doubt, but if we have inherited Black Oaks and Chestnuts and Beeches which have left not even a stump, I reckon we can leave one little persimmon tree to posterity!

Chapter
11 ⁄ ⁄

When Henry gave Sale Coffey a check for $10, which was the standard fee for a small surveying job, it just about scraped the bottom of the bank account. We were now living about as cheaply as people can live. Short, that is, of Thoreau's simple life on Walden Pond. We had no rent to pay, and no utility bills. The roof over our heads, tin though it was, was ours and paid for. Our utilities were the well we had dug and the wood we had cut from our own wood lot. Plus a little kerosene for the lamps. This we bought from the huckster by the five-gallon can, at fifteen cents per gallon. Five gallons lasted a right smart time too. There were no other bills. We didn't owe a dime, but we had precious few left to spend, either. And even though a garden may be bearing heavily, there are always a few things you must buy. Sugar, flour, coffee, and cigarettes. It was along about this time that I learned to roll a bulky, but perfectly adequate, cigarette from

Bull Durham tobacco. In the summer of 1949 it still sold for a nickel a bag.

Henry added to our garden diet with squirrels, which cost only the effort and time to hunt them and the price of shells. And fish were for free. We also had an occasional chicken, for they were selling at an all-time low of fifteen cents per pound. Otherwise we did without. We did without everything except the absolute necessities of life, and we stretched every dollar just as far as it would stretch without snapping back.

We quit driving the old car, except in emergencies, for the water pump was in such a state that every time we started it Henry was afraid it was going to let fly and go through the radiator. Also we had no money for gasoline. So we bought what few things we had to buy from one of the hucksters.

Forty years ago the huckster made his weekly trip around the ridge in a covered wagon, peddling such things as country people buy. Dried beans, baking powder, salt, coffee, flour, lard, a few canned goods, a little stick candy, thread, needles, pins, unbleached domestic, and cotton batting. Miss Bessie tells me that one man huckstered on the ridge for thirty years. And he never failed to come. The weather never got too bad for him, for his old high-bed wagon could cross the swollen streams, and the mules could pull him through the mud. He brought a full wagonload onto the ridge, and he took a full wagonload away with him, for most of his trade was in barter. Baking powder salt, and coffee, for eggs, butter, and chickens. He also brought news of the outside with him, for in those days there were no radios, few papers, and there has never been phone service back in these hills. Miss Bessie said that during the First World War the news of every battle was brought by the huckster. The folks frequently gathered at one home to wait for him, and he would crawl down off his wagon and spend an hour or two describing a newly fought engagement. He must have been a very articulate person, for she tells me that often he held them all spellbound.

Nowadays we have three hucksters on the ridge, all of them driving their portable grocery stores in great, high-powered trucks. They are not as unfailing as the old covered wagon, for when the winter sets in, the big trucks frequently can't get over the road. And they are not now our news carriers. But they still sell pretty much the same things — baking powder, salt, soda, and coffee — and they still buy eggs, butter, and chickens. We are steady, but not very heavy, customers of all three.

Henry had said, nonchalantly enough, "We'll worry about money when the time comes." It had come. There was no doubt about that. And you could almost see the wheels of Henry's mind going round and round trying to cudgel up some way to make some money. A fellow drove up one day and stopped by the side of the garden to talk to Henry. When he drove on, Henry came in beaming. "That guy wants us to dig him a well."

"Who," I said, "is 'us'?"

"Dad and me."

"How?"

"Spring-pole, of course."

It made me heartsick to think of their spring-poling another well. All that backbreaking work again. But Henry was determined, and he and his dad started out the next morning. They were more fortunate than they had been with ours. The man's home was down in a valley and the water level was high. They hit no hard strata of rock and within a week the well was finished. They were paid the regular well-drilling rate, and at the end they divided seventy-five dollars between them.

I remember looking at the bills of our share when Henry handed them to me. And I remember thinking how he had made almost that much in a day in the city. And I remember wondering if we could last it out. If it was worth lasting out. I remember that Henry looked at me quizzically as if he knew how my thoughts were running, and that he then picked up his old straw hat and put it on and went, whistling, to the tobacco field. All the way across the garden I could hear that whistle. He always whistles or sings the same tune when he isn't thinking of what he's doing. And he never gets farther than the first line or two . . . "Though I labor and toil as I look for a home . . ." I have no idea what the name of the song is, nor how the rest of it goes. It is a hymn, of course, from one of the shaped note songbooks.

But that day, remembering the words as I listened to him whistle the tune, there was a strange lightening of my heart. Let him labor and toil, I thought, if he just whistles and sings as he does it. Let him. And let me labor and toil beside him. All men are looking for a home, and if we have set our feet upon a path that climbs more steeply, perhaps it climbs all the more surely toward the home that we are seeking — the home that only we can recognize when we reach it. For home to each man must be a different thing. If to us it means struggling thus hardly for freedom to do what we most want to do, for peace of heart and soul and mind, let me not, I prayed, be a laggard. Let me not be a faintheart. And above all else, let me not start looking back and regretting.

In September the tobacco was ready to cut. We had pampered and babied that tobacco as if it contained uranium, and some of it was mighty good tobacco, standing shoulder-high, with big, broad leaves now turning yellow under the sun. But some of it, higher up on the slope, hadn't done so well. All told, though, it was a fair crop. Even yet I can tell you that there were seventy-two rows in all, each nearly one hundred feet long. I doubt if I shall ever forget that, because I had helped set every little seedling, had helped hoe them and weed them, and now I helped cut them.

Henry made his own tobacco knife, and it was a wonderful knife. It had a twenty-inch handle, and the blade was tapered and curved just right. Also it was so well tempered that when he sharpened it he could have shaved with it, and it held an edge an amazingly long time. You cut tobacco by taking hold of the stalk toward the top, placing the knife against the lower end, about eight or ten inches from the ground, and pulling steadily against the stalk. You don't slash, as you do in cutting corn. From first to last tobacco must be handled gently. It bruises very easily, and a bruised tobacco leaf is a useless leaf.

Before you start cutting, however, the sticks are made ready and placed. Tobacco sticks are a standard four feet in length, and about an inch in diameter. One end is sharpened. This is to be stuck in the ground. You take a bundle of sticks and go down a row, digging each one into the ground at intervals of about six or eight feet. You can stick an entire field at once if you like, or you can stick one row at a time. The sticks are set into the ground at a very slight slant. We stuck ours three or four rows at a time.

When that had been done, I started down the row, and as I cut I handed each stalk of tobacco to Henry. Handed it very carefully too. Back in the old days the tobacco stalk had to be split with a knife and slid onto the stick. But farmers use what they call a spear today. It is merely a little piece of tin about the size and shape of a small funnel. The large end fits over the stick, and the small end is sharp. The tobacco stalk is held horizontally and jabbed quickly over the sharp spear, which splits it and allows it to slide easily on down the stick. Depending upon how large your tobacco is, a stick will hold from five to eight stalks without crowding. With his eye for neatness, Henry turns each stalk the same way. When you come to the end of a row and look back at the laden sticks, they look for all the world like kneeling ladies with their skirts spread demurely behind them.

You never cut more tobacco at a time than you can handle, for you don't dare leave it in the field to be caught by rain. So we cut eight or ten rows, then stopped and carefully piled it on the wagon to haul to the barn. We had no barn, of course, but we had been able to rent one just a whoop and a holler away. Here the tobacco is hung, by sticks, on raftered tiers. A barnful of tobacco is a pretty sight, the long yellow leaves hanging limply, brushing gently against the tier below. But even in the barn you don't crowd it. There is always that fear of bruising, and in the barn there is also the fear of damp mold if the sticks are hung too close together and the air can't circulate freely.

From first to last tobacco is hard work, and dirty and mean. It oozes a thick, resinous gum which gradually glues your fingers together, each layer of gum hardening as another layer forms. A few hours of handling tobacco and your hands are armor-plated. I know of nothing that will get it off entirely. Turpentine might, if your skin could stand enough of it for long enough. Dirt, just common, ordinary dirt, does the best job of cutting it. It didn't take me long to pick up Henry's habit of catching up a handful of dust every ten or fifteen minutes and rubbing it strongly between my palms. It didn't add much to the looks of my hands, but it certainly helped cut a good bit of that viscous glue with which they were coated.

For some strange reason which I cannot now define, it was my ambition to cut all our tobacco. And I did cut all but eight rows of it. The galley proofs on my book arrived about that time and I had to turn my knife over to Henry. I had enjoyed the cutting. It isn't hard work at all, and by this time my muscles were so adapted to bending and stretching that I didn't even have an extra ache. I did rub a blister on the inside of my thumb with the handle of the knife the first day. But if I'd had sense enough to wear a glove on my right hand, that needn't have happened.

There was a rhythm in the work which pleased me. Bend, cut, straighten . . . over and over again. And the precision and neatness with which the sharp knife bit through the stalk was pleasant. I think I like the feel of things very much: the texture of cloth, or earth, or wood; the depth and plush of fur; the cold, slick sheen of satin; the smoothness of oil or varnish; the cup of typewriter keys under my fingers. And through the handle of the knife there came to me a feel of texture in the tobacco stalk: porous, pithy, sappy. The knife pulled against it, then bit into it and sliced, and the sound and the feel were smooth and silky.

All told, I cannot remember ever having had so strong a sense of achievement as I did when our tobacco was all cut and tiered in the barn. But in addition to the sense of achievement, there was also one of relief. Now, for a brief space of time, six weeks or two months, we were free of tobacco. Now it would hang in the barn and cure. No more weeding or hoeing. No more attention from us. No more worry for fear it was raining too much, or the tobacco worms were getting too thick, or it wasn't raining enough. For a little while, now, peace.

Peace? Well, there was still the state of our exchequer. But at least Henry was free now to do something about it. He heard about some people over in southern Indiana who buy hickory for ax and hatchet handles. He wrote them. Yes, they were buying. They paid forty cents each for first quality white hickory ax lengths, and eighteen for hatchet or hammer lengths. Well, we had a lot of hickory. So he propositioned his dad. Sure, he'd help.

I went along to the woods the first day. I can pull my end of a crosscut saw right along with the best of them, and I thought I might come in handy. I stood aside, though, while they cut down a dozen or so tall hickory trees, and then I spelled first one, then the other, sawing them into lengths. After that my puny assistance was dispensed with, for I sure can't swing an ax. I can't even split kindling wood without getting a black eye. The ax never goes where I want it to go, and the stick of wood always heads for my face.

The two men got out three truckloads of ax handles in about four weeks, each truckload bringing them around a hundred dollars. Our share looked like riches to us. And, as if fortune meant to smile upon us double, there came in September another windfall. The Government, for some reason, figured it owed Henry another hundred dollars — back pay for soldiering or something. Anyhow that check came right on the heels of the hickory money. So we had funds again. "Now," Henry said, "we'll get your typewriter."

We had never bought a typewriter. I had written *The Enduring Hills* on a rented machine, but we were not in the city now and we both knew a typewriter was a necessity we must somehow include in the budget very soon. Already I had been called on to make some changes in the manuscript of the book, and I had had to make them in longhand. One change required rewriting an entire scene, which I had laboriously done with pen and ink. I have used a typewriter for so many years that

I cannot think any other way. Words flow too slowly when I write in longhand, and I long ago gave up writing even letters by that method. That scene is a weak spot in the book, I think, for I wrote awkwardly with a pen. Now, finally, I could have a typewriter again.

We borrowed a Sears, Roebuck catalogue from the folks and pored over the pages listing typewriters. Neither of us likes a portable, so we flipped hastily by them to the standard desk models. Oh, the new ones were so beautiful! But they were also beautifully priced. Slowly we turned another page. Here were the used, reconditioned ones. And here, the very cheapest of the reconditioned ones, was the one we could afford. An ancient L. C. Smith — so ancient, in fact, that the model was not even dated. "Thoroughly reconditioned by our experts," the description said. And the price was $48.95, plus, of course, postage charges. We made out the order carefully, enclosed our check, and sent it off. Almost unbelievably promptly it came, and we tore it out of its wrappings eagerly. We placed it on the desk. Then we had to laugh. There it sat, high and naked as a Model T Ford, old-fashioned and almost antique. "It ought to have brass head lamps," Henry said.

But when we tried it, we found that it worked smoothly and well. True, the type was just the least bit out of line, and occasionally the spools failed to reverse properly. It also had a habit of jumping a letter once in a while, but the reconditioning had been done as thoroughly as possible, and I should be happy to write a testimonial to Messrs. Sears, Roebuck's typewriter mechanics. We have now written several books on that old L. C. Smith, and while our finished copy is done on a brand-new Royal, we still prefer to bang out the first draft on the familiar, noisy old machine that has been so trustworthy.

But September was due to hold more good fortune for us. One day toward the last of the month I went out to the mailbox after the postman had passed. There was a telegram! Telegrams come to us by a devious route. They come as far as Lebanon, Kentucky, fifty miles distant, by wire. From there they are mailed to Campbellsville, and I presume travel by rail. At Campbellsville they are placed in the pouch of the star route carrier, to be delivered to the post office at Knifley. At Knifley they are transferred to the rural route mail delivered along the ridge. Even so, they do reach us much faster than letter mail, because they come part of the way by wire. Libby, for instance, can wire us late one afternoon and the telegram is delivered on the route the next morning. That is true also of a wire from Mr. Swan, our representative in New York.

But it had been so long since I had seen a telegram that for a moment I didn't even recognize it. I thought perhaps it was an advertisement made up like a telegram. Three or four times a week we get "box holder" advertising. The kind on which postage is paid by the advertiser and the rural route carrier must conscientiously place one in each box along the route. They are addressed merely "Box Holder," and they are the bane of our existence.

Then a pang of fear shot through me. When you live fifteen hundred miles from a daughter as dear to you as your own heart's blood, and she has three small sons, ranging from one to three years old, who are equally dear to you, your first thought when confronted with a sudden and unexpected telegram is likely to be that something terrible has happened to one of them. Knowing Libby, I knew it would *have* to be something terrible before she would wire me. So I opened the message with shaking hands, and even after reading it couldn't quite take it in. "Delighted to inform you Family Book Club have chosen *The Enduring Hills* as their selection for May. Congratulations! Olga Edmond."

Olga Edmond was the editor who had patiently and understandingly worked with me all during the writing of the book, making me go back time and time again to rewrite a section until she was satisfied it was the best I could do. In her letter which followed two days later, she told me she had been so excited that she couldn't help sending the wire, even though she knew it would not reach me immediately. It was like her warm, generous heart to know I would be thrilled by it, and to be so thrilled herself that she wanted to share it with me at once.

I read it again and its significance began to dawn on me, and
then the shaking was from excitement and happiness instead
of fear, but if anything it increased rather than decreased.
Henry, I thought. I must tell Henry. He was cutting hickory
over in the woods. Without knowing exactly where to find him,
but knowing I must, I clutched the telegram in a wad in my
fist and tore out across the garden patch, the tobacco field,
and into the woods, yelling unnecessarily every other breath.
It's uphill all the way from the tobacco field to the edge of the
woods, but I know I never stopped running. Sereny told me
later that she saw me take off from the mailbox like something
was after me, and she said she told Elmer something awful
must have happened. She said she changed her dress so as
to be ready to help out when I came back.

I stopped when I reached the edge of the woods to listen,
for I knew the sound of his ax would lead me to Henry. There
it was, faint and distant, but straight ahead. That led me down
the hillside into the hollow and up the other side. I ran and
slipped and slid down the steep hill, yelling again and again
for good measure. As I reached the foot of the hill, Henry
came, on the run, his face as white as paper and his own hands
shaking. "What's the matter?" he shouted before he reached
me. "What's happened?"

I was much too out of breath to answer so I just waved the
telegram at him and panted. He snatched it and read it and
started grinning. Then he sat down on a log and wiped his face.
"Lord have mercy," he said weakly, "I thought the house
was on fire, or you'd half killed yourself!" He began to get
angry. "Don't you ever come tearing through the wilderness
like that again yelling bloody murder every step. You scared
me out of ten years' growth. Why, the least I thought . . .
Hey, let me see that telegram again."

Foolishly we stood there and read it over and over and
grinned at each other and patted each other on the back. You
don't really know what you're doing at a time like that, nor
how silly you can be. "What do you suppose it means?" Henry
finally said.

"I don't know," I said, "but it must be pretty wonderful or

Olga wouldn't have wired. I mean . . . well, it *must* mean the book's pretty good. And I imagine it means a little more money . . ."

How naïve we were! We didn't find out exactly what it did mean until the next August when there came that first nice fat check from the book club. And another nice fat check the first of October, and another one the first of January. That day in the woods when we stood and grinned at each other we thought it might mean an extra thousand dollars maybe. And an extra twenty or thirty thousand copies of the book . . . maybe. And that was good. That was wonderful! But never in our wildest dreams would we have guessed that nine months after it was published the book would have reached out and touched nearly 110,000 people. Figures like that were beyond comprehension.

We read the telegram once more, and then Henry patted me on the shoulder and kissed me and said prosaically: "Well, that's fine. Fine. But it's not getting any hickory cut. I'll be home to dinner around twelve."

And he went back to cutting his hickory, and I went back to the house to cook his dinner. And Sereny, seeing me come back more calmly, decided nothing catastrophic had happened after all and changed back into her work clothes again.

Chapter
12 ↙↙

All summer we had sneaked time from the tobacco and the canning and the improvements on the house to fish and to study birds, and Green River was perfect for both. Green River! Ah, everyone should have Green River flowing at the foot of the ridge as we do. Beautiful, emerald, winding stream, chattering over the rapids, purling around the shoals, stilling over the deep places. "Lonely river, weary water." Henry sings a song that begins with those words, and I never go to the river without thinking of them. Lonely river, weary water.

Only when the tide comes is the water ever muddy, and then quickly it clears to its lovely, cool green emerald again. Someday I'm going to find out why the hill people, a hundred and fifty years removed from their residence by the sea, still speak of a rise in water on the creeks and rivers as the tide coming, but as yet I have found no clue other than the one that applies to so many of their sayings: That's the way their fathers spoke of it, and their fathers before them, and their fathers. "It's allus been that way"!

Green River flows shallow under the bridge where the pike crosses, noisy over the pebbled shoals. Then it tunnels under the willows and deepens, slowing and flowing genteelly, like a lady who has been slightly hurried, but who now preens herself and straightens her skirts. Green, green water, jeweled in the sun. Deep and cool and still. Here it bends around a bank, high-cut and steep. The water is roiled at the edge, disturbed. Then come the rapids, noisy and rushing, water-whitened and restless. And then, the travail past, comes a long, clean stretch of water, slow-moving and sweet. Here the canes grow down to the water's edge, and it is here that we come to fish.

I do not hunt with Henry very often. Not that I mind the hunting, or even the killing of game. I like to eat it too well to be sentimental about its death. It would not be very consistent of me to enjoy the rewards of hunting and object to its methods. I don't enjoy hunting because I am a physically lazy person and Henry goes much too far and too fast for my comfort. When he is hunting, he forgets all about me, as he should, and I am left to fend for myself. We go uphill and downhill, through brush and timber, and my legs are weary and my tongue is hanging out long before Henry has begun to think of turning toward home. I am just a millstone around his neck when I go along. And it may be sheer rationalization, but I think he should be allowed to keep one thing entirely for his own. He seems glad to have me go, on those rare occasions when I want to go. But I know he never has as good a time as when he goes alone, or with another man.

But fishing — now, that is an entirely different story. I am ready to go fishing almost any time Henry says the word. But we drive down to the river and then all I have to do is sit on the bank and hold a pole. That's the kind of thing I do best. Oh, I like to fly-fish too, and I'll work hard at it without even noticing the passing of time. But we don't have much fly-fishing in Kentucky, and I have never got the knack of casting. I can get my line snarled up with a backlash quicker than you can say Jack Robinson. Consistently too. Not many people can do it as completely and as frequently as I. A double-action reel is just beyond me. I never could do two things at once, and casting and thumbing the line are like rubbing your head and patting your stomach, as far as I'm concerned.

Henry was patient with me for a while. "If you can handle a fly rod, you can certainly learn to cast," he said. He just didn't know. But the day I lost two Hawaiian Wigglers for him within thirty minutes he learned, and his patience was surprisingly and suddenly exhausted. I don't know why he can cast millions of times and never lose a lure. And then let me get hold of the thing and if I ever get my line unsnarled long enough to cast at all, the dratted lure snaps off. The first time it happened he didn't say a word. Didn't even look crossly at me. He just fastened another Wiggler on and told me to try again. And it's the truth, so help me, on the very first cast *that* Wiggler snapped off. He didn't say anything then, either. He merely reached out and took the rod.

With a single-action reel I know where I am all the time. I can whip my line out and never once get it snarled — nor in the top of a tree, either. And the feel of it threaded through my left hand gives me a sense of control. The rod is long and sensitive, and I react automatically when I get a strike. The only time I ever caught a fish casting, I didn't even know I had it. I just reeled the dratted thing in. Of course it *was* minuscule in size, but I'd have felt it with a fly rod.

So, fishing being what it is in Kentucky, and I being the kind of fisherman I am, I usually put a worm on a hook, drop it in a still, shadowed pool near the root of a tree, and catch a nice little string of bream, rock bass, bluegill, and sunfish. Henry turns his nose up at that kind of fishing, but he never fails to eat what I catch. Game fish are scarce in the fresh-water streams around here, and while occasionally Henry nets a nice bass, more often than not he comes home empty-handed. I have yet to fail to bring home enough fish for a nice meal.

We keep a boat in a small inlet on the river. It is only an old, leaky rowboat, but it's handy to have when you want to get out in the stream and cast into the rooty, reedy places near the bank. At such times I become the oarsman of the boat, and, if I do say so myself, I am very proficient at the job. I have to be. One splash of the oars, one thoughtless creak, too fast or too slow, and I should promptly be put ashore. I don't know how other people row for a fisherman, but I don't. I paddle. I can use the paddle for a rudder, and an occasional dip, about every five minutes, is enough to keep the boat moving at the snail's pace Henry requires.

We spend long hours that way many summer afternoons, perhaps not speaking the entire time. I don't believe if it were left up to Henry he would ever quit fishing. Always that next cast is going to hook the big fellow. Just around that bend, just there by that gnarled root, just here near the reeds. Now, once more . . . Darkness is the enemy that puts him to rout. We rarely come home from the river before night.

One day he had the moment for which he had been waiting and patiently casting times without end. The water was slow and the day was still and windless. It was about four o'clock. We had rowed up to the rapids and were slowly drifting back to the inlet. The river shoals on the far side along there, and, almost idly, Henry cast toward the shoal. I saw his arm jerk, and then z-z-zing, the reel sang, and Henry was on his feet in that split second. We both saw the big fellow plainly when he arched clean out of the water. He looked as big as a whale! A flash of his sides and the churning water — that was all — but it was enough for us to know that *this* was the fish. My heart ballooned into my throat and I chunked it back down with a gulp, praying and praying that the hook was firmly set, that the leader would hold, and that I should have sense enough to know what to do with the boat when Henry needed me.

But my very excitement almost fouled up the whole works. I dropped the oar! And of course I did what anyone would do under the circumstances. I grabbed for it frantically. That rocked the boat, naturally, and Henry came very near pitching out into the water. He clutched at me to recover balance and got me by the hair, nearly pulling me bald-headed. But it was enough of a hold to steady him, and at the same time I managed to recover the oar. "In a crisis," he said bitterly, "you can always be depended on to be detrimental to the cause."

I could have batted him down with the oar. Did he think I had purposely dropped the thing? And my head still hurt where he'd yanked my hair. "You," I snapped at him, "can get out and walk!"

The line sang again then and we both forgot everything but the whopper. "Thank God he's headed for deep water," Henry muttered.

Oh, it was beautiful to watch that battle — a battle between strength and skill! The big fellow was such a gallant fighter, turning, twisting, swimming deep down trying to dislodge the hook, flashing clear of the water occasionally, angry, frustrated, and strong. But Henry's skill was patient, and in the end the big fellow tired, and when we netted him, he had accepted the inevitable. At such times you feel like giving the tired old warrior back to the water. After all, you've had the hook on your side. We looked at him as he lay in the bottom of the boat, and then we looked at each other. "I'd throw him back," Henry said, "if I thought he wouldn't end up in someone's net or trap."

For all the men who fish Green River are not sportsmen. All too many will use any method at all to catch fish. There are fish traps, nets, baskets, all up and down the river. And men even shoot them on occasion. That this big fellow had escaped a net or trap so long was just pure luck. When we measured him, he was just under eighteen inches, and he tipped the scales at two pounds, fourteen ounces. Not a giant of a fish, certainly, but he was far and away the largest small-mouth bass we had ever seen caught here.

We called it a day, then, for any further fishing would have been an anticlimax. When you've had the best, there's no use asking for anything more. The big fellow made several meals of succulent fillets, and he made fireside talk for many months. "When Henry caught the whopper . . ." and the story is told over and over again. Of course it wasn't long until the fish had grown in size. Two full feet long and a good four pounds. But if a fisherman can't lie about the fish he catches, the world has indeed come to a sad state of affairs.

The people we like best to fish with are Henry's Uncle Marion and his wife, Ider. I don't know why we call him Uncle Marion, but never say Aunt Ider, unless it's because Ider is too cute and too sassy and too everlastingly young to be dignified by the title "aunt." But that's the way it is . . . Uncle Marion and Ider. And Uncle Marion, by grannies, is *not* a Giles. For a change, he is Miss Bessie's kinfolks — her youngest brother, to be exact.

Uncle Marion is a tall, handsome man, with kindly eyes like Miss Bessie's, and a wry sense of humor. He has a nice deep chuckle, but he usually drops his pithy little aphorisms into the conversation with a perfectly dead-pan face. They are deadly, I can assure you, and any time you think you can top him, you're just headed for trouble.

I admire him a lot, but the thing I admire most about him is that he managed to get Ider for a wife, and for forty years has been able to keep her so adoringly in love with him. Never have I seen a man loved so devotedly or so tenderly. Whatever Marion wants, says, or does is gospel to Ider. She has raised a large family of children, kept his home, worked by his side, and waited on him and tended him through thick and through thin — and there's been plenty of thin — and her devotion to him has never wavered. She's the bravest little ninety pounds of humanity I ever ran across. If Marion needed her to help whip his weight in wildcats, she'd be right there until she was clawed to pieces, and even then if there was enough life left in Marion to call for her, she'd keep on fighting until the last breath was gone.

She's tiny, thin, and frail-looking. But that's very deceiving. Ider is as tough as shoe leather inside. She turns out enough

148

work to keep six women busy, and then tells you, mournfully, that she can't hold out to do the work she used to do. When Uncle Marion was desperately ill with peritonitis several years ago, she never left his side, even though he was in the hospital. He was quieter when she was there. The nurses begged her to sleep or to go out and walk and rest. But Marion was fretful without her, and for more than a week what sleep she got, what rest and peace, she got by the side of his bed.

When they finally brought him home, she nursed him by herself, and in addition to nursing him, she fed, milked, and tended the stock, grieved over the way the weeds had taken her garden, and then angrily got down on her hands and knees and crawled between the rows and pulled every weed out by hand. When Uncle Marion was able to sit up and walk feebly about with her help, canning season came on, and it never occurred to her not to fill her usual quota of jars of vegetables and fruits. In between she kept the grass in the yard cut, tended her flowers, and cut the tobacco. He was able to help only a little when it was time to strip. And Ider was afraid for him to be out in the damp and chill of the barn anyhow. So she got most of the tobacco crop ready for the market. And at the end, when Uncle Marion was ready to take over again, when at last she could sit down, Ider's only comment was, "Well, now, it's been a right wearisome time."

I love her to pieces! I love to say something that shocks her just a little bit and watch her eyes widen childishly and her mouth round into an "O" to match. Then her hand flies to cover her mouth and she giggles, "Why, Janice!" I love to drive up in front of her house at some ungodly hour and surprise her. Her mouth flies open, and she gasps, and then she starts flustering around to fix something to eat, for you can't go to Ider's house without eating, and in between she stops and looks at us and shakes her head. "You all are the beatin'est two. Fancy poppin' up here at seven o'clock in the mornin'. Why, I've not hardly got the things done up."

That was the Sunday morning we drove over to Knifley very early to get the Sunday paper. Uncle Marion and Ider live on the edge of the village. The papers hadn't come yet, so we drove out to Ider's to wait, knowing full well that she had been up for hours, that her house would be as neat as a pin, and that Ider herself would probably be dressed for Sunday school.

"We've come for breakfast," I told her when we went in.

Her mouth flew open, and she blinked her eyes, but she grabbed her apron. "Jist you wait," she said, "I'll build up a little fire, an' fry you a little meat an' some eggs in no time. An' they's plenty of coffee done made."

"I'm joking, Ider. We'll eat breakfast when we get home."

"You'll do no sich of a thing. Jist git you a cheer an' set in there an' talk to Marion till I've got it ready. Won't take me no time."

And she was right. In no time at all she had a good, hot meal on the table.

I think she likes to have us come. They are lonely now, Ider and Uncle Marion. All the children are grown and gone, some of them many, many miles away, and one of them never to return. They had three boys in service during World War II, and Edward, the oldest, didn't come back. He was killed on Christmas Day, 1944, in the Battle of the Bulge. Ider showed me the letter his commanding officer wrote her. It was the first letter of that kind I had ever seen, for we were mercifully spared that sort of news in our family. It was the gentlest, kindest letter that could have been written under such circumstances. I wish that man could know how his words comforted Edward's father and mother. If he did not personally feel the death of every man under his command, then I am much mistaken in my knowledge of human nature. He wrote as if he himself were grieving with them. He told Ider, as sweetly as it could be told, that Edward died a hero. That, except for his great sense of duty and his love for his fellow soldiers, he need not have been killed at all. For Edward was safely dug in himself. All he had to do was stay where he was. But about two hundred yards away a little handful of men were all but trapped. They were pinned down by a murderous cross fire in an open field. Edward watched them, and then he inched out of his own foxhole and began creeping across the field toward them. He never reached them, of course. If he counted his chances he must have known he wouldn't reach them. But I doubt if he stopped to think. He must have done what all of them had done times without number before — gone instinctively to the aid of another. Henry has told me how that happened so often in his own outfit. He said they didn't even think about it. They'd been together so long they functioned like members of one body, like fingers and toes with one brain activating them. A man got pinned down with machine-gun fire out on the girders of a bridge they were building. Whoever was nearest crawled out to help him. He has done it, and it has been done for him. They took such things for granted.

So Edward must have acted almost automatically. But his commanding officer recognized it as heroism and so named it in his letter to Ider. During the war death telegrams were not delivered through the mail, as telegrams are usually delivered back here in the hills. A certain man of the village, with a black car, brought them personally. I'm not sure that was a kindness, for his car was known and was watched with dread and fear. To see it turning off the road spelled a moment of heart failure to the people of that home, no matter how friendly his call might have been. Ider was spared that, however. For that man had gone to town that day, and another, unsuspected car turned off the road toward Ider's house. With no premonition whatever she met the driver and was handed her telegram. She has the telegram too — bleak, impersonal, informative — along with the officer's letter and Edward's small parcel of personal effects. And Edward's picture hangs, enlarged and tinted, on the wall over the head of her bed.

Now, Uncle Marion is a fisherman for who-laid-the-chunk. It is said, and with good foundation, that he never fails to catch fish, and he fishes much of the time. We hadn't been having any luck over our way, so we planned an all-day fishing trip with Uncle Marion and Ider on Casey Creek. Ider told me not to bring a thing; she'd take a little grease and corn meal along to fry the fish, and some bread, and we'd have a real old fish fry on the bank of the creek. But I baked a cake and took it along, anyhow. And when we got to their house, Ider sneaked a good mess of fish Uncle Marion had caught earlier in the week and which she had kept frozen in her refrigerator against the occasion. She giggled as she packed them. "Jist in case . . . ," she said. We wouldn't have needed them, it turned out, and don't think Ider actually doubted Uncle Marion's prowess. She just wanted to make sure.

It was a wonderful day. We caught scads of fish — that is, Henry and Uncle Marion did. Ider and I tended the fire and fried them. That's the way a fish fry usually turns out. The menfolks fish and the womenfolks fry. But we didn't mind. The menfolks were having such a grand time, and we were having our own kind of good time talking and frying and making coffee.

I think it was a letter I had received recently from Libby that started us talking along rather morbid lines. Women alone will frequently turn to intimate talk. Libby had written distressfully about a pitiful, abnormal child that had been born to a woman she knew. It frightened her, because she was even then expecting her own second child, and she felt an exaggerated fear and horror over it under the circumstances. I was telling Ider about the child. She nodded her head wisely. "Them things happen," she said. "Why, I knowed of a baby was marked with a snake! Its ma seen a big rattlesnake jist before it was borned, an' when the baby come, it looked fer all the world like a snake. Had a long, thin neck, and little, bitty eyes, and skin that was rough and scaly. They was no doubts its ma had marked it."

"O Ider, babies can't be marked like that. It was just malformed somehow."

"You don't think babies kin be marked? Well, they kin, an' I know they kin. I know of another was marked with a horse's hoof. Its ma was kicked by a horse before it come, an' the print of that horse's hoof was on its cheek as plain as day, an' bloody red too. An' they was one I knowed seen a blind man over in town, an' when her young'un come it never had no eyes at all. Of course they was marked. They ain't no way of explainin' it else."

"But, Ider —"

"Marion never used to believe in sich, neither," she went on.

"He never believed that a young'un borned with a caul could cure the thrush. But when one of ourn got the thrush in its mouth so bad it couldn't swaller, I told him to git Lena Smith. She was borned with a caul, an' I knowed she could cure that thrush in a minnit jist by blowin' in the young'un's mouth. He jist laughed, so I put on my things an' went myself. An' he seen fer hisself what happened. She jist leaned down an' put her mouth next the baby's an' blowed in it, an' that thrush was gone by the next mornin'. They's things we don't know about in nature, but whether we know about 'em or not, they ain't no use goin' agin 'em. Jist take 'em the way they are is best, seems to me."

I had heard about the healing power of persons born with a caul, and I had heard also that this same power was present in the seventh child of a seventh child. Also in a child born after the death of his father. I mentioned these things. Ider nodded again. "Hit's true," she said. "I reckon only the Lord knows why, but hit's true jist the same."

It was sometime during that conversation that Ider told me about the woman who nursed a pig. She laughed when she told it. "I never to say actual seen her doin' it," she explained, "but hit was told on her. They was awful miserly folks an' she'd jist had a new young'un. About that same time their old sow littered, an' she had thirteen. Now you know, I reckon, a sow can't nurse but twelve. Well, the woman, she wasn't goin' to lose a pig jist on account of the old sow not bein' able to raise it, an' seein' she had plenty of milk, she jist raised it herself!"

That story simply stopped me deader'n four o'clock! I was speechless. And it was just as well that the menfolks joined us about that time. I don't know yet whether Ider was trying to see how big a tale I'd swallow, or whether she was telling it for true. There was a mischievous twinkle in her eyes when she told it, but later when I asked Miss Bessie about it she said she'd heard the same thing.

Well, we ate like pigs that day. And never did food taste so good. We fried four big skillets of fish and there wasn't a crumb left. We made two gallons of coffee and didn't pour out a drop. And we ate every smidgen of a huge, three-layer chocolate cake. On which Uncle Marion impolitely choked.

It was while we were sitting around the fire eating that the conversation turned to an elderly man we all knew who had recently married a woman, his second wife, who was much, much younger than he. Uncle Marion had a word to say about it. " I jist up an' told Jed," he says, " that he was too old to be so pa'tickler. Man needs a woman, I says, an' with Suse dead an' gone he'd best find him another'n right away. I says to him a man his age couldn't afford to be picky an' choosy. He'd jist better tetch an' take. Reckon that's what he done."

Ider hadn't heard of the marriage and her eyes were as round as a puppy's. " Why, I never heared the beat," she said. " Hit must of happened awful sudden."

" Met her on a Saturday and married her the next Saturday's the way I heard it," Henry put in.

" Well, I never! " Ider sputtered. " Why, Jed White must be all of sixty year old, if he's a day! "

" Sixty-five," Uncle Marion said laconically, spitting a fishbone to one side. " He put in fer his old-age draw last month."

" An' she ain't but twenty-five? "

" That's what they say," I affirmed.

" My land! " Ider thought for a moment. " Reckon she's a good cook? "

Uncle Marion blew on his tin cup of coffee, and then, out of the stillness . . . " Ider," he said gently, " that ain't what he married her fer! "

Chapter

13 ✒ ✒

We began to make a serious study of birds almost as soon as we moved to the ridge. There were so many, and they were so beautiful, that we wanted to know more about them and their habits. Henry, having been raised in the country, could identify many of them, but he knew only the more common ones. So we sent to the University of Kentucky for bulletins, and during the summer we began an intensive study of the birds native to Kentucky.

We learned that there are three distinct faunal areas within the boundaries of the state. The greater part of it lies within the Upper Austral zone, which includes the great northern area from Pennsylvania to Nebraska and from North Carolina to Kansas. In the east the mountains lie within the Transition zone, which runs along the Appalachian range from Canada southward, and in the southeast we are within the Lower Austral zone, which extends upward from Louisiana, Mississippi, and Tennessee. Thus we have birds common to three areas. In addition, Kentucky is on the great migration route, and along the Ohio the route branches, some birds going on directly north, others going northeastward. But that gives us nearly all of the beautiful migratory songbirds in season.

We are still very amateur bird watchers, but we are learning, and the little we have learned has opened such treasured doors of beauty to us that we constantly study and watch for more opportunities. We are trying very hard to get rid of the pesky English sparrows which are such an enemy of the songbirds, for which we keep feeding stations in the winter, baths in the summer, and the seed-bearing plants the year round. We have made no new discoveries, nor have we even seen any rare birds, but we have learned to enjoy the ones that are around us all the time. There was a little wren this year who built in the tool shed in a paper sack of staples. I think she actually became so accustomed to us that she wasn't afraid of us at all. She fluttered a good bit and scolded when we first discovered her eggs, but more and more often she would allow us to stick our heads inside and talk to her, and finally she only blinked her eyes at us when we opened the door and walked in to get a hoe or rake or some other tool. That was a proud moment for us.

We have chimney swifts and bull bats, whippoorwills and hummingbirds all around us. The swifts build in the chimneys and we can hear them twittering as they settle down for the night. And the call of the whippoorwill is as familiar as the summer evening itself. You can hear it along about dusk, from the woods, or the head of the hollow, or the meadow, clear and distinct. Once we were sitting in the back yard in the early twilight. We were both tired and were not talking very much. A whippoorwill flew low across the yard onto a stump near the fence, not twenty feet away from us, and we could hear the little cluck it gives before each call just as plain. You have to be very close to hear the cluck. We hardly took a breath while it sat there, for fear of frightening it away. And we were rewarded by hearing it call a dozen times or so. It would call a few times and then wait, and from 'way over in the hollow there would come an answering call. That answering call was too much for our little bird eventually, and he flew away to meet the young lady who was so encouraging.

I pulled a big boner in my first book. I had a whippoorwill giving the chuck-will's-widow's cry. I didn't know there was such a bird as a chuck-will's-widow, and while I had heard its call all my life, I thought it was a whippoorwill. But while they are of the same family, they are two entirely different birds. The whippoorwill says over and over again, and very rapidly, "Whip-poor-will, whip-poor-will, whip-poor-will," and the chuck-will's-widow says something that sounds like "Cheap butter in the white oak," or, if you must be literal, "Chuck-will's widow," and not nearly so fast. The only person who called my hand on it was a cousin of mine who lives in Mississippi. He wrote me that we certainly had unique whippoorwills back here in Kentucky.

We have many birds around the house and yard. There are the martins, of course, who are friendly, cheerful, beautiful purplish-black birds that chatter constantly. No home on the ridge is complete without its martin boxes, facing west, naturally. I don't know of any scientific reason for building the boxes to face west, but there is a very good practical one: the birds won't use the boxes otherwise. Not our ridge martins, anyhow. And I'll bet our own martins have the ritziest apartment house in Adair County. It's made of cherry, no less. I bought an old three-cornered cupboard one time, fondly cherishing the hope it was cherry underneath several coats of paint. The doors were, but the rest of it was just plain poplar, and very rat-eaten at that. Henry took the doors off and we stacked them away in our always-bulging storeroom, to use at some later date. I should have known better, but I had no premonitions, not even when the martin box was being built. It had been up several days before I missed the cherry doors. There was quite a to-do when I did. Henry pretended he thought I'd decided not to use them. But I strongly suspect he was glad to saw them up and get rid of them, for it saved him the work of cleaning and rubbing them down. I look at that martin box occasionally and think how beautiful the cherry doors would have been on a cupboard in the chimney corner, and I feel a little bitter about them. But I must say the martins are very fond of their de luxe home, and it may be true I never should have got around to doing anything with the doors anyhow.

We have the catbird, which sounds so much like a cat mewing that if you don't know you'll go looking for a cat in trouble. There are bluebirds, blue jays, yellowhammers, flickers, the mockingbird, the oriole, the meadowlark, the tiny, ruby-throated hummingbird. Did you ever see a hummingbird go courting? He flies back and forth, back and forth, back and forth exactly like a hammock swinging in front of his lady love, dazzling her with the speed of his motion and the beauty of his humming wings. It's a sight to see. We have had to teach Honey to leave the hummingbirds alone. She thinks they are giant insects darting into the cup of the morning-glories or the four-o'clocks, or " pretty-by-nights," and she resents their freedom with the flowers she has been taught to guard against the neighbor's chickens.

We have the woodpecker too. In the summertime we are frequently awakened by one persistent fellow who drums on the roof right over our heads. Why he doesn't break his bill on that tin roof I don't know. But no alarm clock is needed when he is on duty. He can bring you on your feet out of a sound sleep.

Then there are the little slate-colored juncos, the snowbirds, which stay with us all winter. We have seen the entire front yard covered with them, and they benefit greatly by our feeding stations, of course. The chickadee stays with us all winter too. He is a friendly, cheerful little fellow with a shining black cap. He tells you who he is very plainly — "Chickadee-dee-dee."

We see an occasional nuthatch — silly thing — wandering up and down the trunk of a tree upside down. The first time I saw one he was walking right down a tree trunk headfirst. He didn't seem to care at all whether his head or his feet were up. "What kind of bird is this?" I yelled to Henry.

He looked. "That's a nuthatch."

"But look at him! He goes all around the tree, upside down."

"Wait until you see one hanging from a limb upside down before you start thinking he's so remarkable," Henry laughed.

The only other bird I have ever seen who is as much of a clown as the nuthatch is the female diver we see in New Mexico when we are fishing. She sits on a rock in the middle of a rushing stream, doing one knee bend after another while she quarrels with her laboring spouse, who is knocking himself out diving for minute larvae under the rocks in the icy cold water. We watched a pair of them one day move slowly upstream, and never once did that little lady exert one single effort to feed herself, and never once did she stop doing those monotonous squatting exercises of hers. Up and down, up and down, up and down. It was like perpetual motion. We got tired just watching her.

But it's when we are on the river that we are really treated to a symphony of song from the birds. Birds love the woods along the banks of streams and you'll find the rarer ones there. There, most often, we hear the killdeer. He says, "Killdee, killdee, killdee," over and over on a high, clear note. And we hear the wood peewee most often there too. He says, "Pee-a-wee, pee-a-wee." And there we watch a brash young redbird try to pick up a young lady winging by. He tilts his head as her wings flash and calls to her, "Pretty, pretty, pretty." If she's a properly brought up young lady bird she gives him the brush-off by answering: "What's it to you? What's it to you?"

We find the peter-birds there also. Actually the peter-bird is a titmouse, and he has no song except that high, clear, ever-repeating cry, "Peter, peter, peter, peter." We also call him the tomtit.

I have learned about most of the birds we see on the river at great disadvantage. In spite of my best efforts at studying the bird book, comparing the description with the illustration, it was difficult for me to identify many of them. There are so many birds that are small, brown, with black markings on their heads, with white stripes on their outer wings. I would take the bird book along when I was due to play gondolier to Henry and study the birds during my enforced silence. I row a few feet and then take a peek at the book. But the birds in the trees along the bank were never the birds in the book. So again and again I have risked anathema by hissing at Henry. " Ps-s-t! What's that bird? "

" What bird? "

" That one. Oh, he's gone. No . . . over there."

" That's a peewee."

" Oh."

I turn to the page on peewees and study it furiously. A half hour goes by. " Ps-s-t! What's that bird? "

" Where? "

" There! "

" That's a peewee."

" But it doesn't look like the other one! "

" It's a female."

Not only do you have to learn to identify the make, but you have also to learn to identify the model.

But by persistence, and mostly by Henry's patience, I have now learned to identify, and positively, the male and the female of most of the species native to our own woods and streams. That doesn't qualify me as any great shakes of a bird watcher, but I'm very proud of it just the same.

Our most beloved bird, however, the one whose song always makes us stop to listen, is the wood thrush. It is another small brown bird, with black spots on its breast and sides. We hear it most frequently on the river. However, our hollow has a tiny, spring-fed stream channeling down its rocky bed, and the thrushes come to the head of the hollow. That is near the house. From there, their song is very clear. They sing in the very early morning, or late in the evening. But we rarely hear them in the morning. I don't mean that as any commentary on the time we get up, either, for we are usually up fairly early. They just don't seem to sing as often in the morning. But I don't mind. I have more time to listen in the evening.

The tone is liquid, full and round, and the opening notes are sweetly flutelike, pure, clear, and lyrical. I associate the song always with the afterglow of a summer sunset, the west sky banded with gold and crimson, the trees standing sharply clean against it. We are most often sitting outside at the time, and as first dark begins to settle down over us, a thrush lifts its song from the head of the hollow and lets it fall like a golden shower about us. I never hear it that a sad, lonesome feeling doesn't catch me by the throat. But it is a sweet sadness, for it is the feeling that all great beauty brings . . . the beauty of a sleeping baby, or the sweep of violins in concert, or the sight of a loved figure after an absence.

We were sitting one such evening that first summer in the cool and the quiet of twilight, tired, tired, as we so often were, but blessedly tired and knowing it. Not talking. Just watching the night come on, and the first fireflies puncturing the dark. And a thrush began to sing. We listened. A brief song, and then he was quiet. In the quietness Henry chuckled. "You know," he said, "when I was a little boy I thought I was the only person on the ridge who could hear the birds sing."

"Why, Henry!"

"Yes. No one ever mentioned hearing them. No one ever spoke of the birds at all. So I figured I must have different ears or something. I really thought I was the only one who could hear them."

Somehow that made me inexpressibly sad. All children, of course, keep many of their inner feelings and emotions to themselves. I remember some of mine. But the little boy Henry kept locked within himself so many, many things. He was so sensitive, so timid, that laughter hurt him unbearably. And the ridge has a cruel way of laughing at a child's fantasies. So he learned early to say nothing of the beautiful things he saw and felt. The song of the thrush was so lovely that he ran away from it sometimes, because he couldn't bear to hear it. But he ran away in loneliness and said never a word.

When we went inside that night, I went straight to the typewriter and wrote the first chapter of *Miss Willie* — the chapter about the boy Rufe and the song of a thrush and how Rufe didn't think anyone else could hear the birds sing.

Chapter

14 ↙ ↙

It happened that shortly after we came to the ridge the whole settlement was thrown into a seething kettle of resentment by the addition of two questionable families to the community. One of these was the Tooneys.

We all thought they ate pretty far back on the hog, especially since they were on the draw, but we also felt it was none of our business. We talked, of course. We always talk on the ridge. None of us approved of people drawing sixty dollars a month as indigents for the schooling of their children and then not sending their children to school. Furthermore, we thought it mighty fancy of them to spend their draw on boloney, bubble gum, and soda pop instead of good, solid food. Oh, they bought meat too. Plenty of it, for Mrs. Tooney said the old man had to have meat. He couldn't live without it. We said that for folks on the draw they had right high and mighty notions.

But none of us ever figured to get mixed up with them. After all, they lived down at the far end of the ridge, and to those of us who count the center of the ridge the main settlement, that was almost like living in another town. News of them trickled down the grapevine, of course, and we heard how they bought so plentifully of the delicacies the hucksters carried; how they ran up big grocery bills at Knifley and in town; how they were always sick and having to be carried to the doctor; how lazy the woman and the girls were and how dirty the whole family was. We heard, and we talked, and then we dismissed them from our minds. The Tooneys were actually no concern of ours.

The Tooneys were renters. It is no disgrace to be a renter here in the hills. Plenty of good farmers have got their start by renting. But you don't ever want to rent any longer than it takes to get a start, of course. A piece of rocky land, a leaky roof, anything at all if it's your own, is better than renting. So the fact that the Tooneys were renters didn't count against them. But the fact that they had always been renters, and probably always would, did. "Do-less" is the term we use about people like that. So we labeled the Tooneys do-less and skipped them.

We skipped them, that is, until Simon brought them right smack into the middle of us. Simon needed help on his farm badly. We all knew that. His own sons had long since grown up and left the ridge for the cities, and Simon had been managing alone for several years. But he was growing older, and in the past year he had been ill frequently. We knew he couldn't work his farm alone any longer. But the Tooneys! Couldn't he have got another family to rent? Evidently he couldn't. A good tenant is mighty hard to find, and Simon's wife, Jennie, told us that Simon tried to find someone else, but the season was getting late and he had to have a renter, and the Tooneys had to move, so he had taken them. Jennie told us this apologetically, knowing we were critical.

So here they were, spang in the midst of us. The lazy, dirty, do-less Tooneys. We all congregated and talked. And we hoped. "Maybe," we said, "maybe they'll make good this year. Maybe they won't be a burden to the settlement. Maybe they'll manage better. Maybe they'll make out for once." And they came to live in Simon's old rent house.

This much may be said for Simon. His rent house was no worse than many another hereabouts. For that matter it was no worse than many another home in which the owner lived. Simon and Jennie had lived in it a good many years until they built their new home. But it had run down considerably since then. The roof leaked, the floors sagged, and the house itself tipped at a gaunt angle into the wind. Folks said, well it was a better house than the Tooneys had been used to at that. They'd lived in a two-room log cabin down at the other

162

end of the ridge. 'Way off the road too. Simon's house sat right on the road and it had three rooms. Anyway, the Tooneys moved in with a pitiful, pathetic wagonload of house plunder.

It may be true, as some said, that the Tooneys would have wrecked a brand-new house. I don't know. But it certainly is true that they did nothing for Simon's rent house. In no time at all it was a crazy litter of junk, bugs, and filth. It smelled when you passed in the road, and there it sat, right in the middle of us, and we had to pass it every time we went anywhere. It was a constant reminder and a constant threat to all of us. We had the Tooneys on our necks now, and we sort of tiptoed for fear of disturbing the delicate equilibrium to which we were accustomed.

There were six of them. There was the old man — and we called him that because his wife and children spoke of him thus — the old man, who, the talk went, had been a good worker in his time, but who was a sick man nowadays. He had the high blood, Mama Tooney said proudly. "When his blood gits up," she sighed, " he ain't good fer nothin'. Jist plumb gives out. He ortent to ever do a day's work in the sun. But," she reflected tiredly, " a body's got to live."

He was a tall, powerfully built man, beefy and bulky, with a red face and gray hair that stood up all over his head as if it had been starched. He was a good-natured man, slow-moving, still willing to work when he was able. But more and more he depended on Olaf to carry the heaviest load.

Olaf was a strong, oversized boy of fifteen. He was the oldest of the four children. He could do a man's work and ask no quarter. Generally he had it to do too. My guess is that Simon rented to the family largely because of the boy. There appeared to be nothing he couldn't do. We watched him plow, cultivate, disk, rake, fell timber, cut and strip tobacco — all the things it falls a man's lot to do on the farm. If he questioned his right to any of a boy's privileges, such as hunting and fishing, we never heard of it. We always saw him at work, and hard at work. There is little doubt that Olaf was the mainstay of the family.

There was Mama Tooney, then. All two hundred pounds of

163

her. She had beautiful dark, naturally curly hair, and lovely, soft, doe eyes. She must have been a very beautiful girl once. But now her beauty was larded over with layers of soft fat, and the reason was evident. None of us ever saw her turn her hand to do a lick of work. All spring and summer she sat on the porch or under the trees, her hands folded over her ample stomach, her mouth puckering a lip of snuff. When we went past, she spoke pleasantly, mentioned the weather or some ailment she had, her face placid and dull, her heavy body quiet. And she never seemed to notice the accumulation of junk and filth all around her.

There were two older girls, Noonie and Stella. They did what work was ever done: the cooking — and very little cooking they did, for they lived out of cans mostly; the dishes; an occasional sweeping up; and once in a great while they made a vague attempt at doing a washing. The clothes hung slattern and gray on the line, ragged, shameful, and almost obscene. We turned our faces from their wash on the line.

Noonie was the older, and she had a look of frail fairness about her when she was clean enough to see. I don't recall ever seeing her with her hair combed. I doubt if she could have got a comb through it, it was so tangled and matted. She was thirteen or fourteen, and she could neither read nor write. For that matter, no one in the family could read or write. All of us were called on at various times to read their mail to them, and to write their letters for them.

Stella was a strong, pudgy young twelve-year-old, with stocky, sturdy legs and arms, and a ready, friendly laugh. Her face was always ruddy under its crust of grime, and her mouth was always full of snuff. Noonie seemed to carry most of the burden of the housework, for Stella frequently was out in the fields with Olaf. She could pitch hay all day long, swing an ax as well as any man, and I have even seen her behind a plow. Her voice was hoarse and strong, and her laugh was raucous and thick. You had the feeling that Stella would always get along — but not Noonie.

Then there was the baby, a girl of three or four, who was the darling and idol of the entire family. She ruled them with an iron thumb. Big and as fat as she was, the older girls still swung her to their hips and carried her everywhere, for she didn't like to walk. She was a badly spoiled, terrible-tempered little brat, and already she was smoking cigarettes and using snuff. The family thought it cute of her and encouraged her in it, laughing at her and boasting of her to any who would listen. She badly needed the back of a hairbrush where it would do the most good.

For a time after they moved among us things went along fairly well. The slow summer days went by and Olaf made a good crop of tobacco for Simon and laid by an ample crop of corn and hay. The old man's blood stayed down and it looked as if they were going to have a good season. We were all anxious. We watched them and we said: " The tobacco looks fine, and with their half of it and the corn and the hay, and with their draw, they ought to make it through the winter in good shape. If they just don't spend it on foolishness! "

They didn't. But they had to spend it all just the same.

It was September. Our tobacco was cut and tiered in the barn. The canning season was over. I was writing again. My mind was a thousand miles removed from the Tooneys when I went over to spend the afternoon with Miss Bessie that day. We talked of this and that, and then, almost casually Miss Bessie said: " Noonie's sick. She's got the tonsilitis."

" Oh? Very bad? "

" Pretty bad, they say. I've not been up. But Stella says her throat is swelled up an' she cain't hardly swallow."

I felt no premonition of disaster. A swollen throat is typical of tonsilitis, and all ridge children have it often, for none of them have their tonsils out. " Have they taken her to the doctor yet? "

" Not yit. If she ain't no better by tomorrow, they're gittin' Elby to take 'em."

Elby Giles is Henry's cousin. He had the only other car on our part of the ridge at that time. I remember feeling relieved that they were asking Elby instead of Henry. Our old water pump was certainly acting up and we didn't drive the car except in an emergency. But you don't ever turn people down when they need to go to the doctor. If your car will run at all, you run it. Nine times out of ten it is panic that sends our folks to the doctor after they have already done all that can be done for their sick, but there is always the threat of that tenth time when death may be beckoning from around the corner. Out of pure humanity you answer that panicky cry: "My baby's sick! I've got to git my baby to the doctor!" No matter what time of day or night it is, you go, and no matter whether your car can be trusted or not. We wish sometimes they wouldn't wait until night to go, but we understand why they wait. A woman can be calm enough about her sick child during the day, ordinarily. It's when dark draws nigh that fear closes in — when night curtains the familiar with strange, ghost shapes and hovers with strange, ghost fears. Panic sets in then, and the woman who has gone about ministering to her sick child with a measure of calmness all day loses her calmness and becomes terror-stricken. "I've got to git my baby to the doctor!" she cries, and her fear spreads through the whole family, and an equally terror-stricken father or older brother is sent flying for Elby or Henry. And they go, quickly, for they understand that fear. We are that close, at least, to the medical profession. We never turn folks away.

It was a week, I suppose, before I heard anything more about the Tooneys. Again I was at Miss Bessie's. We were sitting in the late sun in the yard when Stella came flying down the road, fear and horror written across her face and terror in her voice. "Miss Bessie! Miss Bessie! Come quick! Ma says come quick! Noonie's chokin' to death!"

Now Miss Bessie is not well herself. She rarely leaves her home and she never walks anywhere. Her strength is much too frail, and under excitement her heart pounds up into her throat until she is near choking herself. I saw her hand go to her throat, and I knew her heart was beating hard. "I'll go," I said quickly, for I knew she would try to go, no matter how she felt. "You stay here, I'll go." And I flew back up the road with Stella pounding heavily beside me.

How shall I tell what I saw when I entered that house? There are no words with which to tell it . . . to tell about the dirt, the sourness, the millions and millions of bugs crawling all over the house, the beds, the floors, everywhere, and the awful pervading smell, the horrible, horrible smell! It was only late September and the weather was mild and warm, but, for fear that Noonie would take cold, they had already put up the heating stove and had sealed out every breath of fresh air. The thick, hot room, dark from only one shaded window, struck at one and rode down one's defenses, and fear and horror and nausea overtook one. I remember stumbling against something and reaching out to steady myself against the wall. As briefly as my hand rested against the wall a roach ran over it, and my flesh crawled and pimpled to the shoulder. I shook the roach off, frantically. "The bugs is bad," Mama Tooney said dully.

Noonie sat in a rocker near the stove, and the stench when I drew near her was so terrible that I could hardly breathe. The choking fit was evidently over, but she sat with her head thrown back still gasping for air. Her throat was swollen to a strut and there was no telling where her chin and jaw line had been. Her face was swollen and her eyes were almost hidden in the puffy mattress of her cheeks. She breathed in fevered, pus-filled gasps, which rasped out of her distorted throat, and her thin little chest heaved with the effort of drawing air into her lungs. "She's been gittin' better," Mama Tooney said, "till she takened worse this mornin', an' then she takened that chokin' spell an' she like to coughed up her insides! I thought shorely she was adyin'!"

The bucket in which Noonie had vomited and coughed still sat in the middle of the floor. I summoned every ounce of courage I had, and it wasn't much, and looked. "That's pus," I said. "That's what's been collecting in her throat and choking her. All of that should have been swabbed out long ago. Haven't you taken her to the doctor yet?"

"Oh, yes. We takened her last week. He give her a shot of pencil an' said take her to the nurse at Knifley for another'n in a few days."

"Have you taken her?"

"No. We thought she was gittin' better. She's been stirrin'

three or four days now."

I was new on the ridge, but not so new that I hadn't seen with what delicacy Henry and his family tread when it comes to interfering with someone else's business. You don't make suggestions. You don't give advice. You don't step in and take over. You wait. You stand by, ready to help. But you wait until you are asked before you say anything. You may go in and cook and wash dishes and keep the house going, but you don't take over the sick. Miss Bessie had followed slowly down the road and she came in now. She said Noonie might get better now that she had rid her throat of the phlegm. She said, thoughtfully, that it might be a good thing if Noonie were taken to the nurse. Just to make sure. She said if they needed her to let her know.

I had the crazy feeling of wanting to bundle the child up and drive her to the hospital at once. Get her some place where she would be clean, and where medical attention could be given her constantly. I didn't want to be gentle with the Tooneys. I wanted to *do* something for the child. Right now. And I wish I had.

I ranted a little to Miss Bessie as we walked down the road. "She doesn't have tonsilitis, Miss Bessie! She has a strep infection. She should be in the hospital. She needs nursing. That throat needs draining, and she needs feeding. Why don't they take her to the hospital?"

"Likely they will. But it's fer them to decide," came her calm reply.

We were all uneasy then. Anxiously we asked each day, "How is Noonie?" and, generally, they said she was getting some better. She did seem to get better. Some of the swelling went down, she laughed a little and talked, and she stirred around the house more. Not even at her worst, though, had she stayed in bed.

And then one day — she had been ill almost three weeks now — they sent for Henry again, frantic and in terror. "Noonie's bad agin. Git the nurse!" Henry went, and while he was gone I talked to Mrs. Tooney. My conscience would not let me keep quiet any longer. "Take her to the hospital, Mrs. Tooney.

When the nurse comes, let Henry take her to town with Noonie and put the child in the hospital. She needs professional care."

"I doubt Noonie'd go. She don't even want the doctor or the nurse the way it is. She begs us not to git 'em."

"A sick child never wants the doctor or nurse. She is scared and ill. You have to decide what's best for her."

"Yes . . . but I wouldn't rest easy with Noonie over there by herself, 'thout me to do fer her. I'd ruther she'd be where I kin keep watch." The big, soft-spoken woman twisted her hands and the tears rolled down her fat cheeks. " She's awful sick. She's awful sick, an' don't seem like nothin' kin he'p her."

"Take her to the hospital."

"They ain't no money to be payin' the hospital."

"The money can be found."

She turned away, the tears still runneling her cheeks. "Hit's trouble that's come. Trouble. My pore sick little girl, an' us with no money. An' she'd die at the hospital 'thout none of her home folks clost. She wouldn't stay. I know she wouldn't."

What should I have done?

The nurse came, as she always does. Oh, she looked so competent, so efficient, so cool and calm, in her starched white uniform! We sat outside in the car and waited for her. I felt comforted, just knowing she was inside, doing for Noonie. When she came out finally, Henry took her back to Knifley. She told him that the child was very sick. She would not eat, and they would not make her eat, nor did they know how to fix tempting things to try to get her to eat. She wanted only cool things to drink, and they gave her soda pop, frozen, fruit-flavored ice from Simon's refrigerator. I suppose they hadn't the heart to try to make her eat soups and broths, even had they known how to fix them. The nurse said her bowels hadn't moved in over a week, and that she had told them they *must* give her an enema. It never occurred to any of us that they didn't know what an enema was, and that Noonie in all probability wouldn't have allowed such an indignity to be forced upon her anyhow. The nurse had swabbed out her throat, asked what the doctor had said, given Noonie a shot of peni-

169

cillin, and told them to feed her, bathe her, make her eat, get her bowels to move, and that was all that lay within the realm of her jurisdiction. She could not prescribe, she could not diagnose, she could not recommend further. She could only allay the pain, and, under the doctor's orders, give her penicillin.

Now, of course, some of us went daily. We took food, we sat with Noonie, we talked with the Tooneys, we tried to be hopeful. We sat around in that hot room, for not even the nurse had convinced the Tooneys that the child needed fresh air. And we watched her die a little more each day.

For Noonie died. At seven o'clock one evening she died. "Ice, ice!" she kept crying, and Jennie kept the refrigerator making ice constantly to provide it for her. They could not keep enough to satisfy her burning thirst.

Miss Bessie and I were there that afternoon. In addition to calling for ice, Noonie complained that her feet were cold. When we left, Miss Bessie said, "She's goin'."

"How do you know?"

"Death always commences in the feet."

They said she rolled and tumbled on the bed the last hour, thrashing from one side to the other, not knowing any of them. She turned finally toward the wall and flung her arms over her head. "Ice," she mumbled, "please, I want ice." And then she died.

Ridge folks sit up with the bodies of their dead, for the undertaker can rarely come until the next day. It was a tragic deathwatch that night with Noonie. Mama Tooney went hysterically to pieces and the women put her to bed. The old man sat frozen in his chair beside the bed all night, and the other children wept noisily and crept tearfully about the house, their own throats now swollen and sore, for the infection had spread to them. But the most ghastly thing about the watch was the bugs. They were bad enough during the day, but at night they swarmed in legions over every surface. In horror the people watched them creeping up on the bed where Noonie lay. Soon they were thick on the bed, for the little figure under the tightly drawn sheet was very still and could no longer brush them away. With a sob one of the women ran out of the house to her own home. She came back with a spray gun, and she sprayed the bed, the floor, and the walls around it, and then, tenderly, she sprayed the small, still figure to keep the filthy, creeping, crawling things out of the still open eyes and mouth of the dead child.

When I went the next day, with food, Mama Tooney was still weeping and wailing. She sat in her rocker, her arms folded across her bosom, the tears flowing, her voice hoarse from crying, still talking, still telling again and again how Noonie had died. Still telling what her last words had been. Still telling how they had tried to do for her. " The last thing she ast fer was ice," she sobbed, "an' Stella was jist agoin' to Simon's fer some more. But she was gone 'fore Stella got back with it. An' before that she wanted milk. Not cow's milk — that we've got aplenty of. She wanted canned milk. An' I walked all the way down to Charlie's store to git it fer her. I would have walked twicet as fur. God knows I wouldn't of denied her ary thing she wanted. She ast fer a apple two days ago. I was afeared hit would hurt her, an' I never give it to her. I wisht I'd of give it to her now. Hit's on my soul that I denied her ary thing she wanted. I done the best I could, people. I done the best I could."

And the circle of ridge folks gathered in the room wept with her and nodded their heads. " God knows. You done the best you could."

I put the food on the kitchen table and left. I couldn't bear any more. I felt as if we had all killed her. All of us. Why hadn't we done more? Why hadn't we spoken more plainly? Why hadn't we walked in and bundled Noonie up and taken her into our own hands? No. You don't do things like that. You mind your own business. You don't give unasked advice. You don't barge into other folks' affairs. You just stand there, minding your own business, and let a child die. After she's dead, you may say, if you dare, " I knew it wasn't tonsilitis." You may say, if you dare, " I sat by and helped kill her." In whom may a child trust? In folks. And none of us was worthy of Noonie's trust.

She was buried the next day, and even as Noonie was buried,

the rest of the children were ill of the same infection. But they were stronger than she and the disease touched them lightly. In a week or two they were well again. Then, as if trouble had spread its wings over them and meant to hover there forever, the old man had a stroke and was laid helplessly in bed. The men went, now, to sit up and help. The old man was too heavy for a woman to turn in bed, for women to help, and, besides, it was more seemly for men to wait upon him. The Tooneys. The Tooneys. It was as if each one of us had the Tooneys, ailing and bedridden, in our own homes. All of us worried about them. All of us went. All of us carried them, a daily burden, on our hearts and minds. The Tooneys. We carried them to the doctor, all of them, time after time. And when they didn't need the doctor, they needed medicine, and we carried them to town for that. And when they didn't need medicine, they needed food, and we carried them to Knifley and to town for that. Elby and Henry. Elby had driven his old Model A tirelessly during the time Noonie lay dead, making trips to the next county to bring Mrs. Tooney's people back. He had driven in the funeral procession the next day, back to that same county where they buried Noonie. He did not go to bed for thirty-six hours, and his car wheels never once stopped turning. Then when Noonie was at peace at last, and it was the old man who lay abed, it was Elby they sent for, when they were frightened about him. At midnight, at four in the morning, any time. Sleepily he got up and went.

But winter was coming on and Elby's old car had most of the windows out. He had no heater. Still it had served the Tooneys faithfully. Then one day Mrs. Tooney told Miss Bessie she believed she'd get Henry to take her from now on. His car was nicer. It was warmer. All the windows were in, and it had a heater. It rode easier. We gasped. Can people choose? Elby was the worm that turned. He said, "I'm through." So then it was Henry who drove them. Oh, yes, all of us got very much mixed up with the Tooneys after all.

And what were they going to do, we asked. Where were they going to go? We said: "Surely she will go back to her own folks now. Surely she will not want to stay on the ridge now. Surely she will see that Simon can't possibly keep them another crop year." They owed all their tobacco money. All their corn money. All their draw. As a matter of fact, the hucksters took corn to settle the big grocery bills they owed them. We said, "How can they get through the winter?" And we wanted them to move away where we wouldn't have to watch them get through the winter. We wanted them off the ridge. We were fearful, uneasy, anxious. Their draw would now be forty dollars, instead of sixty, for with Noonie gone they would lose twenty dollars.

And some of our fear was righteous indignation. They had been so do-less. They had more cash money than many of us, but they spent it for boloney and bubble gum and soda pop. They had nothing laid by. The woman had been too lazy to can up her garden stuff. She said they didn't like it, anyway. It wasn't right we should all have to help carry their burdens. We had made ready for the winter. We had taken care of our things. And when we bought from the huckster we bought beans and meat. Good, solid food. "But the old man," Mrs. Tooney said, "he don't like that there side meat. He'd ruther have boloney or salmon." Well! Who was the old man to have his ruthers!

We waited to see what Simon would do. Waited and talked. Would he rent to them another year? Could Olaf, alone, handle all Simon's crops? And then, to our relief, we heard that a relative of the woman's had offered them a small place over in Taylor County and they were going. They said they didn't want to go. They said they'd rather stay on the ridge where folks had been kind to them. "I tell you, people," Mrs. Tooney wept, "money don't count in this world. Hit ain't money'll git you through. Hit's folks with hearts. An' we've been alivin' amongst 'em up here. How'll we git through the winter amongst strangers over there? How'll we make out?"

How, indeed!

And as we watched them pack and make ready we thought guiltily of how relieved we were that they were going. That someone else would have to read their letters for them, and write them, and carry them to the doctor and nurse them through their illnesses. For one thing was certain. Folks with hearts would always have to help the Tooneys.

The last I saw of them they were packed like sardines into our car. They had sent for Henry to move them. All their house plunder had gone ahead in a wagon, and Olaf had gone with it to drive. But the rest of the Tooneys had no way to go. The old man had partially recovered the use of his legs, but it had taken Henry and Elby and Elmer to lift him into the car. Then came Mama Tooney, the spoiled brat, Stella, the two dogs, the old man's rocking chair, an armload of quilts, a box of odds and ends, and they were ready to go. They drove past the house and I looked out. Henry was lost among the Tooneys. I could barely make out the top of his head, for Stella was hanging over one shoulder and one of the dogs was dangling over the other. I waved, and Mama Tooney waved back. "We'll come back to see you," she yelled. "We'll come back!"

But they have never been back. We hear of them, or see one of them in town occasionally, but that's all. Oddly enough, we are all glad to have news of them. "I saw Mama Tooney in town today," we say, and it travels around the ridge, and everyone wants to know: "Are they makin' out all right? Has the old man got his health back? Is Olaf still doin' the work? Has Stella growed clean up?" We talk about them for a while, laugh a little over the boloney, bubble gum, and soda pop, and grieve a moment for Noonie. Then we pass on to other things.

I doubt if we'll ever fail to be interested in the Tooneys. I think we put so much of ourselves into them, and took so much of them into us, that we shall never forget them. The Tooneys will live on the ridge a right smart time yet, I shouldn't be surprised.

Chapter
15 ⸝⸝

Then there was the Mary Magdalene of the ridge, Lacey
Stokes, who posed a neat problem to the more, shall I say, vir-
tuous — or do we then get into a discussion of the definition of
virtue? — women of the settlement. If among those who looked
with indignation upon Lacey there were some who remembered, darkly and fleetingly, that their own first-born came a
mite too soon after the wedding, theirs was but the more vin-
dictive virtue. Theirs the more scornful tilt of the head, the
more lashing tongue, the more biting sneer. Water over the
dam is soon out of sight. Swiftly it flows away and its troubled
foam around the spillway is dissolved into the current.

But when Lacey and her brood of mismatched children
were deposited in the little shack down the road from our
house that summer, the entire settlement was indignant. Her
presence there was an affront to every decently married woman
on the ridge. An affront, and a threat.

The shamelessness of Lacey is ever-present, with her regularly increasing clutch of children. We pass by and look
askance, but we eye the children furtively. Does that youngest
one look a teeny bit like . . . well, *someone* fathers them. If
Lacey knows, she never tells. Quietly, darkly, she goes about
among us, the stumps of her tobacco-stained teeth showing
when she smiles timidly. Her attitude is timidity. She never
knows whether to greet you or not. It may be that if she speaks,
her greeting will be turned back on her. It may be that if she
smiles, it will curdle on her lips. So she reserves her spoken
word, her smile, until we speak or smile first.

I do not know her age, for she is now but a wreck of a once-
handsome woman. She is tall and strong still, rawboned and
sinewy, able to do the hard, harsh work of any man in the
woods and fields, but time and life have gaunted her and
honed her down Her skin is leather, her dark, curly hair is

thin and coarse, her fine black eyes are dull, and there are heavy shadows lying under them constantly. When I look at her, I think I can see past the woman to the girl she used to be. I know that she stood tall and slender, and that her eyes must have been warm and sparkling. I know that her hair curled sweetly on her neck, for it still escapes her bonnet to corkscrew into wispy, straggly tendrils. I know that she was shy and timid, big for her age, perhaps blunderingly awkward, for she is shy and timid now and there is awkwardness even yet in her big-boned frame. I think she must have been eager to be liked, eager always to please. She still is. But all the odds are against her. They always have been, and some of that accounts for her becoming what she is. The rest of it was due to circumstances.

She came of a family about whom no good was ever said. Worthless. Shiftless. Do-less. That's what the ridge said about them, and about her. Nothing good ever came of that family. Nothing good was ever expected of Lacey. She never went to school and she does not know, to this day, how to read or write. She cannot even write her own name. She worked in the fields with her father and brothers, her back and arms as sturdy and as strong as theirs. She was kicked and cuffed and beaten. And at fifteen she married a man three times as old as she in order to get away from home. He was a man close-lipped, dour, and unlovely in every aspect. As shiftless and do-less as her own menfolks, but at least he took her away from them. That's about all he ever did for her, for in his broody, sour way, he took her youth and used it and ground it down to further misery and hopelessness.

They had four children, and then he went completely and totally insane and was put away. There were two boys and two girls. Of the boys, one is badly mutilated by a malformation of his face. The other is normal in appearance, even handsome. The two girls are as lovely to look at as young girls ever get to be. Dark, beautiful eyes and hair, lush womanly figures already. Ridge women look anxiously at Lacey's two young daughters. Especially ridge women with almost grown sons.

176

That the sons, and maybe the fathers, call at Lacey's in the dark hours of the night, most of us know. For the husband has been put away these many years, yet the children continue to appear regularly. There have been four since she has been without a husband. They are not the daughters'. We know that. For we see Lacey before their birth. We know who the mother is. It is the father that provokes our curiosity, and our unrestful glances. Is there one father of them all, or is their birth simply the accident of numerous chances? Numerous and uncertain chances. We do not know. Lacey keeps her counsel, if indeed she herself knows.

For a short space of time she lived near Henry and me. She is constantly shifted about, for no one will have her near very long. Her oldest sons are nearly grown now, old enough and strong enough to do a man's work, so they hire out and Lacey lives in whatever shabby and empty house she can find. An absentee owner rented to them on a share-crop basis. No sooner were they settled in the rent house, however, than he sold the farm. The new owner was confronted with a grim wife: "I'll sign the papers fer you to buy that place on one condition. That woman has got to go."

Sheepishly the man began to look for a place for them. He'd paid his money. The farm was his, but he had to get the woman off the place. A two-room shack down the road from us was empty — had stood empty from time out of mind. It hadn't been occupied in so long that it had fallen into ruins and a sad state of disrepair. He rented it for them, and they moved their bedsteads, cookstove, and other few pieces of house plunder into it and took up their abode therewith. The ridge drew in its breath. "Right in the middle of us! Right in the midst of decent folks! How did he dast! Well, they'll not last long there. Hit's not to be put up with."

The night they moved, one of the smaller children, a boy about eight years old, knocked on our door. Henry opened it. "Ma says will you take her back to the holler to git her chickens." He had on a torn sweat shirt, and a pair of man's trousers lapped over and roped about his waist. It was a chilly evening and he was barefooted. He stood and twisted one ankle about the other, rubbing his feet together.

I had been cooking supper and the kitchen was still warm. "Tell him to come in, Henry," I said.

The boy stood by the stove, but he refused to sit down. "Ma says will you take her back down to the holler to git her chickens," he repeated.

"No," Henry said. "You tell her to wait until the boys come home Saturday. One of them can go after them for her."

"We need the eggs," the child mumbled.

Henry sighed. "We'll loan you some eggs."

And the little boy left, clutching a sack of eggs in his hands.

"Why wouldn't you take her?" I asked.

Henry looked at me steadily. "Because," he said slowly, "because if I took her back down to the hollow tonight, every living soul on the ridge would know it tomorrow. And every last one of them would say I had done it for one reason only."

I was aghast. "But how could they? Everyone knows you! They surely wouldn't think . . ."

He shook his head. "No one is ever given the benefit of the doubt with Lacey."

"You mean you can't even do a decent, common kindness for the woman without being suspected of ugliness?"

"That's exactly what I mean."

And he never did. He never did a thing for her unless I was along, or one of her older children. He knew his ridge and he stuck to what had to be. When, later, Lacey's varicose veins began to trouble her, and she had to go to town to the doctor, she sent for Henry to take her. He took her, but only with a car full of company. "Take Suse along," he would tell her. Or, if the boys were at home, "Jim, you or Link come go along."

During the brief time she lived down the road from us she stayed entirely to herself. Not once did she come up to my house, and I did not go to hers. Henry said it would make her uncomfortable if I went. Frony was visiting me one day shortly after they had moved. She looked down the road and shook her head. "Ain't it too bad!" she said. "Jist too bad!"

"It is," I said. "The children are all so pretty, and whatever you say about Lacey, she keeps them as clean and neat as anybody's."

It is a fact that her four young children are handsomer than the average child on the ridge. Three of them are dark, like she is. The youngest one is fair. They all have beautiful eyes, teeth, skin, hair. And she does keep them cleaner than most.

Just then the eight-year-old boy passed — Dode, they called him. "That'n, now," Frony said, eying him sharply, "he looks a sight like a Warden, don't he?"

I didn't say anything. I'd always thought he looked a sight like Frony's own son-in-law.

"I hope," Frony said severely, "you don't go mixin' an' minglin' none with 'em. You git turned in with 'em, an' they'll borry you outen house an' home."

I didn't get turned in with them, and I didn't mix and mingle, and they didn't borrow me out of house and home. But I did share the garden with them. Lacey sent for Henry one day to take her over on the other side of Campbellsville to see her second son. With three of the children to chaperon, he took her. When he came back, I was curious. "What did she want?"

Henry was short. "They haven't anything to eat. She went to see if he'd got paid, and if he'd give her enough to buy food."

Well, ridge or no ridge, hungry children were something I wasn't going to stand idly by and let suffer. Our garden, big and plenteous, was in full bloom. There was corn, green beans, lima beans, cucumbers, squash, tomatoes, rhubarb, and potatoes almost ready to dig. I went down to their house. I couldn't find words but the blunt truth. "We have plenty. Come help yourselves."

And they did.

Lacey is on the relief rolls. Once a month she gets a check, which she always owes. The check is based on the number of children in the household, and it is increased each time her family increases. She may, therefore, welcome each new baby joyfully. I do not know whether the men who visit her so stealthily after night has fallen ever pay her or not. I have my doubts. Not many of them would have anything to pay her with. Oh, they may bring her a turn of corn, or a chunk of meat, or even leave a dollar occasionally. But one thing is certain, she makes a mighty poor living that way.

She was arrested not long ago for giving a bad check. She said she had never signed such a check, and we on the ridge believed her for we knew she couldn't have. One of the men interested himself in the case, and went her bond. He and Henry investigated, and they learned that she had owed a large grocery bill to a certain man for a very long time. When the grocer became insistent, the two older boys agreed to pay it off five dollars a week, and that was satisfactory to the grocer. Evidently the boys had begun to skip payments. One of the girls was in the store one Saturday and the grocer filled out a check for the balance, some ninety dollars, and had the girl sign the check for her mother. The girl did not know what she was signing, not knowing people did business by check, except the official welfare check with which she was familiar. Then he gave her a nickel in change to make the transaction a Federal offense. When the check came back, as naturally it did, he swore out a warrant for Lacey, believing that in the face of going to jail she would borrow the sum and he would be paid the entire amount.

But it didn't work out that way. For once she had some people on her side. Witnesses who could swear the girl was only fourteen, couldn't have known what she was doing, and had no authority to sign her mother's name at all, were found. The whole thing was finally thrown out of court, and the best the grocer got was a promise that the payments would be taken up again. I do not excuse Lacey for the bad debt. But in the face of a shabby trick I was glad to see her come out ahead.

We are not ones to keep an eye on our neighbors. We tend to our own business and allow those who live near us to do the same. We have neither the time nor the curiosity to do otherwise. I have often chuckled over the remark Sereny made to me a few months after we had moved to the ridge. " I wisht," she said one morning, " I wisht that there old pear tree was outen the field betwixt us. Spring an' summer I have the worst time makin' out what you all are doin' down at yore house! "

But we could not help being aware of some things that went on down at Lacey's. It was summer and we liked to sit outside in the yard long past dark. It was often ten or eleven o'clock before we went into the house. With no lights in the house, ourselves in the dark, we sometimes saw things that doubtless we were not intended to see. Like the shadowy, dusky figure of a man slipping down the hedges of the road past our place, turning in at Lacey's, silhouetted very briefly and momentarily against her lamplight in the doorway. Or the slow chug of a car trying to ease quietly along the road, stopping at her gate, and discharging two, three, or four persons. Persons? Men, then. Or the clop-clopping of a horse in the dust, and the sudden quiet when the horse was halted at the big tree in front of Lacey's house. But there was never noise, never loudness, never the signs of drunken rowdiness. There was simply the quiet, stealthy coming and going. And the quiet and the stealth carried their own shame.

There was even humor occasionally. One Sunday evening just at dusk, to my surprise I saw Elmer's wife going down the road, and I saw her turn in at Lacey's. She had been one of the most vicious in her denouncement of the woman, one of the first to cry out against her move among us, and one of the ones to cry longest.

" Why, Sereny's gone to Lacey's! " I told Henry in amazement.

He laughed. " There's two horses hitched out back. Her curiosity's got the best of her. She's gone to see who's there this time of day."

It *was* unusual for someone to be there so early. We lighted the lamps and turned the radio on, but we had hardly got settled when there was a knock at the door. Henry went, but instead of inviting the person in, he stepped outside on the porch and pulled the door to behind him. He was outside quite a long time, I thought. But so many people come to ask for something — to drive them somewhere, to borrow a little money, to borrow a pack of cigarettes, to see if he wants some wood cut. I went on reading, the radio making a pleasant accompaniment. It must have been thirty minutes before he came in, and the expression on his face was a mixture of exasperation, anger, and laughter. "That was Stew," he said.

Stew was a very distant cousin. "Why didn't you ask him in?"

"Didn't want him in. I'm not going to have him coming in here three fourths drunk."

"Oh."

He laughed. "He was down at Lacey's and Sereny came, so he lit a shuck out the back door and came up here until she left. She's just gone back up the road."

"Why would he care for Sereny knowing he was there?"

"Because she's the biggest talker on the ridge and it would have got back to his mother by daylight tomorrow morning."

We both laughed, for we knew Stew's mother thought he was a little angel straight from heaven.

The Stokeses didn't live near us very long — just a few, short months. Then the house, that little ruin of shack, was sold and they moved farther on down the ridge, out of our sight and hearing. We had dug the potatoes the day before and I knew we could never use them all. So we filled a bushel basket and took it down to them, thinking they could move it with the rest of their belongings. Everything was stacked in the yard, ready to go. And all the children were milling and swarming around.

One little fellow whom I had not seen before except at a distance came around the corner of the house, pulling the baby in a small red wagon. When he saw us, he stopped and shyly stuck his finger in his mouth. He looked to be about three or four years old, and I think he was one of the most beautiful children I have ever seen. His head was a mop of dark, chestnut curls, tightly screwed to his scalp. His face was oval, with clear, olive skin drawn sweetly over the bones, reddened brightly on each cheek. He was pudgy and chunky, with fat little hands dimpled on the knuckles. His knees were dirty and skinned. I went over to him and spoke to him, and he ducked his head in unbearable embarrassment. So I got down on my knees to see into his face. He looked at me then with the roundest, brownest eyes in the world, fringed with lashes that curled half an inch up from them. "He's beautiful," I said to one of the older girls, "he's just beautiful!" And I wished I could have him. I wished it so much that it was an ache inside of me. I put an arm around him and he leaned against me, warm and sweet and babyish.

"What's your name?" I said. "What's your name?"

He didn't answer.

"Tell her yer name," prompted his big sister.

He took his thumb out of his mouth and grinned at me. "My name's Junior."

"My name's Junior"! Junior, who?

Chapter

16 ↙ ↙

It was along late in the summer that we met Miss King and Mrs. Bierly. Our hills are a mission field not only for the White Caps but for another church group called the Evangelical United Brethren. On Barnett's Creek, about nine miles from our ridge, they have established a church, a parish house, a clinic, and headquarters for their work in the hills. Perhaps some of you are members of that Church and have given clothing, money, books, or medicines to the Barnett's Creek Mission. If so, the next time you pack a missionary barrel remember that I wear a size 14 dress, a 6½ shoe, and I am badly in need of a lightweight, rainproof coat!

Seriously, I have great admiration for the people over at Barnett's Creek. The Evangelical United Brethren Church is old in this area, an organized church at Bear Wallow dating back to 1834. But the actual mission work was started around 1930 with something like one hundred twenty-five members left in the entire area. In the earlier days there had been as many as twenty or twenty-five groups worshiping either in union churches with other denominations, or in private homes.

But the work had run down for lack of money, equipment, and preachers, only a faithful few followers hanging together. In 1930 a great effort was begun to organize again, and now there are thirteen churches in the area comprising six counties; there is a total membership of around 750, and there are three pastors and three staff members.

But it is about our friends Ethel King and Mrs. Mary Bierly I want to tell you. Miss King is a registered nurse. She is a big woman — big, hearty, handsome, good, and kind. She radiates confidence, happiness, and skill. I know that she has only to walk into a sickroom for the ill to feel immediately better. I have heard our people say: "Miss King's better'n a doctor. I'd as lief have Miss King as ary doctor in the world!"

And, to tell you the truth, I'd as lief have her myself. I would put my life in Ethel King's hands without a moment's hesitation, for she is a skilled nurse and I would trust her skill, but, more than that, I would know she would lift me up in the arms of her own faith and never, never let me down. Our people feel the same way about her.

She was reared in New York State and took her nurse's training in Buffalo. She wanted to be a missionary, and she was ready to go to Africa when the war broke out and all new missionary placements were stopped. So she came to the Kentucky hills instead. And here she has stayed. She is now an ordained minister of her Church and, in addition to running the clinic and doing her full share of parish work, she is acting pastor of a new church just being started in Columbia. When she talks of her work, her enthusiasm sparks every word and her eyes light up with a fine glow. You can tell she loves every minute of it. You can tell she is dedicated to it, and that it absorbs every thought and action.

I had heard of Miss King. Had heard of her constantly, for that matter. Everyone in the hills knows her and how she never turns down a call, no matter how far away it is or how hard the place is to get to. But we had not visited the mission at Barnett's Creek yet. I wrote her a note expressing interest in her work and she promptly asked us to come have lunch with her. We set a time and went.

It was our good fortune to meet Mrs. Bierly that same day. For the two women, Miss King and Mrs. Bierly, are largely responsible for the mission as it is today. Together they directed its work for seven years and inaugurated the wide, full program that the mission has undertaken. It was their thought, and that of the Mission Board, that the church should undertake a program that was all-enveloping. They thought of its areas as being economic, physical, spiritual, and educational. They realized very early that merely to minister to the spiritual needs of a people ground down by poverty and illiteracy was not enough. They felt they must offer a larger ministry than that.

So, groping for a way to help the people to help themselves, they began with the making of corn shuck dolls, such as the mountain mothers had once made for their children. We looked at them that day and were amazed at the skill and artistry shown. They gave us a pair, made of corn shucks with buckeyes for heads. Each doll is about six inches tall and is complete in every detail. The man wears a pair of overalls and a straw hat, and the woman is amply folded into a gay apron with a headkerchief tied around the kinky wool glued to her buckeye scalp.

Still trying to find creative things for the people to do, Mrs. Bierly went to Berea College, at Berea, Kentucky, in the summer of 1943 to learn hand weaving, another old handicraft of the pioneer mothers and housewives. Miss Harriet Howard, weaving instructor at the college, became very much interested in the project and came twice to Barnett's Creek to help in getting it started. Looms were secured from the old N. Y. A. agency, and when the women had become sufficiently interested, several of them went to the college to the opportunity school held each winter.

The result has been far-reaching. There is now a program of economic importance to the people of Barnett's Creek. The women weave beautiful rugs, handbags, towels, napkins, scarves, and such things, which have an outlet through the church. When Miss King goes to one of the general conferences, she takes along a good display of these hand-woven articles and they are sold far and wide over the country. I thought they could enlarge the program by magazine advertising and probably triple their output, but when I suggested it to Miss King, she told me that it would require full-time work of the people, which they are not yet prepared to give. Most of them are farmer's wives, and the weaving and handcraft program is still a spare-time project. The church furnishes an adequate outlet for what they produce. I was especially taken with the rugs. I am hoping to have in the living room someday a full-sized handwoven rug made at Barnett's Creek.

Mrs. Bierly is the one who has been greatly responsible for this handcraft program. She is from Ohio, near Dayton, and she is a teacher. She is no longer at the mission, having now retired, but she was visiting Miss King the day we were there. She is a gracious, charming, intelligent woman, with a generous heart and mind. In addition to starting the handcraft program she was instrumental in starting the small library which the church supports and she also gave much time to the vacation Bible schools which are conducted every summer.

Thus two women with imagination and big hearts have established a fourfold program 'way back in these hills. Their first cornerstone was spiritual, so for seven years, without a man to act as pastor, they kept the church open and preached and conducted services; their second cornerstone was physical, so they maintained a clinic, and those who were able to come came and brought their sick and ailing. Those who could not come sent, and the two women went to them, riding horseback many times over rough ridges and hollows. Their third cornerstone was educational, so they started a library, and they held vacation schools in different parts of the hills all summer each year. Their fourth cornerstone was economic, so they began a handcraft program and opened a market for the finished products.

I do not like to see any agency throw wide its arms and say: "We have come to help you. Here we are. It is all free and open to you." For I feel that in the long run it will probably contribute, as too often the well-meaning welfare boards do, to the further delinquency of the people. It is very difficult to help people without making them more dependent. And our people need to recover a lost pride and independence. Their forefathers would not have accepted relief. Their forefathers would have gone hungry before going on the county welfare roll. Their forefathers would have died before taking castoff clothing from the missionary barrel.

So I am doubly grateful for Miss King's and Mrs. Bierly's past work. For they have showed the people how to make use of their own resources, while encouraging them to develop new ones. They have said: "Here are some things which your grandparents used to do and which still have value on today's market. Learn them and profit by them."

And, knowing full well that free things are held in contempt, they have required the payment of a small fee for clinical services. If the fee cannot be paid, the patient is not turned away, but the people know they are expected to pay if they can.

The people are also expected to help maintain the mission program. It is not entirely financed by the denomination. The program belongs to the people and they must support it. If they get the use of it, they must pay for it, and keep on paying for it so that it may build and grow.

In the long run that is the only kind of help you can ever give people that is worth a dime, either to them or to you as the giver.

Chapter

17 ↙ ↙

In October the moon is a hunter's moon, full, fat, and yellow. In October the night wind rattles through the drying leaves and the foxes bark hoarsely down in the hollow. In October the horns blow, mellow and deep, over the hills. In October the dogs thump restlessly under the floors, sleepy blood stirred by some ancestral haunt. In October, Honey stands before the door with amber eyes shuttered against our love. Gone is the comfort of the sofa. Gone is the luxury of her feeding plate. Gone is her devotion. We are forsaken for the primeval urge of the chase.

Henry takes down his gun and slips into his hunting coat. Honey capers wildly. She comes over to me and jumps high to lick at my chin. She dashes to Henry and paws madly at his coat. She runs in circles around the gun, sniffing and smelling. "See!" she says, "See! We're going hunting!" And she flies to the door, scratching in her hurry, tail fanning up a storm. Henry opens the door and a jet-propelled bundle of honeyed fur streaks off to the woods. October! And Honey has gone hunting.

We call her Honey because that is the color of her coat. Soft, satiny, marcel-waved honey. She has a white collar and vest, white feet and face. But the rest of her is the color of new honey, fresh from the comb. She was given to us when she was about a year old by some people who were moving to the city. Until then we did not know how much it is possible to love a dog. She is our child, our sweet-tempered, devoted, intelligent child. We have spoiled her, as much as she will spoil, because we cannot bear for her to be unhappy or uncomfortable. She is the only dog on the ridge who stays in the house. She is the only dog who is counted so much a part of the family that all food is divided three ways. When we have steak, Honey has steak.

As a matter of fact, she has a very finicky appetite. She likes bacon and eggs for breakfast. But she prefers them fed to her piecemeal while we ourselves are eating. We have often suspected that if we placed a chair for her and tied a napkin around her neck she would eat at the table with us. But though folks on the ridge laugh at the way we have spoiled her, they all love her. And, being a well-mannered little lady dog, she is nice to everyone. She suffers the affection of all. Patiently she stands and lets strange hands pet her silky fur. Then gently she moves away to stand near Henry. For Henry is her real love. Next to Henry she loves me best. She even prefers to have me scratch her, but she does so apologetically.

188

She says to Henry, with a cornerwise look out of her eyes: "You understand. She has her uses. Even *you* know that!" Then, the scratching over, she moves back to drop at Henry's feet and to lay an adoring nose on the toe of his boot. She says very plainly to me: "You're nice. You've been very kind to me. I like you. But here, here, is my beloved."

Honey is restless when Henry is out of the house, going again and again to jump up on the sofa and peer out the window. He takes her with him nearly everywhere. But occasionally, when he is going to town and will be busy for a long time, too long a time for her to stay peacefully in the car, he has to leave her at home. She doesn't sulk then. Never that. But she is sad. She crawls into a corner and watches me with great, mournful eyes. We never command her. We try to explain. We say: "We're sorry. But you'll have to stay here this time."

She knows what "stay here" means, and when she hears those fateful words, she accepts them. She knows the tone of regret in our voices. She never begs or tries to disobey. But she is not to be denied her restlessness or her unhappiness. And she hears the car long before I do. When I see her prick up her ears, turn her head to the side, listening, when her tail begins to thump joyfully against the floor, I know Henry is coming. I have not yet heard the car, but Honey has, and long before he turns into the driveway, she is waiting impatiently at the door.

She rides on the bucket seat in the back of the car. Our car is a 1939 Oldsmobile. It was built as a business coupé, and the rear seat was never installed. For convenience we put in the folding seat that came from an old Chevrolet. That seat is Honey's. She rides in state, breathing down our necks, head stretched to the breeze and paws resting on the door. She has clawed great rips in the upholstery of the door where a sudden turn or bump in the road made her slip. I don't know what we shall do if we ever get a new car. It would be too bad to let her tear the upholstery like that. But Honey would never learn new riding habits at this late date.

She likes to nip at bushes along the side of the road. The

ridge road is very narrow, and there are places where the vines and bushes overhang and make a tunnel. Honey knows every place like that on the road and she gets ready for them before we reach them. As we pass she nips, gets a mouthful of leaves, drops them in a hurry to nip again before her chance is gone. We don't understand why she likes to do this. We don't know why nipping the bushes is such fun and so important to her, and we went through a time of trying to break her of the habit. We were afraid that thorns would tear her mouth. She obeyed us, but she missed so much fun and was so grieved that we finally gave it up. "Go ahead and nip," we told her, "just be careful of thorns." And gleefully she picked up right where she'd left off.

She likes to go squirrel-hunting, but she isn't much of a rabbit dog. She is infallible at treeing squirrels. When she trees, you've got a squirrel for sure. Of course he may be in a hole you can't get to, but Honey isn't responsible for that. She's treed. The rest is up to you. She even knows how to be very quiet when the leaves have fallen and are dry. When Henry sits by a hickory to wait for a squirrel, she will lie patiently beside him for an hour or more. Once it was almost too much for her, though. An impudent little field mouse came out to play right under her nose. She switched her tail and the leaves rattled. "Quiet," Henry warned. Obediently she held her place, but her breath quickened, her nose twitched, and her feet jerked impulsively. It was a terrible ordeal for her, but discipline won over instinct.

She goes rabbit-hunting too, of course. But rabbits have such a tiresome habit of running into brier patches. And Honey is too much of a lady to enjoy getting her beautiful self all stuck up with cockleburs, sticktights, and thorns. When the rabbit runs into a brier patch she hesitates, comes to a full stop, looks around in anguish, then she points her nose toward the meadow. "He went that-a-way!" she says, and she runs wildly *around* the brier patch.

There are some things we do that bore her very much. Fishing, for instance. Oh, she wants to go, terribly. She always wants to go. She prances around in great glee while we are getting the tackle ready. She's so afraid she might be left behind. But when we get to the river, she can't see a bit of fun in it. She clumps along behind us, sighing gustily, and she flops to the ground at the first opportunity and eyes us with disgust. "Now, I ask you," she says, "what fun is there in this?"

Each time one of us comes to the tackle box or minnow bucket she jumps up eagerly. "Now?" she says, "now, are we going?" And she runs excitedly up the bank. When we shake our heads, she comes back and flops to the ground again and puts her head between her paws sadly. "Weary woe," she says, heaving a big sigh, "more of the same."

And she does not like to go visiting. The going, yes. The car wheels never turn but she wants to go. But when we drive up in front of a house, she peers out, then settles back in her seat. "I'll just stay here," she says. When we insist that she get out, she rises, taking plenty of time to do it. "I'd just as soon not," she implies. When we are still insistent, she crawls deliberately over the seat and out, and stands there hopefully. When we go through the gate, she follows at her leisure. When we get into the house, she stands at the door, her nose poked hard against the screen. Knowing that most people don't like dogs in their houses, we can't allow her to come in. She does not understand this. She frets, fusses, begs. When we are firm, she finally turns away and lies down on the porch. But every five minutes or so she is back at the door. "Let's go," she pleads. "Please, let's go. There isn't a thing to do out here. I'm bored to tears. Let's go home." And we have cut more than one visit short in answer to her pleas.

She doesn't enjoy going to the garden in the summer. She sees me come out of the house with a basket over my arm. She knows full well I am going to the garden. I always go to the garden when I have the basket on my arm. But she pretends she doesn't see the basket. She scampers ahead. She runs hopefully up the road a piece, stops, and looks back. "This way?" she asks.

When I don't turn *up* the road, she does a fast rightabout-face and flies *down* the road. "Oh, *this* way!"

When I keep firmly on my way, she tears past me and runs down the garden fence on the outside. "To the blackberry patch? To the woods? To the persimmon thicket?"

When I go through the garden gate, she comes sadly and forlornly back to my side, her tail drooping, her eyes reproachful. "Saints preserve us! This dull spot again. With the whole world to choose from — the open road, the woods, the thickets — you choose this place!" And there are times when I agree with her entirely. I'd like the woods, the road, the thickets, myself. But, I remind her, we've got a man to feed. You know, the one you love so much. He eats. Three times a day. We can't always be chasing off to the woods.

Dogs so often have almost human reactions to situations. Honey can be just as embarrassed as any human being you ever saw. Once she was chasing a ground squirrel in the back yard. It had been raining and the ground was very slippery. She was flying along when suddenly all four feet flew out from under her and she nose-dived into a soft place, scooping the mud up with her nose. We whooped with laughter. And an amazing thing happened. She picked herself up with all the dignity in the world, stood very still, looking off in another direction, deaf ears turned to our laughter. Muddy nose, muddy feet, muddy coat, she ignored. She pointed her ears, lifted her tail stiffly, and gazed intently across the field. "Not a thing has happened," she insisted. "Not a thing. Just pay no attention, please." And there was reproof too. "How unkind of you to laugh! How ignoble of you to notice a lady's shame!"

Very chastened, we called her, and the pose broke. She scampered happily toward us and, with all the good will and forgiveness in the world, allowed us to clean the mud off her face and feet and coat. We have seen that happen several times since. But we never laugh now. Always when she falls, slips, skids, comes to grief somehow, she picks herself up quickly, looks hastily around to see if we have noticed. If we are looking at her, she pretends. "Oh, I meant to slip then! I thought it would be clever." And we have learned. "Sure," we say, "that was a cute backslide you did. Not many dogs can do that." And she grins and wags her tail a mile a minute.

Besides going places in the car, and hunting, Honey likes next best to go sang-digging with us. "Now, that's fun," she says, frisking out through the woods ahead of us. "Up and down hill, through the woods, and away." And, with her tail flying an excited banner, she leads the way.

Ginseng grows thinly on our hills now, having been carelessly dug and gouged out over the years. The root, dried, is sold for its medicinal value and it brings fifty or sixty cents an ounce. Ridge folks have never been able to resist that excellent price, so it has been dug much too small, much too often, so that the seedlings are dying out and it has become scarce. But sang, as it is called locally, is still to be found occasionally on a north or east hillside. It does not like a southern slope. It wants shade and coolness to do well. And yet it likes a rich soil. It stems up proudly from dank leaf mold or the rotted dust of long-dead trees.

The root is unusually large, being tough, fibrous, gnarled, and wrinkled, and looks very much like a parsnip. From this root one slender stalk stems upward, fragile, delicate, thin. It stands alone for six, eight, or ten inches, and then, beautifully and proudly, it forks into two, three, or four prongs. The age of a bunch of sang can be determined from the number of prongs. A seedling has one. A plant two or three years old has two. It branches into three prongs when it is around five years old, and then it is grown. A four-prong plant is a hoary old man. There are not many four-prong plants any more.

The prongs bear the leaves, which lie flatly and thinly veined, like the palms of your hands lifted in supplication. They are a dark, dark green, smooth and satiny. During the spring and summer I can never find it. There are so many other plants that grow from one slender stalk with leaves lying flat on three or four prongs. A small hickory seedling greatly resembles sang to the beginner. Young May apple plants bear a resemblance to it. And I am not yet an expert at identifying sang anyhow. I usually tag along at Henry's heels with the top of a bunch clutched tightly in my hand to help me, peering at every bunch of weeds or every seedling sprouted through the undergrowth. I rarely yell "Sang!" triumphantly in the spring or summer.

But, ah, in the fall, in October, I am infallible. For then, in the center of the several prongs, the seeds have clustered into a bloom of berries, and the berries have turned scarlet. Like holly berries they are. Bright, glossy, brilliant. In the fall I have been known to find more sang than Henry. Led by the bright red berries, it's as easy as following a flag.

We do not dig sang for its commercial value. We are trying to cultivate a bed of our own in the yard, and we have managed to transplant enough of it so that we now have a small bed about the size of a blanket. It repays us for all the walking, all the peering, all the climbing of hills and hollows. For no bed of flowers is more lovely than our bed of sang, dark and green and proud, with its scarlet patch of berries bosomed closely in the center. It is so lovely that I have transferred two three-prong bunches to pots and brought them into the house. No house plant could be more beautiful — not even poinsettia with its brilliant red leaves.

But the aesthetic side of sang-digging is lost on Honey. She is no good at finding it. She does not stand, as we do when we have found a bed, with indrawn breath at its fragile beauty. She sniffs, and lifts her head to tell us: "Not a sign of scent. Not a thing here. What's all the excitement?" And if we don't watch her, she will dash carelessly through it, breaking the stems and leaving a trail of wreckage behind her. "Come on!" she says. "Just over the top of the hill there may be a squirrel. Come on, let's find him!"

Honey gets into scrapes occasionally. We went gathering walnuts one October day. Honey disappeared while we were picking up the nuts. She likes to go off exploring on her own when we are in the woods. After a time we heard her scratching around in some bushes nearby. About the same time I got a whiff of something *very* ripe. "Phew!" I said to Henry, "there's something dead near."

He sniffed too. "Yeah. Probably a coon or possum."

We went on picking up the nuts. Honey scampered into the

cleared space under the tree then, and the smell was almost overpowering. "It's on *her!*" I cried, grabbing my nose.

"Damn!" Henry yelled. "She's rolled in it!"

I don't know why it is, but let dogs find a ripe carcass — coon, possum, hog, calf, anything that has died and rotted — and right in the middle of it they must get. The stench on Honey was so terrible that we could not stand her. And poor Honey, of course, could not understand why we would not allow her to come near us. She slunk off and grieved, following us through the woods. "Come on," Henry told her, "you've got to have a bath."

He took her down to the pond and heaved her in, then scrubbed her with laundry soap. She doesn't mind water when it's obviously a lark. But to be lathered and scrubbed was something different, and she didn't like it at all. She was constantly escaping him and before Henry finished with her he had got about as much soap on himself as on her. And he needed it. When he started to come into the house after the job was finished, most of the smell on Honey had been transferred to him. "Don't come into the house!" I yelled. "I'll hand you some clothes and hot water out there." He had to strip and bathe in the back yard, sneaking looks up and down the road to be certain no one was coming.

When we go to Santa Fe, we have to leave Honey with Henry's folks. It is always heartbreaking, for her and for us. We take her over the night before, and we do not try to fool her. We tell her we have to leave her. We say, "You'll have to stay here." She creeps dully under the porch floor and peeps out at us, head laid sadly on her forepaws. It is almost more than we can bear. But there is no place for her in Santa Fe, and she cannot go. Miss Bessie tells us that she never ceases to watch for us. Day after day she stands at the gate and looks up the road. They can never make her happy, although they are infinitely good to her.

Oddly enough, she has a different set of habits over there. As if she knew she must adjust herself to the difference in the two places. The folks' dogs are not house dogs. So Honey does not insist on coming into the house when we are gone. She stays with the other dogs. She is not finicky about her food. She eats what is put before her without question. She makes no trouble, accepts the entire situation quietly, and even tries to be helpful. Kenneth, Henry's young brother, taught her to help him bring the cows up at night. She never does it when we are there with her. It belongs to the time when she has been left behind. Each night, then, she goes out into the pasture with him and rounds up the cows, barking, snapping at their heels, corralling them vigorously and firmly. Unless they are too far off. In the edge of the woods, maybe. Then she pretends she doesn't see them. "What cows?" she says. "Where? I don't see any cows."

Then when we come home she has hysterics. She is all over both of us, whimpering, crying, licking at us, pawing us. "Oh, you're home again! Heaven be praised this exile has ended! You're back. Let me smell you! Let me taste you! Let me feel you!" It takes an hour or so for her to calm down. Then she runs to the car and jumps in. "Come on! Hurry! Let's go home!" And, swearing we'll never leave her again, we take her home, where promptly she must be in the house all the time, sleeping on the sofa, eating from our hands, finicky again about her food. She knows we are clay in her hands, and she takes every advantage of it.

Recently we have acquired another dog — just a plain, common, ordinary coon hound. Henry hopefully calls him Drum. He hopes he will have a deep voice when trailing.

Honey wasn't very much taken with Drum at first. The first day she ignored his awkward, puppy antics with something of disdain. "Who is this wiggly, embarrassing creature?" she asked. "Nothing good will ever come of him, I assure you. He's all over feet and head and tail. And besides, he looks pretty dumb to me."

Henry fixed Drum's bed in the doghouse which Honey could never abide and which she had never so much as once even sniffed at. He made him a nice, thick mattress of straw, covered it with canvas, piled some old coats on top of that, and for good measure threw in one of his shoes. We had heard that a pup will be comforted his first night in strange surroundings if he can snuggle up to an old shoe or hat or glove. We expected to have considerable trouble that night.

We did.

But not with the pup. He slept like a log all night long. It was Honey who gave us the bad time. We had no more than got to bed when she came whining to the foot of the stairs. "Let's go see about that animal you brought home," she said; "he's probably freezing out there."

Henry got up and went out with her. She ran to the doghouse, sniffed around it, stuck her nose inside the door, and was satisfied. If only she had stayed satisfied! All night long Henry was up and down with Honey's concern over the pup. Just as we'd drift off to sleep here she'd come. "Pop, I just know the pup's got his covers off."

The next morning we were both sad sacks, with drooping eyes and dark circles. "You," Henry told Honey at breakfast, "can move out in that doghouse with the pup if you're going to stay up nights with him."

And that's just what she did, believe it or not. She moved bodily into the doghouse with him. No more Honey under our feet all over the house. No more Honey on the sofa, or stretched out on the hearth. She never even asks to come inside any more. Of course there is a very good practical reason for that now too. We now have *five* dogs. Honey and Drum have provided us with an embarrassment of riches in the way of offspring. You know anybody who wants a pup, mixed shepherd and coon hound? We have three we can spare!

Chapter
18 ✒ ✒

Living as we do in the extreme north end of Adair County, we feel almost as much at home in Taylor County, and we take both county newspapers. The Campbellsville *News-Journal*, which is the Taylor County paper, is a very vigorous organ, modern, progressive, alert. It has repeatedly taken state awards on make-up, editorials, news reporting, and so forth, and it has even, once at least, won the coveted prize of being named the state's best rural newspaper. The editor is a twenty-three-year-old boy by the name of George Trotter, who is a graduate of the University of Kentucky's School of Journalism, and who is as smart a newspaperman as you'll find anywhere. The *News-Journal* is a rural newspaper. It has to be to appeal to Taylor County, which is a farming county. But it is definitely not a hillbilly setup. It has a fresh, young, modern approach, and its editorials are shrewd, timely, and steady.

The *Adair County News* is a smaller paper in both size and circulation, and it is more what you expect in a rural newspaper. It is a folksy, homey little paper, not trying to cover the whole world, since radios and city newspapers already do a very good job of that, but bringing to Adair County, instead, the news about its own folks. We notice that four of the Columbia teachers attended the meetings, in Louisville, of the Kentucky Education Association. Mrs. John Sparks fell last week and broke her hip. The Columbia Book Club met Saturday at the home of Mrs. Jane Smith and Ernest Hemingway's new book was reviewed. The high school band will give a concert Tuesday night, proceeds to go toward buying new uniforms. The Columbia Wildcats will play Turnersville Friday night in the college gym. Warm, friendly, folksy items.

The advertisements in both papers are always interesting. Here is one by a local firm, reminding us that they buy horses, dead or alive! A drugstore runs a quarter-page ad offering: Hadacol, Lydia E. Pinkham's, Wampole's Preparation, Cardui, New Peruna, Retonga, Pursin, Creomulsion, Musterole, Vick's Salve, Syrup Pepsin, Ex-Lax, and Feen-a-mint. Right in the middle of the list they offer new alarm clocks at $1.98, and summing up the ad is the warning against winter colds and an urgent suggestion that we buy our vitamins now.

There are six "At Auction" ads in the two papers this week. I have just counted them. I read every one of them, for I love to go to auctions, and there are always several in each issue of the papers. You run across some of the doggonedest things at auctions, and I am forever cluttering up the place with old washstands or china cupboards which turn out not to be cherry, as I so fondly hope, but the cheapest sort of gum. But I still love auctions. Here is one over on Casey Creek. " At auction. 140 acre farm. Located on Casey Creek near Knifley. 140 acres good strong land, lying well, level to rolling, under fair fence. 1 acre tobacco base. Good orchard. Improvements: 1 five-room dwelling with porches in good state of repair; water at house; feed and tobacco barns; smokehouse; chicken house; woodshed and other outbuildings."

But it is the *personal* property I am most interested in. It includes: " Some antiques, 1 six-year-old mare (Tenn. walker), saddle and bridle; few farming implements; some corn and hay; lawn mower, garden tools, 12 bushels of Irish potatoes; 1 buggy and harness; 1 Ford car, 1938 model; 1 kerosene refrigerator; 1 organ; 1 Victrola; 5 parlor chairs; 1 sewing machine; 1 hall mirror; 2 couches; 3 dressers; 2 washstands; 1 square top table; 4 beds, springs and mattresses; 1 radio; 1 rocking chair; 1 bureau; 1 flour and meal chest; 1 cook table; 1 dining table and 6 chairs; 1 gasoline iron; 1 pressure cooker; 1 sausage mill; 2 cookstoves; dishes, cooking utensils, canned fruit and preserves; many other articles from around a farm."

I shall certainly want to go to *that* auction. Imagine, 1 organ; 1 flour and meal chest; 2 couches! I have been looking for a flour and meal chest ever since I came to the ridge. I have also been looking for one of those old-fashioned leather couches with the raised headrest. Maybe I'll find both at this sale.

The ad ends with the usual statement: " Terms, cash. Reason for selling, Mrs. Doaks is removing to the city and has instructed us to sell this property at the High Dollar." And it informs us that the sale is in the hands of the Johnnie Ruble Auction Company, with Col. Jim Ruble as auctioneer. It also tells us that the sale will be held on the premises, rain or shine, beginning at 10 A.M. And that lunch will be served on the grounds.

If we have been reading the paper carefully for some time,

we will remember that several months ago it carried an obituary notice about a Mr. Doaks. This, then, must be his wife, left widowed, and going now to the city to live with one of the children, probably. Likely she has already gone and the sale is in charge of her son, or brother, or some other male relative, who will spare her the heartbreak of watching her life's possessions go under the hammer. She is doing what's best, no doubt — doing all that's left her to do. But those stoves have cooked many a meal for that man now laid away, and doubtless the couches still bear the imprint of his head. That old flour and meal chest — how many batches of biscuits have been mixed up at it? If I am fortunate enough to buy some of your things, Mrs. Doaks, I shall remember those things. And I shall take good care of your belongings.

In the "Personal" column there is a small notice: "Lost: 1 change purse wrapped in a chamois skin. Contains $2.00. Please return to Mrs. Starlight Harper." I don't know Mrs. Starlight Harper, but I can tell you what she looks like. She is a small, weathered old woman, who rarely comes to town. She had probably sold her eggs that day to have two dollars in her tiny change purse. It was very important to her, so she wrapped it tightly in an old chamois skin. Probably the change purse was badly worn. A nickel or a dime might have slipped out otherwise. She was going to buy, with her two dollars, a little coffee, maybe — the cheapest kind; a box of soda, a package of needles, and, if there was enough left, she might get a bottle of Retonga. She'd heard it was good for the "stummick trouble," and her "stummick" had been bothering her a heap of late. And then, somehow, she'd lost the purse. Laid it down, perhaps, while she looked at a piece of goods she'd like to have a dress off of. Sighed, maybe, because she couldn't get it, but, reconciled to the more pressing needs, she'd turned and walked away. And not until she'd gone to pay for the coffee had she missed it. Trembly and anxious, then, she had gone to the newspaper office and worded her ad. I hope her purse was found and returned to her.

And then, in both papers, there are the reports from the outlying districts. From White Rose, Cane Valley, Basil, Bear

Wallow, Oak Hill, Pellyton, Gradyville, Ella, Eunice, and Christine. I have always wondered about the names of those last three settlements. Did one of the early settlers name each of them after a daughter, perhaps? A beloved Ella, Eunice, and Christine? The columns are short and full of homey doings. The scribe from Pellyton, for instance, warns all who visit there to do so cold sober. Pellyton folks don't want any drunks disturbing their peace. Over at White Rose the Abner Barneses have celebrated their fiftieth wedding anniversary. All their children and grandchildren, to the number of thirty-five, were present. Dinner was served on the grounds. All wish Mr. and Mrs. Barnes continued good health and happiness.

At Bear Wallow, Mr. Lucius Swink died last week. He was ninety years old, the founder of a family of more than fifty members, a respected and honorable member of the settlement for more than seventy-five years. He was a good man and all will mourn his passing.

At Basil the Homemakers' Club met at the home of Mrs. Carrie Stephens. Members were instructed in making aluminum trays by the home demonstration agent, and a talk on landscaping was given by Mrs. Jasper Dugan. Tasty refreshments were served at four o'clock. Also at Basil a mad fox ran amuck and bit five people, several dogs, and an unknown number of hens! The folks were taking the rabies shots.

I love these local columns. They are so everlastingly human. And they are so nearby. We take the city paper also, the Louisville *Courier-Journal*. I would not dream of trying to get along without it, for it stands very high among the list of influential papers in the nation, and I depend upon it a great deal to help me interpret the national and world news. But when I have read the *Courier*, which comes every day, and have been saddened by the state of things, saddened and depressed and cast down, it is a relief to turn to the weekly county papers and to read about folks who are close by, who are still growing things, making crops, raising stock, going to Homemakers' meetings, reading the new books, going to educators' conventions, giving birth to new babies, burying their ancient dead. It reminds me that life *does* go on, steady, sure, and even serenely, in spite of everything. That it remains important, and that each of us has a part to do. If my part seems feeble to me, I remember that the whole would not be complete without it, so long as I live and breathe and can do it. I take heart from the county newspapers.

But even here they have their arrow of hurt. Here is an item I found the other day tucked down at the bottom of an inside page of the *Adair County News:* "The commissioners voted the usual allotment of $70 per month for the eight pauper idiots in the county." Seventy dollars per month to be divided eight ways.

Pauper idiots! Barney is a pauper idiot, although we do not call him that on the ridge. We say Barney is just natural. Squinting at you, drooling his snuff, he will tell you his mind is kind of weak. He roams the ridge like a stray dog, dirty, ragged, and unkempt, teased and tormented by the boys, tolerated by the adults in a mixture of pity and shame, and carried as a heavy burden of responsibility by his family.

He walks all over himself. All his joints seem loose and they knock together when he goes down the road. His knees go one way, his feet another, and he stumbles over his big shoes which turn up at the toes. He swings his arms high and his head doddles on his neck. He is thin and scrawny and ageless, although Henry tells me he is somewhere in the middle thirties now. He is the filthiest person I have ever seen in my life. He wears the same clothes for months on end, never taking them off, even to sleep. The same overalls, the same shirt, the same denim jacket. They become slick with grease and dirt and the droolings of snuff and tobacco from his mouth. He rarely has his hair cut, and it hangs beneath his cap and over his ears in long, greasy strings. His eyes are vacant and weak. He cannot see very well. In fact, he is more than half blind. His mouth is loose and his lips hang stupidly. His face is smooth of beard.

He is not happy with any of his people. His parents, who pitied him so deeply that they spoiled him terribly, died some years ago. They had shielded and protected him all his life and had allowed him to grow up uncrossed in his tantrums and cruel rages. When his father died, thinking to continue his care for Barney, he willed his meager property to an older son, with the proviso that he should pay Barney six hundred dollars for it in time, and that until he had paid for it he should divide the income from it with him. He was also to provide a home for Barney, always. So Barney knows he is a man of property, and he holds this over the head of his poor, troubled elder brother. " Ifen you don't do right," he'll threaten, " I'll put you offen the place! "

Come to think of it, I don't know how Barney is entitled to draw even $8.75 per month as a pauper idiot. That he is an idiot no one can doubt. But is he a pauper?

He is never contented to stay very long with either of his brothers, or with his sister. His poor, frail mind is constantly troubled for fear they are trying to cheat him out of his draw, or some of his property. And since they are a bickering, quarreling family, one member plays on his easily aroused fear to set him against the other. They are all forever at war with each other, Barney in the middle.

So far as I know, his older brother has always played absolutely fair with him about his third of the crop money, for it goes without saying he has never been able to pay off the six hundred he owes Barney for the farm. When the tobacco is sold, one third goes into the bank for Barney's use, whether he is, for the time being, loose on the ridge or in the asylum at Danville. Every so often someone gets weary of having Barney sleeping in the hayloft and goes to the county seat and swears out a warrant for him, and he is taken away. But the family are not happy with him in Danville, so, inevitably, after a time they go get him out, one of them signing the paper that makes them responsible for him. Since he is not insane, just congenitally feeble-minded, the institution will release him. And he is always ready to promise that he will not wander off and be troublesome. He forgets that, of course, in less than a week.

The last time he came home from Danville there was a little accumulation of money for him. So he decided to buy a cow and some chickens. No one ever knows why Barney decides anything, but his brother humored him and helped him buy both. And for a time, a very brief time, Barney was happy. He felt big and important to own stock. Of course he had nothing to feed the cow or chickens, but his brother did, and it was all right. His brother had the use of the milk and the eggs, so it was probably a fair enough deal.

Then Barney got it into his head that they were trying to sell the cow and keep the money. Trying to sell the chickens and keep the money. Trying to cheat him and gyp him. Where he gets these ideas no one knows. They may simply rise like clouds on a summer day in his poor, unbalanced mind. They may be put into his head by other members of the family. It is not farfetched to imagine them, jealous of the older brother's right to live on Barney's property under the father's will, whispering to him: "He's atryin' to git ever'thing you got! He'll do you outen yer land, outen yer cow, outen yer chickens, ever'-thing. You better come stay with us an' let us look after you."

So Barney goes up and down the road asking: "You seen the deed on my place? Have they took my name off?"

We tell him: "No, Barney. No one can take your name off the deed."

But he wants to see for himself. "Take me to Columbia! Take me, Henry, so I kin see."

And Henry, or someone else, takes him.

He ponders the whispers and he watches his brother and the family. And inevitably he decides they *are* trying to cheat him, so he gathers his pitifully few possessions together, tormented, suspicious, frightened. He rolls up his extra shirt and overalls, takes his feather bed off the iron cot on which he has been sleeping, makes a bundle of his old, ragged quilts, goes and hauls down from the shelves some fifty or so empty fruit jars that belonged to his mother, heaves and tugs at an old cupboard that was also his mother's, sacks up a bushel of potatoes he dug for someone on the halves, even empties the coffee can because he bought the last coffee out of his draw, and he piles everything by the side of the road. Then he ropes up his cow. He is ready to go. But he must find someone to move him. He is so frightened by now that he will not leave the cow, the most prized, the most expensive possession of all, while he finds someone to move him. He pulls and hauls on the rope around her neck and trudges down the road, the cow reluctantly following after. He comes first to Henry. "I'm goin' to move," he says, "over to the other place. These is tryin' to cheat me. They want my stuff. They don't like me." The easy tears run down his cheeks.

Henry sits by the side of the road and listens. "Now, Barney. No one is trying to cheat you. No one is going to take your stuff. You oughtn't to move off like this. Go on back to the place and settle down there and help make the crop and be a good boy."

But Barney shakes his head and gives the cow's rope a tug. "They're tryin' to git my stuff. I got to move." And he wanders on down the road, pulling the cow along behind him.

He goes first to one man then the other, and each tells him just what Henry has told him. "No one's trying to cheat you. You oughtn't to drag that cow up and down the road like this, Barney. Take her home and stay there yourself."

But Barney will not. On down the road he goes. Feebly he understands that no one is going to move him and his cow and his other worldly goods. No one dares. Barney is committed to the care of his family, and we can't interfere. But he is a pitiful, pathetic sight trudging so wearily down the road, his poor old cow getting hotter and hotter, and tireder and tireder. No one will take him, of course.

The day reaches noon, and then three o'clock, and four o'clock and Barney has not yet come back. "Henry, maybe you'd better go see about him," I say.

"His folks have gone. Just saw them pass."

Long after dark they came back with Barney and the cow, the cow now lowing at every step, her tongue hanging out and her legs wobbly. They found him over on the pike headed toward Knifley. When Barney got to the pike, he didn't know which way to go. He's never been off the ridge anywhere, except as he's been taken. The road running two ways confused him. Instead of turning left, which would have taken him eventually where he wanted to go, he turned right and kept on trudging.

Well, his other brother comes after him, promises Elmer to look after him, and he leaves the ridge for a time. For a very short time, for no sooner has he got settled over at Juney's than he begins to suspect Juney is trying to cheat him. His torment is begun all over again. He comes back and pours out his troubles to Elmer. And Elmer patiently moves him back to the ridge again. We see this happen dozens of times. It goes on constantly. Barney will not stay anywhere.

When he is at Elmer's we are all uneasy, for he won't sleep in the house. They say he has sense enough to know it worries them for him to disappear and wander off. And they say he's mean enough to want to worry them. I don't doubt it. He has sense enough to know he owns a few things. He has sense enough to step out of the road when a car is coming. He has sense enough to chop wood, to work in the fields, to do manual labor under supervision. But he doesn't have sense enough to know a one dollar bill from a ten dollar bill. He can neither read nor write, and he does not know the value of anything except that which he clutches to himself. All he knows is that he is driven by some weird, haunting memory of peace to wander like a ghost from Juney's to Elmer's to Danville. And he is happy nowhere.

We are uneasy for fear he will either come to some harm on our property or do some harm to it. He sleeps in our woods, for instance, and, since he smokes almost constantly, we are deeply afraid that he will set the woods on fire during the dry season. Also the south slope of our ridge field is a copperhead area. What if he is bitten by a snake while ambling around over there?

He sleeps in Elby's corn shocks, and Elby is uneasy for the same reason. He cannot afford to lose his corn in the field. He sleeps in another person's barn, and he narrowly escaped being killed by so doing once. The man was forking down some hay, and only his quick action kept him from sending the pitchfork through Barney's body when he started to run it into a bundle of hay and it stirred and Barney emerged.

If you leave a wagon out in the yard, Barney is apt to make it his bed that night. If you leave your car out in the open,

Barney will pop up under the wheel the next morning. If you hear a peculiar noise under your house in the night and get up to investigate, flash a light under there and you may flash it right into Barney's startled eyes. You never know where he is going to sleep. Or what he is going to do.

He came to Henry one day. "Henry, you got any work I kin do? I'll work awful cheap. But I need me some money to buy some snuff."

"You can chop up that rick of wood," Henry told him. "Cut it in stovewood lengths."

Barney works with a will — you have to say that for him. With a sort of reckless will. I looked out later that morning and the stovewood was flying. Without looking to see where it was going, Barney was chopping and heaving. "Don't go out in the back yard," Henry warned when he came in to dinner. "You'll get hit in the head, sure."

Because he is so nearly blind he has to bend far over to see where his ax is going to hit, and he works all day crouched and bent like that until you think surely he will never be able to stand straight again. He puts all he has into his work. He works all over, just as he walks all over. Every muscle is in action and every joint is moving. He reminds me of a marionette whose strings are being pulled very jerkily.

It took him two days to chop the wood. "You got arything else I kin do?"

We were beginning to accumulate the rocks to build our fireplace. "I'm going after a load of rock," Henry told him. "You can go along and help load."

But that was a mistake. Two others went to help also. When Barney started letting fly with rocks, Henry had to intervene. Someone was likely to get knocked out with one of Barney's slugs. Henry set him to stacking rocks for the others to load. But he will work just as long as you'll let him. And he'll tackle any kind of job. Later that fall Henry let him help while he was building the fireplace. He told him not to lift the biggest rocks by himself. "I'll help you," Henry told him. But he had to watch him constantly.

He sifted the sand from the gravel. Henry had made a balanced, meshed-wire sifter, and it rocked from one side to the other. Barney shoveled in the gravel, grabbed hold of the handle, and rocked so vigorously that the gravel and sand both flew in every direction. The faster, the more furiously he can do a thing, the happier he is.

He decided then to sell his cow and chickens. The huckster bought his chickens, but he doesn't deal in cows. So Barney came to Henry. "Henry, buy my cow. I give a hundred forty for her, an' I'll let you have her fer a hundred. Buy my cow, Henry."

"What would I do with a cow, Barney? I haven't got any place to keep her. I don't need a cow."

But he doesn't understand. "Henry, buy my cow. I give a hundred forty fer her, an' I'll let you have her fer a hundred."

When finally he is made to understand that Henry is not going to buy his cow, he wanders off. He goes up and down the ridge. "Buy my cow!"

In the end someone bought her. And Barney gave money to all of his friends, bought moonshine and got drunk, scared everyone on the ridge half to death, and wound up sick and broke.

When he is feeling particularly tormented and desperate, he sings. He doesn't know the tune or words of a single song, but he is not discouraged. He shambles aimlessly down the road, his head thrown back, his voice lifted in a tuneless, shouted song. He waked us along about daybreak one Sunday morning, singing. We waited, thinking he was passing. But the song kept on and on, right in front of the house. "Is this a serenade?" I asked.

"I'll see what he wants," Henry sighed, and he got up and dressed and went outside. I peeked out the window. There they sat side by side on the road bank. And I could see that Barney was crying. Soon his voice was lifted until I could hear the words. "Henry," he said, "Henry, I want you to promise me that when I die I'll be buried alongside my mammy. My mammy said that's where I was to be buried. My mammy knowed I had the weakest mind of all of 'em, an' with her dyin' breath she said I should be buried alongside of her.

An' they'll not do it. Jist fer meanness they'll not. Henry, they don't like me. They don't like me. Don't nobody like me."

Don't nobody like him. And they don't. We are all afraid of him a little bit, bothered by him more than a little bit, provoked with him constantly, ashamed of him always. It would be nice if I could say here that Barney is a sweet, childlike person, a little simple, a little feeble-minded, but docile and harmless. I don't know that he is actually dangerous, but I do know that he is ugly-tempered, mean-natured, and cruel. When I feel so terribly sorry for him, am inclined to be mawkishly sentimental about him, I remember watching him one day catch a butterfly and deliberately pull its wings off, and then stand there laughing idiotically at its desperate, agonized struggles. I remember seeing him kick Honey once when he thought we were not looking. I remember seeing him impale a worm on a sharp stick and hold it, fascinated by its slow, wiggling, tortured death. And I shudder at those memories, for suppose he should decide he wanted to watch a child struggle in such agony? or one of our young ridge girls?

So I say, along with the rest: " Why don't they leave him at Danville where he belongs? Why do they ever bring him home? "

We know they bring him home because they are ashamed to have him in the asylum, and because they are always hopeful he will be better after a stay up there. To the family he is Barney, weak-minded, perhaps, but not harmful. He's just Barney whom they've always had to look after. The rest of us can only hope and pray that's all he'll ever be.

Chapter
19 ↙ ↙

My heart is sad, almost beyond being lifted up, and I think I cannot bear to look at life on this ridge another day. Let me, I cry while weeping, go back to the anonymity of the city, where I can hide myself among people and turn my eyes away from ugliness and bitterness and sadness! Let me turn my face away from them! Let me not see and hear and be aware of them! Let me go away from this place where things happen like what is happening to Calline today!

But even as I cry, I think as Rufe thought when he cried out against Miss Willie. It's there in the city too, but you didn't notice it. You didn't look for it. You didn't go out of your way. You could let it alone. You could pretend it wasn't there. You could surround yourself with softness and beauty and ignore the ugliness. But it was there all the time. Here on the ridge you've *got* to notice it. You can't ignore it. You can't look the other way. It's right under your nose. It's, maybe, your own kinfolks. It's, maybe, something you helped cause. And of course that is why I weep.

Calline is not kinfolks, except as all of us who live here on the ridge are kinfolks. We are bound together, we cannot get away from the closeness of our lives, knit as we are on one long strand of yarn. We *have* to share each other's lives. There is no escaping it. We *have* to weep and grieve, laugh and rejoice, hate and love, together.

She was shy and quiet that day we moved to the ridge. She came as the movers unloaded the furniture, as so many others did. But Calline slipped through the door with no noise, her mother's newest baby astraddle of her hip. She was little and thin, her hip sagging under the fat load of the baby. She had soft, pale hair which drooped about her face; blue, blue eyes; and a timid, afraid little smile. I don't recall that she spoke a word of greeting. She just smiled and shifted the baby. "Won't you sit down?" I asked.

She shook her head and continued to stand, the baby restless on her thin, young girl's hip. She looked around the room at the furniture banked against the walls. Her eyes took in the piano, the desk, the beds and dressers, the long sofa, the big lounge chair. "Hit's purty," she said finally, and then she slipped away.

In time I learned who she was. She was the oldest of a horde of children that swarmed in and out the doors of the shack they called home. It sat sprawled near the road, leaning crazily into the wind, its sides boxed with battened boards and rolled siding. The doors sagged, half the windows were broken out, the steps to the porch were missing, and the porch floor itself gaped where boards had been pried loose for firewood. In the yard dogs, junk, weeds, children sprouted indiscriminately. Flies swarmed over all in a solid mass. Hogs rooted under the floor and the hounds fought with them. The vacant-eyed children fought with the hounds, and the vacant-eyed mother fought with the children.

The nurse told me once that she had seen many awful things since she came to these hills, but that nothing, absolutely nothing, could compare with what she saw the night she was called for the birthing of one of those children! The woman was sitting up in bed, on a mattress spread with newspapers. The house was deep in filth and clutter and children, and only a smoking lamp without a chimney lighted it. There was not a sheet in the house, and not a single garment for the new baby when it arrived. The nurse went home and brought back bedclothes and clothing for the baby, out of her own store. Shortly after she returned, and before she could make up the woman's bed, the woman squirmed on the newspapers, like an old hen making herself a nest in which to lay an egg, grunted a couple of times, and the baby was born. She did not even lie down.

That was Calline's mother, and that scene was one Calline watched every other year, and at which she officiated. Except for its nursing, the new baby became immediately Calline's charge. One after another she took over the new babies and washed them, changed their diapers, and tended them. She swung them easily onto her hip when they were old enough to carry with her, and took them wherever she went. I never saw her without a baby on her hip.

One bitter cold day she came, shyly as usual, and sat by the fire. She made the baby comfortable and then she warmed her hands, which had never known the touch of a glove. They were blue with cold and raw and chapped. She sat for ten or fifteen minutes without speaking. "I brung the baby," she said then, "to git warm. I knowed yore house is allus warm."

Oh, I built up a tremendous fire! My heart melted and I

wanted to warm them enough to last out the winter.

"Don't they have any wood?" I asked Henry when she had gone.

"They have timber like all the rest of us," he said. "If they don't have wood it's because they're too shiftless to go out and cut it."

I had seen the man dragging up one log at a time. Never more than that. And not until that was burned down to the last scrap of bark did he drag up another. "Maybe if someone helped —" I began feebly.

"You can't begin that, Jan. They would take all you gave, and keep on reaching for more."

But I couldn't help thinking of Calline's hands, and the baby.

Where did Calline get that soft, pale hair that was so silky to touch? Another day she came and sat quietly by the fire. I had made a big pan of candy . . . chocolate fudge, rich with butter and cream and thick with black walnuts. Shyly she took a piece — one piece — when I offered it to her. She would not have another. It took thirty minutes for her to find the courage to tell me why she had come that day. Finally, in a breathless rush, as if she must get it out quickly, she said: "I've come to git you to cut my hair. Jist like yore'n!"

I wear my hair cut very short in a careless, wind-blown sort of way. I learned to cut it myself soon after we moved to the ridge. You can't be running to the beauty shop every week when you live 'way back in the hills. I have learned to snip here, there, everywhere, rather recklessly, and the result is comfort and, oddly enough, the prettiest hairdo I have ever worn. Now, Calline wanted her hair cut just like mine.

We propped the baby in a corner of the sofa and I draped a towel around Calline's shoulders. I ran the comb through her hair and touched it tentatively to get the feel of it, its texture and body. It was so clean that it shone, and so soft that it clung to my hand. Soft, soft as baby's hair, clean, shining, pale as honey. It curled around a finger, and I knew when it was cut it would turn easily and sweetly up and out into little duck tails around her neck and ears, and frame her oval face enchant-

212

ingly. It was a joy to cut her hair, and it was a joy to see the clean, round shape of her head emerge as the too-long, tangled locks fell to the floor. Her ears, when revealed, were small and pink, and the line of her hair on the back of her neck was sweet and childlike. She looked like a little blond elf when I had finished. I handed her the mirror. "Calline, you're so pretty!"

She looked at herself in the mirror unbelievingly. Then she laid the mirror down hastily, grabbed up the baby, and fled. Herself, revealed so beautifully, was too much for her.

Where did Calline get those beautiful, deep-blue eyes, and that smooth, white skin? Where did she get the small, fine bones of her wrists and ankles? Where did she get the quick mind that learned so rapidly? Where did she get her knowledge and wish for cleanliness? For Calline was always clean herself. In the midst of filth, she kept herself as clean as she could. I have seen her in the summer out in the yard, washing her hair. I have seen her scrubbing out the clothes, and hanging them, clean, on the line. Like a lily rooted in mire, Calline bloomed in the midst of her environment.

Her visits to me were rare. Once she brought me a paper rose she had made. Something of beauty she wanted me to share. Once she asked me to play the piano. When I had finished, she touched the keys timidly. She didn't say anything, just touched the keys, and then she smiled her quick, shy smile and slipped out the door. Something of beauty I had shared with her.

I was always going to do something for Calline. I thought about her much and talked to Henry about her. "When we have more room," I told him, "I'd like to have Calline come stay with us. Do you think her folks would let her?"

"If you pay her enough."

"Oh, I'd pay her!"

"Just so they could make something off her, they wouldn't care."

"She's different, Henry," I would say. "She's so lovely herself, and there's something inside that needs helping. If she could live where there was more beauty and — well, niceness — maybe . . ."

I don't know what I meant. Only that Calline pulled at something inside me and I wanted to help her. I thought if she could be got away from her home and given a chance, if she could bring her own loveliness to something equally lovely, if she could touch beauty more often . . . I thought about it, and talked about it. "When we have more money," I said. "When we have more room."

We would drive past Calline's house and she would wave and smile. Always she smiled and ducked her head. And her thin little hip rode the baby heavily. And I never saw her that my heart didn't ache for her and that I didn't promise her silently . . . someday, Calline! It's not practicable yet, but someday.

But Henry has just come home and told me Calline was married yesterday. I didn't believe it. "Who?" I cried. "Calline doesn't know any boys!"

"Lacey's oldest."

Lacey's! The oldest! Quickly my mind sought him out. "Not the one . . ." Surely, surely not the mutilated one!

"Yes. Him. He works at a sawmill camp now, and he thinks he makes enough to get married."

"But when did he get to know her? How has he learned . . . ?"

Henry shrugged. "They moved onto that same spur of ridge, remember?"

And then I *do* remember that Lacey moved over on that piece of ridge where Calline's folks live.

Henry went on. "He's seen her pretty often I reckon. Took her to a show once. Now they're married."

So. He saw her around home pretty often. He took her to a show once. And then Calline married him and now she has gone to live with him at the sawmill camp. Calline, Calline, what beauty will you find now? "He's goin' to take me to Louisville with him, an' places," she told Miss Bessie. "I've not never been no place. Now I'll git to see ever'thing."

I started crying. Henry rumpled my hair. "Don't," he said. "Don't cry."

"But I was going to help her!"

Henry picked me up as if I had been about two years old and held me. "You couldn't have helped her, Jan. Don't you know that whatever you might have done would only have hurt her in the long run? You'd have made her discontented with life as she would have had to live it. You'd have taught her about things she couldn't have, and she'd have always been unhappy. It's best this way."

He meant to be comforting, I know.

But the thing that I cannot bear, that makes me turn my face to the wall and weep blindly, is this: Calline will not be fourteen until next May! And the first signs of her womanhood have not yet appeared.

Chapter

20 ✦ ✦

It was in October, during the breathing spell between cutting tobacco in September and stripping it in November, that we decided to build the fireplace. We knew just what kind we wanted. It must be rugged and big, built of field stone. You can, of course, go out in the fields and gradually accumulate a supply of stone with which to build a chimney, and that's the way the early settlers did it. But it is much simpler to scout around until you find a deserted one.

We started looking. We spent all our spare time wandering over the country looking at chimneys, and finally we found what we wanted. It was on a Sunday afternoon, and we had been walking through the woods back of Miss Bessie's. Down a steep hollow and up another ridge. When we topped the ridge, we came out in a clearing, and there stood an old abandoned house with two beautiful field-stone chimneys still standing. The owner was a third or fourth cousin of Henry's, naturally. We went to see him about buying them that very evening. He looked at us as if we had suddenly gone out of our minds. "What in tarnation you want with them two old chimneys?" he asked.

"Want to build a fireplace with 'em," Henry told him.

He laughed long and hearty. "You kin have 'em," he said, "but if it was me I'd ruther have a good heatin' stove. Ain't nothin' but a hole in the floor puts out less heat than a fireplace."

"Not the way I'm going to build it," Henry said stoutly.

We had a book on how to build chimneys. We knew exactly how to build one. We knew all about throats, smoke shelves, arches, and so forth. Our fireplace was going to be one fireplace that threw out some heat.

In spite of laughing at us (and I may as well confess that the whole settlement laughed at us for building a fireplace), he sold us the chimneys for a very moderate sum. Henry tore them down and moved them, and then he cut a great hole in the living room wall. I had a bad moment at that time, for the hole was so huge I didn't see how he could ever fill it up again, and I remembered that this was Henry's first fireplace, and, even with the book, I wondered if he knew just what he was doing. For a time I don't think *he* knew how he was going to fill the hole up, either.

The foundation was laid a full two feet below frost line, and he laid every stone from the base to the actual hearth level as carefully as if it were going to show. He had a lot of advice during that time. If you want a sidewalk audience in the country, just build a chimney. People flock from miles around, and each person will be very forthright with his counsel. "Ain't no use you layin' them rock so keerful, Henry," he was told several hundred times. "Not 'way down there noways. Jist throw 'em in an' pour yer concrete on top."

But Henry is a meticulous builder, and he went right on laying his rocks carefully. He knew, better than his counselors did, that the two-story height of that chimney was going to require a mighty good foundation. The hearth itself was laid with the hearthstones of the old chimneys, which Henry had handled as carefully as if they were eggs. They were worn slick and satiny smooth from use. I love to run my hands over them and feel their cool, polished surface. The day the hearth was laid, Mr. Frank, who was helping, said with a twinkle in his eye, "Bet Suse wore them rocks slick warmin' her backside."

I bet she did too, and I keep them pretty well shined up myself.

It took a mort of rocks to build that chimney. The old house had been only one story, and even with two chimneys Henry ran out of good, solid rocks about halfway up. Then we had to go hunting another chimney. We asked so many people, and looked at so many chimneys, that it got so everybody we knew joked about it. Long after we'd located the extra chimney, folks would say, "Henry, found you another chimney?" It was a sort of community joke how many rocks our fireplace was taking.

It was with a great deal of relief that I saw those layers and layers of rocks mount higher and higher until the hole in the wall was covered. It wasn't until then that I could quit being haunted by the vision of snow and sleet bedding down with us during the winter.

I can't take credit for anything but the idea of the fireplace. The rocks were much too big for me to handle. There was just one way in which I tried to be of any practical help. Instead of buying sand, we hauled loads of gravel from the river, and I was fairly good at operating the shaker Henry devised. I could throw a shovelful of gravel into the shaker, grab the handle, and agitate like mad until all the sand was free. Barney and I were of about the same degree of efficiency at the shaker. And I mixed a little of the concrete. Not much. Henry is such a doggoned perfectionist that I never could get it the right consistency to suit him. Finally I told him to mix his own mud pies and I went back to my knitting.

It was something, though, to watch him and his father meet every emergency with that ingenuity that is so native to some men, especially men around here who have been compelled to devise ways and means all their lives. Nothing stumped them. And somehow they always found the simplest, easiest way of doing things. They built a scaffold around the chimney when it reached shoulder height, and then instead of lifting the huge rocks themselves, they fixed a kind of pulley and hauled them into place. They selected the rocks for size, then chipped them into shape and laid them carefully in place. There were some scraped fingers, some mashed toes, a great flinging of mortar, and more than a little profanity, but slowly and steadily the chimney rose.

Until November. Blithely enough, Henry had said it would take about three weeks to build it. At the end of the month it was almost two thirds of the way up the house, and he was thoroughly sick of it. I think he was glad to spread the tarpaulin over its top and leave it to the weather while he turned once more to the tobacco. For now the rains had commenced, and tobacco was in case, and stripping must begin.

This is the way we strip tobacco. In the morning the mist hangs low in the hollow and the fogs come up from the river to drape whitely over the ridge. The fog and the mist drip from the trees, bead the bushes, whiten the deadening grass. The damp is chill. The skies are gray. The days are short. And Henry says one morning, "We'll start stripping tomorrow."

The tobacco has been hanging in the barn since early September, curing in the mild, dry days of Indian summer. Now it is dry, sere, crisp. It is ready. But you cannot handle tobacco when it is dry. It will break and crumble in your hands. So, now when the slow mists and fogs rise over us from the river, and the sky comes down to meet them, and the air is damp and chill, now, we can strip tobacco. It hangs limply in the barn, all its crispness fled. We can handle it without tearing or bruising. Now it is in case.

We get up early the next morning. Henry wakes first. He looks out the window. "Fog is holding," he reports. "It will be a good day."

We have breakfast and then Henry says: "Bundle up well. The barn will be cold."

So I put on a wool shirt, a heavy sweater, cap, and gloves. Henry laughs when he sees the gloves. "You'll not need those."

We start to the barn. Across the garden, across the stubble of the tobacco field, up the pasture path, around the edge of the woods. The widow Gibbs's barn is a good half mile from our house. Henry goes ahead and in the fog he is only a wraith before me, weaving through the bushes and the weeds marking the edge of the path, scattering drops of water behind him. There is an eerie feeling in being out so early in the morning in the fog. As if we were not real ourselves. As if we were two ghosts haunting a path. All is gray. All is weeping. I shiver.

We come to the barn. Henry was right. It is cold. The tobacco hangs like damp brown cloths from the tiers. Henry climbs up on the lowest tier. "I'll hand the sticks down to you and you stack them on the ground over there in the corner." One by one he hands me the sticks until we have a great stack in the corner, taller than our heads. "That will do," he says. "That's about all we can handle by noon. If the sun comes out it will be too dry to work later than that."

Now he shows me how to take a stick and slide the tobacco off. "Like this," he says, skillfully running five or six stalks of tobacco off the stick onto the ground. I try it. Mine hang on the splinters of the stick. After trying half a dozen I realize there is a deftness I don't possess. "I'll have to slide mine off one at a time," I say.

Henry nods. He doesn't care how I get them off. Just so the sticks are emptied. We throw the empty sticks in another corner of the barn and they pile up as we slide more and more tobacco off. The tobacco makes still a third pile in the center. When we have all the sticks emptied Henry begins to lay the tobacco on one end of a long table. He motions for me to pull up one of the tall stools and he takes the other one. Quickly he explains the stripping process to me. He holds up a stalk of tobacco. "The bottom leaves, these, are the trash, or flyings. I'll take them off. Then I hand you the stalk and you take off the long red leaves that come next. Here. See?" I nod. "Then put the stalk down between us. On the next go-round I'll take off the golden, and then you'll take it again and take the tips. You'll only be working with one grade at a time, so you can't possibly get confused. Pile your red 'hands' on the ground next to you. Then we'll move them and make room for the tips. Take your gloves off. You can't strip tobacco in gloves."

All right. I watched him strip the light, lacy lower leaves quickly and easily from the stalk, turning it, looking closely for spots and burns, casting everything out but the good leaves. Then I find the stalk in my hand. Suddenly I am afraid. "How do I know when to stop? What if I get some of the yellow mixed in with the red? "

"We'll just lose about thirty cents a pound."

" Why? "

" The red isn't prime tobacco."

" I can't do it! I can't tell the difference."

" Yes, you can. After a few hands you'll know."

But I don't know *how* I'll know! Timidly I begin. The tobacco is cold. Cold and wet. The chill from it strikes through to the bone. And the torn stalks drip gum which clings sticky and thick to my fingers. The cold, the dirt, the gum. My hands are like steel wedges in no time. I cannot keep up with Henry. The red leaves are bulky and heavy and my hand is full in a few seconds. I watch Henry bind a bunch with a discarded leaf. I grab one and bind mine. "Not like that," Henry says, taking it from me. "Neatly. Round two or three times, over and under. There." I see. Like tying a tie.

" And that's what you call a hand of tobacco," I say, proudly laying mine on the ground beside me.

" That's it."

We don't talk much, except my occasional question, " Is this too yellow? "

But soon I don't need to question. Henry was right. After a dozen or so stalks I *can* tell the difference. I can see just when the red begins to be tinged with yellow. One more leaf after that can go in the red. The next will be almost pure gold. Now I work faster, but my hands are numb. " Can't we have a fire? "

Henry shakes his head. " Dry out the tobacco."

So I keep on. The last hour is torture. But I am determined not to cry quits. It isn't pleasant for Henry either, and it's my tobacco as much as it's his. When he says the word, and not before, will I give up. But it's touch and go. I keep one eye on the steadily diminishing pile of tobacco, the other one on the mounting pile of finished hands. The one grows less, the other grows larger. Does he mean to do all we got down this morning? Can my frozen hands keep on reaching and stripping?

Like Henry, I reach down for a palmful of dust every so often to cut the gum. The dust is cold too. I can feel nothing with my hands now. But the pile is almost done. My shoulders ache with a steady sharp knife of pain between them. My nose drips. A ripple of cold shivers down my spine. I think I cannot stand another minute of this cold, this damp, this heavy brown weed we have struggled with for so long. Cigarettes, I think bitterly. Who wants cigarettes? Who wants pipe tobacco? Who wants to chew the vile stuff? "All this work," I say to Henry, "just so people can smoke and chew tobacco!"

"No," he says, "all this work so we can eat and keep a roof over our heads."

The pile of tobacco is finally finished. I wonder if I can ever straighten my back. I wonder if my hands will ever thaw out. I wonder if my nose will ever stop dripping. And I look at the endless tiers still hanging in the barn. I groan. "How long will it take us?"

Henry appraises the tobacco. "If we're lucky and get a run of damp weather, about three weeks. If it dries up and warms up," he shrugs, "no telling."

Three weeks. Three weeks of numb hands, of shivering spine, of knife blades in the shoulders. Three weeks. I can't take it. I want to sit right down and howl. Henry moves around the table. "Hand me your tips," he says.

"What are you going to do?"

"They have to be hung on the sticks again."

"Again!" I yelp. "We just took the dratted stuff off."

Henry straightens. He has the most incredible way of expecting me to measure up to what the situation demands. He is completely merciless. He won't allow me to be weak. "Jan," he says quietly, "I am not just thinking up work for us to do. Believe me. Hand me the tips."

Wearily I bend and hand. And Henry parts the hands carefully in the middle and drapes them over the stick. When he has a stick full he hangs it again on the lowest tier. But there is a difference now. This is stripped and graded. And when the last hand is hung, we are through for the day. The sun has chased the fog away and we could tell as we handled the last few stalks that it was drying fast. Just in time, we finished. Henry squints one last look at it. "Pretty good tobacco," he says expertly. "Pretty good."

Oh, that makes me feel better! Please let him be right. Please let it be good tobacco and bring a good price.

I follow him outside the barn. We look at the sky. It is clear and blue. "It looks like it's fairing up," I venture to guess.

Henry lights a cigarette and it smells foul to me. "Ugh! How can you stand it?"

"Nuts," Henry says. "How you feel?"

"I'll tell you if I live till morning."

"You'll live. You're tougher than you think."

He should tell *me* how tough I am! But I must be. For the fog rolled in the next morning and I rolled right out into it. Back to the barn again. Back to the tobacco. And it went better the second day. My hands got cold again. My nose still dripped. But I worked faster, more efficiently, with less wasted motion, and at noon my shoulders weren't so achy.

We were lucky. We had three solid weeks of heavy morning fogs and Henry hit it right on the nose. Three weeks to a day we stripped the last stalk. Glory hallelujah! Like a victor, I surveyed the ranks of hands hanging from the tiers. Well, drat you, I felt like shouting, we licked you! Now hang there and get as cold and as damp as you like. We don't have to handle you again until the market opens. We don't have to touch you until we load you onto the truck. And then we're rid of you, until we buy you back again in little white tubes.

"If people knew," I told Henry, "how much work goes into raising tobacco, they'd appreciate their cigarettes and pipes a lot more."

"Would they?"

"Well, wouldn't they?"

"I suppose, when you put your wool shirt on in the morning, you always stop and give thanks to the people who raised the sheep — out in all kinds of weather, up at night during lambing season, uneasy about foxes and wild dogs. And when you lay a cotton cloth on the dinner table, I suppose you remember how the seed was planted, how the long rows were hoed and plowed, how somebody picked it with an aching back. And when you roast a chunk of beef, I reckon you think how somebody rode herd on it, fed it, watered it, and raised it from a calf."

I was humbled. "I didn't say a word."

Henry grinned. "Well, don't take it so hard. Nothing is for free."

Nothing is for free! Wool, cotton, meat, vegetables, metals, lumber, cars, radios . . . The list is endless. Nothing is for free. Back of all of them is a great, toiling world. Toiling for necessities, for commodities, for luxuries. But toiling. I toiled in tobacco. Perhaps you toiled in cotton, or sheep, or cattle. But whatever comes to each of us in the way of material things has back of it the toil and the labor of hundreds of people. When you light a cigarette, think of me! And I'll try to think of you when I put on my wool shirt, or set my dinner table.

Chapter
21 ↙↙

Now once again we could forget the tobacco for a while. The ridge year is always geared to tobacco. From March, when the plant beds are cleared, burned, and seeded, to December or January, when the crop is sold, it occupies practically all the time, the energy, and the thought of ridge people. We watch the skies anxiously all spring for fear it will rain too much; during the heat of the summer we watch them just as anxiously for fear it won't rain enough. Then when the tobacco is cut and housed, we wait anxiously for the rains again so that we can strip and bulk it down. Not until then may we breathe a sigh of relief. Our part is done. But even yet there is some anxiety. Suppose the market is down. Suppose, after all that work, the price is lower than usual. All the cash for clothing, for new equipment, for doctor's bills, for the food necessities we can't grow, depends on the market price of the tobacco crop.

We were as anxious as everyone else, but we turned back to finishing the chimney while we waited for the market to open in December. I began to wonder about andirons and hearth implements. No brass or fancy ornamented things. To go with our rugged and wide-mouthed hearth we needed solid, heavy, down-to-earth iron. "I wish," I worried, "there was an old-fashioned blacksmith around here somewhere. He could make exactly the kind I want."

"There is," Henry told me. "Mr. Holcomb over at Knifley used to be a blacksmith, and he's still got his forge and anvils."

"What are we waiting for?" I said.

Knifley is our post-office address, and it lies only 4.5 miles from our house by the speedometer. But there are times when we might as well be a hundred miles away. Three miles of the distance is covered by the ridge road, and when it has rained for, say, a week, the road is so muddy that no car can travel over it. If, in December, when the weather is alternately freezing and rainy, you are lucky enough to get over that three miles to the top of Dunbar Hill, then the road from there is graveled. But we have one last barrier before we can reach the village. Chelf Branch is a small, winding creek, shallow and fast and clear, which twists itself, unbridged, across the road after you have gone down the hill. A few years ago you had to ford it three times within a distance of several hundred feet. But now the road veers to the left and it is necessary to ford it only once. Normally it offers no real problem to traffic. But come a freshet, or what we hereabouts call a tide, in the spring or summer, or after a long, dismal rain in the winter, or even after a freeze-up and thaw, Chelf Branch is not to be fooled with. It spreads angrily all over the lowlands, rushes deep and wide while it is up, and no one who knows the creek would dream of driving into it. Strangers occasionally do, and come to grief. Cars have stalled in it and been washed down thirty or forty feet. The current is swift and deadly when the tide is up.

We struggled down the road, Knifley bound, on one of Whittier's "brief December days" and got as far as Chelf Branch. The tide was up, so we struggled back again and I chafed at the delay in seeing Mr. Holcomb. When the mail came through again, we knew the creek had gone down, and we started out once more down the muddy road. This time we made it.

Knifley lies snugly on the bank of this same stream, cold and damp in the winter, muggy and steamy in the summer. The first time I saw the village I thought it was very ugly. It has none of the quaintness or charm so many old Kentucky villages have. It straggles out a long mile or so, houses built near the highway and just off of it, the few stores and business buildings clustered in a knot in the center. Once Knifley was a rather thriving little place. Henry remembers when there was a bank there, several restaurants, a poultry and cream market, half a dozen stores, a skating rink, a theater, and so forth. But Campbellsville is too near, and with the graveling of the pike and the prosperity of the valley farmers so that they all have cars, Knifley has been almost abandoned. There are now only three stores, a couple of garages, one restaurant, two churches, and empty, abandoned buildings make up the rest of the town.

Its general ugliness has not been glossed over for me, but it has been absorbed. I don't notice it any longer. Knifley is the home village. And in the same way you become accustomed to faded wallpaper in your living room, a worn carpet, scarred furniture, because you live with them every day, I have become accustomed to Knifley. And we have some very good friends there.

There are Leon Christie and his wife, Montra, for instance. They own one of the general stores and live close by. Leon and Montra are two of the nicest people anywhere. Leon formerly taught school, being a graduate of Western State Teachers College at Bowling Green. But after several years in the schoolroom his lungs were threatened and the doctor advised him to rest a year and then to get into some other kind of work. Since he and Montra were both reared in Knifley, it seemed natural to them to stay there, and they decided to open a store. I think they have done well. They are friendly, generous folks, always making us welcome, always interested in what is happening to us, loyally reading our books and thinking them fine. When we want something Leon does not ordinarily carry in stock, he is always ready to go to the trouble and bother to get it for us if he can. When we forget to go to the bank, he cashes our checks, or puts five or ten dollars on the books until the next time we come around.

Uncle Marion and Ider live in Knifley, and it is always nice to go to their house. And there is Henry's cousin Edgar Giles, and Annie, his wife. Edgar is a White Cap preacher, and I may as well admit that in *Tara's Healing* I used about Jory a remark that the superintendent of the work in Kentucky had made to me about Edgar. Mr. Dohner told me one time that Edgar, being native to the country, had more influence and accomplished more good than all the rest of them put together. I thought that was an extremely fine thing to have said about one. And I knew it was justified, for you'll look far and wide before you find a sweeter man than Edgar Giles. His face is the most pleasant face I think I ever saw. Clear, candid eyes; frank, open countenance; good, broad forehead and square chin. And he always wears a smile. Always. In the pulpit he is winsome and winning, and his strong, deep voice is firm in its " Amens " to the congregation.

Edgar preaches for love. He makes a living doing almost any kind of honest work he can find to do. He has tried farming, working in a garage, and I don't know what else. Currently he is an electrician. He did a nice job on our house when, eventually, we had it wired, and it was a privilege to have him in our home. The bill for a three-day wiring job, including all materials and fixtures, came to $99.10. It would have been at least three hundred dollars in the city. The White Caps do not believe in making too much profit.

And then, at Knifley, there are also the wonderful, fabulous Holcombs. Nowhere in the United States except in the backwash of small towns and villages will you find folks like the

Holcombs. They have almost left the American scene. But, thank goodness, we still have them in our villages.

Mr. Holcomb and his two sons run a small garage. Mr. Holcomb is the hefty man who was a blacksmith back in the old days and who still has a forge and his hammers and anvil. I suppose he is actually the manager of the garage. His sons are the two best mechanics in the United States, I'll vow. You can look the country over and you won't find two that can beat them. We ought to know. They've kept our old car running for a long, long time now. They've replaced the worn parts piece by piece until they've made it almost a new car. But when the Holcombs go over our car and say it's ready to travel, in spite of its 120,000 miles, we travel! We have no hesitancy at all about starting anywhere in it when they say it'll go. We know it will. The only time we ever had any trouble with it out on the road they had been skeptical about the fuel pump.

There is Dewey who is the older of the two sons. He must be nearly forty now, I should say. He is married and has one daughter who goes to school in the city. Dewey is a big man, as they all are. Slow of speech, always ready to laugh, quiet-tempered, goodhearted. It is Dewey who gives you the final word on your car. When we took ours to them the first time, he told us it needed a new generator, a new battery, new exhaust, and muffler, and a new water pump. We told them to go ahead and put them in. When they had finished, and it took them most of one day, Dewey made out the ticket on the work. "Henry," he said, for of course they have known Henry all his life, "Henry, these parts come to a right smart money. We'll not charge you for the labor."

"Now, see here —" Henry started to protest.

But they wouldn't have it any other way. Now, if I understand the garage business correctly, the income is derived from the labor. So don't ask me how the Holcombs make a living, when half the time they won't charge for their labor. I don't know. For that matter, there's a little story about Mr. Holcomb and the gasoline salesman. The man came around, as he does periodically, to check their pumps for accuracy. "Mr. Holcomb," he said when he had finished, "your pumps need adjusting. They're giving about one quart to every five gallons too much gas. You're losing money. But I'll fix them for you."

"No, you don't, young man," Mr. Holcomb said in a hurry. "You jist leave them pumps be! I may be losin' a little money, but I ain't losin' no sleep. Now if they was givin' *short* measure, you could fix 'em. But you jist leave them pumps be."

And there was that other time when a friend of ours drove by one Sunday in a brand-new truck. When he started to leave, he had a flat. "Lord," he moaned, "I meant to get a spare yesterday. Got busy an' plumb forgot it. An' that truck tire is a mean one to change. What'll I do?"

Henry spoke up. "The Holcombs will fix it. Let's jack it up and get it off."

They had a story to tell when they got back three hours later. Dewey and Dink were away, but Mr. Holcomb went down to the garage with them and opened up. He had the tools to wrestle with the tire, but even with the right tools it was a hard, tedious job. Mr. Holcomb wrestled right with them. Finally it was done and our friend reached for his wallet. "What do I owe you, sir?"

Mr. Holcomb pushed his hat back on his head and scratched. "Well," he said, "that there patch sells fer a dime."

And that's all he would take.

Dink, the younger of the sons, is a husky lad who lives at home with his parents. Dink was in the Air Corps during the war as an air-engine mechanic. His outfit wound up in India, servicing the big planes that flew the Hump. That's where Dink learned to be a really good mechanic, and he brought his knowledge home with him.

Once he told us about the most frustrating moment he ever knew over there, and it had nothing to do with an engine. They had gone a long, long time without any meat to eat. It had been so long that they had almost forgotten what meat tasted like. Then one day when the field kitchen rolled up under the wings of a giant plane to feed them, they had meat balls. Big, giant meat balls, enough for each man to have one. Dink's mouth watered and he thought: "Oh, boy. Now here's where I get fixed up."

He loaded his plate and started off to the shade of a nearby tree to eat. He had his plate in one hand, his cup of coffee in the other. Just then a hawk swooped down and in one swift. motion lifted his meat ball from the plate and zoomed off into space with it. Dink said he could have sat right down and cried. There were no more. Just one to a customer, and a hawk had taken his. He said he brooded about that for days. The injustice of it almost made him sick.

The Holcombs subscribe to all the good motor magazines. They have modern equipment. They buy books on engines and they read them. They study engines all the time. I believe they could build a car from scratch. They themselves drive an ancient Hupmobile which they keep in fine shape. It looks like heck, of course, but they know what its old engine will do. We feel a lot the same way about our Oldsmobile. The Holcombs tell us it is a very good car yet. And they tell us as long as we can drive it and get twenty miles to the gallon of gas, and a thousand miles to a quart of oil, and the engine stays tight, not to sell it. We don't intend to. When you see us driving a new car, you'll know that the Oldsmobile has done like the one-hoss shay — gone to pieces — and the Holcombs can't fix it!

Leon Christie wrote a piece of doggerel about the Holcombs, which may not be good poetry (and he'd be the first to admit it) but it just about expresses the way we all feel about them:

> There was a man in Knifley town
> Who was a smithy of great renown,
> From North Caroliny. He wobbled as he walked,
> He had big feet and he liked to talk.
> > That's Holcomb.

> Accommodatin'? He'd loan you his tools,
> He'd credit 'em all, to heck with the rules;
> He'd fix yer plow, or he'd fix yer fence;
> He'd overhaul a freight train fer fifteen cents.
> > That's Holcomb.

There's Dewey and Dink besides the old man;
If one can't fix her, the other un can.
If yer Lizzie goes dead, and that won't do,
If yer wagon's broke, they'll fix that too.
                    Call Holcomb.

They'll change yer battery, or fix yer clock,
If the old gun's broke, put on a new stock;
They'll work all day without any pay,
And they'll even teach yer baby to say,
                    "Go Holcomb's."

Here's flowers for Holcomb while he's alive.
I hope he'll reach a hundred and five,
Have health and wealth and all of that,
For he's a doggone good old Democrat.
                    Will Holcomb!

We found him in the garage that day we went to see about
the fireplace tools. "Mr. Holcomb," I said, "I want a set of fireplace things. Just as old-fashioned as they can be. I don't know
what kind they used in this section in the old days, but that's
what I want. Will you make them for me?"

Mr. Holcomb has grizzled hair and eyebrows, and a whim-
sical gleam in his eyes. "Now, let's see," he said, shifting his
hat to the back of his head and scratching the red rim around
his forehead. "Now, let's see. You'll want firedogs, I reckon."

"Firedogs?"

"Andirons they call 'em nowadays. We allus called 'em
firedogs. First ones made in these parts had a kind of hook you
could lift 'em by. But they wasn't very fancy. Next ones had
the hook joined so's it made a kind of eye. I allus liked them
best myself."

"That's the kind I'd like."

"All right. I'll make 'em jist that way. Firedogs with a eye.
Then you'll want a poker. An' you'll want a shovel. Reckon
you could use a set of tongs?"

Henry was standing near. "We can," he said definitely. "I
certainly want a set of tongs."

230

"What do you do with tongs?" I asked.

With his hands Mr. Holcomb showed me. "Why, you kin pick up a coal with the tongs an' carry it anywheres you like. Start yer cook fire with a good, hot coal. Spread yer fire around. Lift a log. Do most anything you want with a pair of tongs."

So I seconded Henry's motion. "By all means we must have a pair of tongs."

Several weeks went by. Then one day Henry came home with the firedogs. "Mr. Holcomb sent you these. He hasn't got the rest of the stuff made, but he wanted to know if these suited."

Oh, they suited beautifully! Old, black, cast iron. We put them in the fireplace and there they squatted, fat, short, hunched down close, the eye winking at the top. They were just exactly what I wanted. I sent him word that they were perfect.

Soon the rest of the implements were done. The same sooty, black iron, but he twisted the handles fancily. The tongs open perfectly, grasp a coal neatly, or spread to grip a big log. The poker hooks just right into the wood, and the shovel is quaintly square. Not too wide. Not too narrow. Just right. Henry put nails into the mortar between the stones of the fireplace front and side by side our shovel, poker, and tongs hang there, ready at hand, stout and strong. When we went to pay him, Henry asked, "Well, Mr. Holcomb, what do we owe you for the fireplace set?"

His faded blue eyes twinkled. "I reckon if you pay me what the iron cost, I'll call it square."

"Now, that's not right," I protested, "that's not right! After all, you had to make them. You need something for your labor."

"I've had my pay."

"But you haven't!"

"Yes, I have. Jist the pleasure of knowin' they was still somebody liked the old things best. Most folks don't, no more. Most folks want fancy, store-bought things. Tell you what. Jist make out like I own me a piece of that chimney of yore'n, an' jist give me a welcome if I ever git out that way to set by it."

And he'll have that. He certainly will.

Chapter

22 ✝ ✝

A tobacco auction is still a wondrous thing to me. I can't make heads or tails of it, but I am fascinated by it just the same.

I had to tag along, naturally, when our tobacco went to the market about the middle of December. You never know, when you go, whether it will be sold the same day you take it or not, but there's a very good chance it will be. Not all the farmers here on the ridge take their tobacco to the same warehouse. Some go to Lebanon, some to Springfield, some to Greensburg, and some even make the long haul to Danville and Lexington. But we took ours to the same warehouse Mr. Frank uses, at Springfield, some sixty miles from home.

Early that morning our crop and Mr. Frank's had been packed tightly on an enormous truck and carefully covered with tarpaulin. Mr. Frank and Kenneth, who dotes on an auction as dearly as I, rode on the truck, but Henry and I trailed along in the car. We started early, so it was still only midmorning when we arrived.

The truck was backed up to the platform and workers began unloading at once, stacking the hands on large, round flat baskets that look for all the world like overgrown dinner plates. They graded as they unloaded. Bright on this basket, red there, tips on another, and trash on still another. Each man's crop is kept separate and apart. Some of the baskets are loaded so heavily that they are taller than a man's head. Others will have only a foot or so of tobacco on them. It all depends on the amount of tobacco a man has of any one grade.

Finally, when a crop is unloaded and has been graded onto baskets, it is tagged with the Government grade and the farmer's name. Then the baskets are wheeled into line. The warehouse is a long building, stretching it seemed to me for blocks and blocks, very cold and barren-looking, with almost interminable lines of tobacco baskets arranged in aisles down its length. I lost track of ours, because the auction had started and I was so fascinated by the auctioneer's chant that I had eyes and ears only for him.

Rapidly he moves down an aisle, the buyers from various tobacco companies following him, and the warehouse tabulator at his heels. He sounds exactly like you've heard him on the radio. You can't understand a word he says. That ululating, rapid-fire, staccato song goes on and on, with never a pause or break, the bids from the buyers coming in, but not interrupting. It may be true that some buyers bid by signals. I had always heard they did. And Henry says it is probably true. But I do know that there is also bidding by voice, and I soon caught on that when the vocal bidding lagged, the sale was closed. The auctioneer then, flatly and mechanically, and very matter-of-factly, called a company's name. Not with the dramatic " Sold to American " that I expected. The auctioneer merely announced in an ordinary speaking voice the name of the company that had bought that basket. Liggett's. Reynolds'. American. And he didn't even quit walking. Right on down the aisle to the next basket he went. So much for radio advertising!

At noon we dashed out and bought hamburgers and dashed right back in again so as not to miss anything. I wanted more than anything to watch our own tobacco being sold; then I felt I would have seen it through to the bitter end. It was along about the middle of the afternoon that I got what I wanted. " Ours is next," Henry whispered. And I got goose bumps all over.

I had been listening to the various auctioneers long enough by now to tell when the bids shifted higher. Forty cents is fairly plain to hear. Fifty isn't quite so easy, and what they say when they mean sixty is pure Eskimo as far as I am concerned, but I had caught on to the difference in tone and enunciation. Besides, they don't say sixty often enough to count. I listened with both ears pinned back, but I guess I was too excited. All I could hear was jargon.

Within ten minutes our crop was sold. Ten minutes. I had

the most dreadful sense of anticlimax. It had taken us seven months to raise that doggone stuff, and we had been spared the first work of planting a seedbed. Seven months of backache and sweat and worry. And the auctioneer disposed of it in ten fast minutes. I didn't actually expect him to stop and make an announcement that this was Henry Giles's tobacco, but I certainly thought it would take longer than that. I felt rather indignant that it had been so cavalierly disposed of. And I was horribly afraid that the shortness of the time meant that the buyers had been contemptuous of the quality. I completely forgot that they had been moving just as rapidly all day long.

A handler came along as soon as the sale was completed, took the tags off, and we followed him to the office. Quickly, efficiently, the tickets were computed, a check was made out, and we had sold our tobacco. When we looked at the tickets and the check, we had a grand moment of jubilation. The bright had brought sixty-one cents per pound, and that's a very, very good price. Mr. Frank was almost as excited as we. He told us then what the handler had said to him when the baskets were loaded. That our tobacco was the cleanest graded crop he'd seen on the floor. Golly, that was wonderful! *I* had helped grade that tobacco. I, personally, had helped see to it that no red-tinged leaves crept into the bright to coarsen it and cheapen it. I, with my frozen hands and drippy nose. I had helped make tobacco history, for we learned later that our bright leaf had brought the highest price of the season. Even my first book didn't bring me a greater thrill!

You think we took that money and made ourselves more secure with it? No. Not us. We did a mad, crazy thing with most of it. We took the car to the Holcombs in Knifley, had them fix it up like new, and then we took off for Santa Fe to spend Christmas with Libby, Nash, and the babies. Reckless, impractical, foolish us! But we had learned something. We had gone through a tough time together. Really tough. Really hard. We had worked harder than I had known people could work. We had stripped life down to its irreducible minimum. And it had taught us a thing or two. It had taught us to believe in ourselves — to have faith in our wills·-and our bodies and our spirits. It had taught us not to be afraid. Money? Sure you need it. You can't get along without it. But you can always make it. You may have to pull in your belt between times. You may have to face lean days occasionally. You may have to live very simply at times. But what have you got a brain for? What have you got two hands and a back for? What have you got nerve for?

So we took most of the tobacco money, splurged on marvelous gifts for everyone, and went to Santa Fe for Christmas.

Chapter

23 ⟋⟍

As if everything were working together for our good, when we got home from Santa Fe our affairs took an upward swing. I finished *Miss Willie* and sent it to the publisher. Within three weeks there was a contract and a nice advance in royalty. Henry sold a short story, and he had hardly banked the check before there came a request from a publishing house for him to try his hand at a book-length manuscript. One of the editors had read his short story and had been impressed with his writing style. Henry was aghast at the request. The short story had been his first attempt at writing. "I can't write a book!" he yelled. "I never in this world can write a book!"

"You can!" I told him, "you certainly can!"

And he did. He didn't want to, and he cussed and slaved over it, and I sweated it out with him, driving him to the typewriter night after night. Sometimes we practically came to blows over it, and there were times when separation and divorce threatened. "It's no good," Henry would groan.

"It's wonderful," I would say, "it's a grand book."

And it was. That was *Harbin's Ridge* that he sweated over the balance of the winter.

We looked at our bank balance now with awe. It seemed impossible that we had that much money in the bank. And it was all clear. All to the good. All profit. Not one dime did we owe. Not one obligation were we under. We looked at each other and grinned as we realized that the hardest pull was over. It was a sweet victory and triumph tasted mighty fine.

Promptly we did two things. We had our house, and the folks' house, wired for electricity. And we finished the fireplace.

I shall never forget the night we laid our first fire. Henry rolled a huge backlog into place, laid the smaller logs across the firedogs, made a small pile of kindling under them, and struck a match to it. The chimney drew so powerfully that instantly the flames leaped up and the logs caught, snapping and crackling. Henry pulled his big chair up and stretched his legs to the fire. I drew my grandmother's little rocker near and stretched my own. Honey sighed and curled up on the rug near the hearth.

Have you ever, suddenly and without warning, known a moment in which you knew, beyond any question, that this moment, this present now, was all of living distilled and drained, stopped timeless and still? Full, rich, heavy with goodness, fleeting, yet eternal? It's as if the earth stopped for a second, to let you, for the space of a heartbeat, savor life to see just how good it is. It is perhaps that moment when you become real, when you know yourself in your environment, and know that you are forever. It is perhaps then that you really discover yourself. You may say, I . . . I . . . I am . . . here and now, alive and beating with blood and flesh and spirit. Here in this separate, distinct moment of time and tide, I am all and whole and complete.

I knew such a moment then. I have known it twice before in my life. The night Libby was born and I heard her first cry. That was a miraculous moment of complete and perfect love as I heard my own child, my flesh and blood, given identity apart from me. The second time was the night Henry called me from New York when he landed safely home from his two years overseas. The moment I heard his voice, time stopped and the earth spun and every emotion I had ever felt or could ever feel crowded into my heart and throat and choked me. I couldn't answer him, and it wasn't until I heard him calling anxiously to know if I was still there that I could manage to speak above the tumult I was feeling.

And now again, before the fire in my own home, the moment came to me again. Blinding, transcendent moment, motionless and timeless. And I knew finally and forever the circle was completed.

We settled down for the winter with two books to write, my third one, Henry's first. We had to make nice progress within two months, for we had only January and February, and maybe part of March, before it would be time to burn and seed the tobacco beds again. Only the two months in the heart of winter does tobacco let you alone. Then you may pile the beech and chestnut logs on the fire, stretch your toes toward the crackling flames, sink down inside yourself, and read and dream and write. The sleet hisses against the window-panes; the snow falls feathery and light, piling up in thick, drifted banks until the road is hidden and we can only guess by the fence posts where it lies. The haystacks are frosted mounds in the middle of the white fields; the trees are bearded with whiskers of ice; the electric wires hum in the north wind's blizzard, and the whole world is frozen in and slowed down and quietened. And we are inside, snug by the fire.

So many of you who have read the Piney Ridge books have written to me in a wistful, longing mood, as if in reading about the ridge you recapture something long lost. I know so well what you are feeling. For in writing about Piney Ridge it may be that I have been doing the same thing for myself. I think all of us who live today, in a world that seems to have lost its certainty and even much of its meaning, share that feeling to a great extent. We live in a time and circumstance that breeds feelings of insecurity, not only because of the world situation with its ever-present threat of tensions and war, but because we have created a very complex civilization, fast-moving, noisy, crowded, and nervous, in which we are not entirely at home. It has come too fast and our personalities cannot adjust to it fully. Most of us can remember, or at least our parents can remember, a slower day, a quieter day, and in our memories perhaps, a sweeter day.

My books perhaps revive in you those memories of land that once belonged to you, of lamps that glowed with a warm yellow light, of wide hearths and big logs crackling, of a great, black kitchen range where good things to eat simmered and stewed. And those memories arouse in all of us a longing to go back, which in some of us is almost a spiritual need.

I would not disagree with the psychologist who says that such a longing is a wish to escape the present problems. I think in all probability it is. But I would disagree with him that it is unhealthy. I don't believe for one moment that moving to the country and recovering an old way of life will bring the security and peace for which most of us long. That must come from deep inside the individual, and it can be attained in the flow of city traffic as well as in the quiet of country lanes. But I do believe, and believe it strongly, that if you are hardy enough to strip life down to its simplicities you may be able to create an environment in which you can gain perspective. Certainly you can provide yourself with the opportunity for profound and reflective thinking, and you can give yourself a rest from the tense, nervous expenditure of energy demanded of you every waking moment of your life in the city. I think you must bring with you the ability to use such things, or else it is a wasted effort. But, given that ability, it seems to me that the nostalgia for a simpler life is perfectly healthy and understandable, and in some cases even necessary.

I do not pretend that the ridge and the home we have created here will suffice for the rest of our lives. It seems to me to be rather foolish to say that this place answers all my needs. " Here I will stay for the rest of my life " — is that not denying the possibility of growth and change? When we came to the ridge, we needed its quietness and its serenity. But whether we shall continue to need it ten years from now, five years from now, even next year, I cannot say. Our life on the ridge has taught us to have some very real and some very personal concerns. It never allows you to close your eyes and turn the other way. It sticks your nose right down in the middle of living and holds it there until you come up for air, gasping and struggling, and then it cries to you, " What price beauty? " I think we have learned more of compassion, sympathy, and understanding than ever before we knew. I think we are bigger people and better people for having lived on the ridge, and perhaps that is more important than the peace and the quiet we sought.

And we have had confirmed for us a faith in life that may have been dimming. We have had time to look around us and to take a long view. In this time of fear and panic and morbid pessimism, we have watched these people of the hills walk through the seasons, plowing and planting and harvesting, not ignoring the tensions loose in the world, but rather overcoming them. Here we see a positive affirmation that life goes on, if not serenely, still inevitably. The movement of life is forward, not backward. The purpose of life is still creation, not annihilation. They go on about the business of living with a deep faith in its goodness. Inevitably there comes the conviction that so long as there is a spot of earth left, and one man to plow it, with one woman left to sleep by his side at night, life will go on. Food will be raised. Children will be born. The sun will rise over the hills and the sea, and set behind the reddened clouds. Rains will fall and snows will bank. Tides will rise on the rivers and mists will smoke up from the valleys.

The ridge has given us new faith and heart and hope. And we know that if civilization wrecks itself, if the hurrying, noisy, clattering, neurotic world burns itself into ashes, out of the ashes a man with a plow will rise and lift the yoke onto his own shoulders and walk steadfastly down a new furrow.

That man with a plow is a symbol to us of the great courage and heart of the common man everywhere. He is not merely the hill farmer. He is not merely the American farmer. He is all the little men around the whole wide world. Those who go on hoping and planning and living in the face of all odds. And in that great courage and heart, freshly revealed to us, we base a renewed faith in the indestructibility of the positive values of life. The ridge has given us a mood of optimism, in a pessimistic time. And for that we give thanks.

239